T0293368

THE KUAISHOU WAY

The Kuaishou Research Institute

NEW YORK CHICAGO SAN FRANCISCO ATHENS LONDON MADRID MEXICO
CITY MILAN NEW DELHI SINGAPORE SYDNEY TORONTO

ISBN   978-1-264-26416-2
MHID   1-264-26416-X

e-ISBN   978-1-264-26417-9
e-MHID   1-264-26417-8

The core resource on the Internet is attention.
We hope to draw attention to as many people as possible and
increase every person's unique sense of happiness.

———

– Su Hua, Co-founder and Chairman of Kuaishou

Kuaishou is a connector that can connect each and
every person, especially the oft-neglected majority.

———

– Cheng Yixiao, Co-founder and CEO of Kuaishou

A Mind Map for *The Kuaishou Way*

Popularization of smartphones

Decrease in 4G costs

Convenient payment options

Well-developed logistics networks

China's long-term investment in Internet infrastructure

Kuaishou's principle of inclusivity

Shift from picture-and-text to video

Application of AI technology

The decreasing costs of attention mean that ordinary people can enjoy attention as well

Attention is allocated more inclusively, bridging the "attention gap"

A few people get attention > Everyone gets attention > Every life can be seen

	Being seen	
Every product		Kuaishou E-Commerce
Every talent		Kuaishou Education
Every voice		Kuaishou Musician
Every enterprise	< >	Kuaishou Enterprise Account
Every village		Kuaishou Poverty Alleviation
Every heritage		Kuaishou Intangible Cultural Heritage
Every community and industrial belt		Kuaishou Village
Institutional aid for individuals and organizations		Kuaishou MCN

Increasing Every Person's Unique Sense of Happiness

CONTENTS

INCREASING EVERY PERSON'S UNIQUE SENSE OF HAPPINESS

—Su Hua
Co-founder and Chairman of Kuaishou

I. THE EVOLUTION OF HAPPINESS

Happiness has meant something entirely different to me depending on the different stages of my life; from childhood to adulthood the definition of happiness has varied with the seasons of life.

When I was five, my sense of happiness was centered upon having light.

I was born in a small *Tujia* (a Chinese ethnic minority found in Hunan, Hubei, Sichuan, and Guizhou provinces) village in Xiangxi, Hunan Province—a mountainous place at the tail end of China's "capillary network." It is beautiful, but inaccessible and backward. Because there was no electricity in the village at that time, nothing could be done when the sky turned dark.

Without electricity there were no lights, not to mention television. With few recreational activities at night, we listened to stories and gazed at the stars under a big tree. The only electrical appliance we had at home was the flashlight, but because batteries were very expensive, I was often reluctant to use it and instead used a pine branch as my torch when going out at night. As there were no roads in the mountains, getting our living supplies was a trek—to buy soy sauce, for example, meant a two-hour walk down a dirt path into town and another two-hour walk back.

My greatest desire at that time was to have light when the sky turned dark. Having light would mean being able to play and seek joy. This was a most peculiar source of happiness for me. Later on in my life, I developed a bad habit: Sleeping with the lights on. I had grown afraid of darkness and could not fall asleep without the lights on. This habit was only broken for good after I got married.

When I was in my teens, my source of happiness was to get into a good university.

While a student, I moved with my parents into the county seat. Besides the local magistrate, the most prominent people here were the students who were accepted into Tsinghua University and Peking University (the top two universities in China). Every July, the list of students who were admitted into universities would be put up at the entrance of the county's only movie theater.

The National College Entrance Examination (known as *gaokao*) is a very good system that offers everyone the opportunity to change their fate through their own efforts, thereby promoting social mobility. As a result, the poorer parts of China often place even more emphasis on education—it was in such an environment that I managed to get into Tsinghua University.

In my early 20s, my source of happiness was to have a good job.

Early on in my university days, one of my teachers raved about a senior student who had just found a job with an annual salary of 100,000 yuan (about 15,400 US dollars). So, at that time, I thought it would be an awesome thing if I could likewise find a job paying 100,000 yuan per year. Later on, when I heard that the salaries at Google were high, I went there for an interview and they offered me an annual salary of 150,000 yuan (about 23,100 US dollars)—50 percent more than the senior who was seen as great. That was a very satisfying moment for me. A year later, I was granted options that soon doubled in value, causing my sense of happiness to explode.

Toward the age of 30, my sense of happiness came from doing outstanding things.

While working for Google, I spent more than a year in Silicon Valley. What hit me the hardest was my discovery of the structural differences—both deep and superficial—between China and the United States. In 2007, there were not as many cars in Beijing as they are now, but Silicon Valley was already full of cars. It was at this time when I felt that my earlier achievements might have been too shallow. I thought I should be able to do and achieve more, but I did not know what I could be outstanding in.

During the second month of the 2008 financial crisis, I left Google to start a business. I wanted to validate my ideas and find out what I could contribute to society or gain out of it. In less than two years, however, my venture ended disastrously.

The next year I joined the Chinese search engine, Baidu, and did a lot of interesting things. In particular, when I was working on the Phoenix Nest machine learning system, I found that the skills I had grasped related to AI, parallel computing, and data analysis had great potential.

I got promoted, received a higher salary, started a family, and bought an apartment. But still I had a persistent anxiety. Why was I not satisfied after attaining all that I wanted? This was because my ideas on happiness had undergone significant change at a certain point in time. Previously, my sense of happiness came from myself—I wanted to have light, to get into a good university, to have a good job, and to do outstanding things. These were all about giving myself a sense of achievement, making my wife and children happy, and bringing honor to my parents. Although these are indeed things to be happy about, there surely has to be a greater happiness to be found in life. Later on, I discovered that rather than satisfying my own desires and benefiting myself, it would be better to explore how to benefit others. If I could become a pivot that brings happiness to more people, my own sense of happiness would multiply.

Altruism is not simply about helping someone to do a certain thing but is also a process of gradual exploration. When I was working at Google, my mindset was to help everyone using my individual strength. As an engineer with strong technical skills, many teams would seek my help on things ranging from web servers to machine learning systems to large-scale parallel computing. I was like a firefighter who went around putting out fires wherever I was needed. But reality is harsh: because my energy was divided, I could not gain promotion when it was time for evaluation and failed to gain recognition from others.

After working for some time at Baidu, where my technical skills received validation, I went back to starting my own business. At first, our small team was like a mercenary army that went around helping others to deal with technical issues so as to increase our scope of impact, but we later realized that we could not help many people in this way. I became aware that altruism should be engaged not by relying on individual strength but instead by making use of the power of systems and values, and that the best form of altruism is that which is able to benefit everyone. Therefore, instead of judging people based on our own perspectives, what we need to do is understand more people from broader perspectives. What are their common pain points? Why are they lacking in happiness? And what are the greatest common denominators of happiness that can be satisfied? We must become able to find the greatest denominators that increase every person's sense of happiness.

II. WHAT IS UNIQUE ABOUT KUAISHOU

Kuaishou actually has a very simple concept: to store the snippets of life recorded by everyone and allow others to view them through our recommendation algorithm. However, the thinking behind this concept is a little different from that of other entrepreneurs.

First, Kuaishou cares very much about the feelings of all people, including the neglected majority. According to the National Bureau of Statistics of China, as of 2018, only 13 percent of China's population had received higher education, whereas 87 percent of the population had not. Judging from this perspective, the people that we think about and follow on a daily basis come from a very skewed section of the population. We thus made several decisions to help the 87 percent express themselves better and be followed online.

Second, the allocation of attention. A key issue regarding our source of happiness is the allocation of resources. The core resource on the internet is attention, yet it might be even more unequally allocated than other resources. On the whole, the number of people followed by the entire society is probably a few thousand per year, with a handful of people rising to the top every two to three days on average—all media platforms pay attention to and promote news regarding the same handful of people. Given China's population of 1.4 billion people, most people will never garner online attention throughout their lifetimes.

In our allocation of attention, we hope to do our best to help more people to get attention, even if this might reduce the viewing efficiency slightly. In terms of values, there remains a high chance that fairness and inclusivity can be realized. As a type of resource and energy, attention can be showered onto more people just like sunlight, rather than be focused on a small group of people like a spotlight—this is the simple idea behind Kuaishou.

III. USER-DRIVEN COMMUNITY EVOLUTION

The most important thing about building an online short video community is its underlying values. But how can they be reflected in the online community?

Kuaishou's community has changed tremendously in atmosphere, feel and experience over the past few years. What is most unique about us, as the guardians of this community, is that we have defined it as little as possible. Something that we often do is to allow our users to evolve the community using their own wits, talents, and ideas, as well as the "chemical reactions" among themselves, after we have designed the rules. In fact, every transformation in Kuaishou's history has been user-driven. We are instead responsible for watching on from the sidelines to see what our users are happy or unhappy about, what is done right or wrong, what is out of line with our values, and what is in line with the needs of today.

Let me share with you a few stories of user-driven community evolution.

The first story is about Aunt Chen. Back in 2013, online communities and media were only interested in refined and polished content, but Aunt Chen was different. She was once a foreign student in Japan. Although her looks were okay, she did not like to dress up—after all, she was far away from home, had just broken up with her boyfriend, and was in an unfamiliar land.

However, she would post all kinds of snippets on Kuaishou every day. She was especially fond of flaming herself, revealing her own shortcomings, talking about what she did badly, her experiences of being bullied, and so on. She discovered that one did not necessarily have to rely on good looks or meticulous dressing up to become popular in this community—people would accept you as long as they felt that you were genuine and that your life was relatable. Most overseas students would only share the glamorous side of their lives, but Aunt Chen instead had the courage to show the ugly aspects of her life and the things she did badly to everyone. Therefore, a certain style has taken shape in Kuaishou's communities. Here, great emphasis is placed on authentic and interesting things—among the three values of authenticity, kindness, and beauty, it is truth that we demand the most of.

The second story is about Zhang Jingru, a vlogger who was highly popular on Kuaishou. Many of her videos were uploaded to Weibo (a Twitter-like social media website in China), where many netizens would ask about who she was and which city she was from. Because her Kuaishou videos were heavily forwarded, her fans would tell others on Weibo that she could also be found on Kuaishou. She is proof that the external sharing of Kuaishou content on other platforms can bring in more fans to Kuaishou. Many of her fans on Kuaishou spread her videos to other platforms, thereby creating a cycle—the more they spread, the more people would know about her, and in return, more people would look her up on Kuaishou. And the more fans she gained, the happier and more energetic her loyal followers became.

The third story is about Huang Wenyu. As a person with great emotional intelligence, he filmed many videos that related to people from all walks of life, especially women. He would also express his viewpoints using different concepts such as zodiac signs and blood types.

It was then that our users found out that, more than self-flaming and posting authentic things, Kuaishou could also be used to care for others in society and the world. Thanks to Huang Wenyu, the atmosphere on Kuaishou underwent significant change.

In the past two years, the more intuitively felt changes in Kuaishou's communities have had to do with livestreaming. Many Kuaishou users have a deep understanding of livestreaming and a huge desire for this kind of real-time interaction. This was why the promotion of our livestreaming features went especially swimmingly.

We discovered that livestreaming on Kuaishou has many differences from that on other platforms. The biggest difference is that Kuaishou users regard livestreaming as a part of their lives rather than work. Many Kuaishou users livestream after they get off work. For example, a wedding emcee whom I have followed for the longest time is usually busy hosting weddings until midnight, and so it is past midnight by the time he starts a livestream or films a video. His video series is called "Time for a Meal" because he would go for a dinner gathering after he gets off work at midnight. Being a late sleeper, I would watch what he eats every day—his dinner gatherings are always a treat by the newlyweds, and so the food is always high-quality and non-repetitive. This has gone on for several years already.

Another example is a female bar-top dancer whom I have also followed for several years. She would livestream and chat with everyone while putting on makeup before going to work, and then livestream and chat with everyone again while taking off her makeup after getting off work. Many people fail to be understood by others in the real world; she is one of those people who have an indecipherable inner world. You might think that her life must be chaotic, but the truth is that she has a family and bar-top dancing is her means of supporting them. She has shared many snippets of her real life—both its sad and happy aspects—online, and derives joy in doing so.

Once, I saw on Kuaishou a mother whose child was still very young, and so she could only begin livestreaming after lulling her child to sleep. Because her child slept in short naps, she could never go very far outdoors. While staying home to take care of her child, the thing she most desired was to chat with people. Often, her child would wake up while she was in the middle of a livestream, and so she would have to turn off the livestream that may not have lasted even 10 minutes. In her view, livestreams and short videos are a means of connecting with the world, and also a means of gaining the understanding and recognition of others.

These are all stories from within our video sharing communities. To any community, the form of content presented, the methods by which people express themselves, and the methods by which people express understanding, approval, or disapproval would inevitably evolve along with changes in society, in social order, and in internet speeds. Therefore, Kuaishou is still in the midst of evolving.

IV. EVERYONE HAS THEIR OWN STORY

Everyone has their own story—some work in a city, some raise wolves on a prairie, while others chop wood in a forest. Every person's life appears to be insignificant, and their living conditions vary greatly from one another's. We are constantly dealing with all kinds of problems, conflicts, contradictions, and suchlike—everyday life is full of challenges.

I love playing the *erhu* (a two-stringed bowed musical instrument also known as a spike fiddle), and once played the instrument until two in the morning. When my next-door neighbor, a tofu seller, bumped into me the following day, he complimented my playing skills. At that time, I did not realize that he actually meant I had disturbed his sleep. After all, in the small town that I lived in, nobody ever scolded me. The tofu boiler he had at home constantly made an audible gurgling noise, but I had never complained about it to him. This reflected the tolerance we had for each other in a folk society.

I also follow on Kuaishou an old man who plays the *erhu*. All of the videos he posts are of him playing the *erhu* alone. Because his hands are reversed in the videos—his right hand presses the strings while his left hand holds the bow—it is apparent that his videos were taken by himself using the front camera of a mobile phone. That can only mean he does not have a companion at home. What is an old man like him most afraid of? The answer is a lack of electricity and light when the sky turns dark, a lack of companionship, and loneliness. However, he was fortunate to find out about Kuaishou early on. Because of our principle of inclusivity, we do our best to help everyone find their fans or people who like and understand them. On Kuaishou, this old man found more than 90,000 fans (as of October 2019), including myself. At seven or eight every night, 20 to 30 fans would accompany him and listen to him playing the *erhu*. All he wishes for is the companionship of others; even if they criticize him for playing poorly, it would be better than not having any attention at all.

The loneliness of old people is a very serious social problem that is difficult to solve. Kuaishou is actually able to provide a solution that is applicable to this entire group of people rather than a specific individual. Loneliness is a major contributor to many people's sense of unhappiness.

Let me add on the story of a woman from the Dong ethnic group. She comes from Tianzhu County, Guizhou Province. Her real name is Yuan Guihua, but she calls herself "Xueli" on Kuaishou. At first, she uploaded to Kuaishou many videos depicting the scenes of rural life: The thatched house that she built herself, the bows and arrows she handcrafted, and the red spider lilies she saw—a flower that can be found all over the mountains and fields nearby her village. These scenes were very well-liked on Kuaishou because many urban dwellers do not have the chance to see such idyllic and poetic sights in real life.

At 18 years old, Guihua did not do well in the national college entrance examination and thus returned home to do farming work. In her spare time, she would film videos and upload them for everyone to watch. She later found out that many fans enjoyed seeing the scenes of her life. While many people were enthused about going to visit her, she would put them off by saying that her home was too shabby to accommodate them. One day by a pond near her home, she surveyed a small semicircular valley and decided that she could build houses there for fans to stay in when they visited. With that, she started building houses so that her fans could visit her. There seems to be nothing this woman cannot do—she once uploaded a video of her cutting bricks with one hand and another video of her carrying an entire log up onto a roof.

Guihua had suffered a huge setback when she failed to get into university and thus could not leave the rural life behind. However, Kuaishou provided her with an opportunity—if she could not walk out of this life, then she could bring people in instead. She is now the most influential person in her village, organizing the whole village to build houses for visitors. She also guides her fellow villagers in selling their specialty agricultural produce and publicizing the village's idyllic scenery. In doing so, she has improved not only her own life but also that of everyone in the village.

You might think that Guihua is an isolated case, but the reality is that 87 percent of China's population have not received higher education and thus, for the most part, have to seek employment and opportunities in their hometowns. How can Kuaishou help them in seeking these things? When Kuaishou provides them with attention, they will be able to find their own solutions and improve their lives. At first, Guihua only improved her own life, but she slowly began to provide for her family and is now able to lead the development of tourism in her hometown. The solution that she implemented is based on her interaction with her Kuaishou fans, and it has brought her to where she is today.

By showering attention onto more people using inclusive methods, we can help these people to find individualized, focused, and efficient solutions that suit them best. Zhou Tiansong, a tour guide in Zhangjiajie, is one such example.

My own hometown is in the southwestern corner of Tianmen Mountain, near Zhangjiajie. Zhou Tiansong has a very enthusiastic personality. He has filmed videos that introduce the natural scenery of Zhangjiajie—snowy winter views, frosted trees, and early morning mists—and posted them on Kuaishou. Many people like his videos very much and he has thus gained numerous fans.

Because of his popularity, he started his own company that now hires dozens of employees. Although he counts among the 87 percent, he has found his way in life by combining Kuaishou with the local scenery and resources.

By making the allocation of attention more inclusive, we are able to help more people to start their own businesses. Kuaishou's principle of inclusivity has created more opportunities, albeit it was not Kuaishou that chose Zhou Tiansong to do what he did—instead, he seized this opportunity himself.

Xiaoyuan is a woman from Fengyang County, Anhui Province, who sings among the outdoor street food vendors in Hefei City. I have followed her on Kuaishou for nearly four years and witnessed her gradual changes over time. Early on her fans would ask her things like: "Xiaoyuan, what is your ambition?" Her answer was simple: "My ambition is to sing 10 songs today and earn about 200 to 300 yuan to support myself." Last year, I asked her the same question. This time she said, "I would like to buy an apartment for my mom." In three years, her ambition had changed from feeding herself to showing filial piety to her mother.

Xiaoyuan's greatest change over the past four years is in her self-confidence, which writes itself on her face, in her words, and in her behaviors. Where did this self-confidence come from? We can see it on Kuaishou. For example, her fans might casually mention to her: "Xiaoyuan, your eyebrows look like caterpillars today," and the next day she would make up her eyebrows better. Or they might say: "Xiaoyuan, you look slim in this dress," and she would thus learn what kinds of clothes are most flattering for her. Through such interactions, she kept improving herself little by little and became more and more confident. Women who sing among roadside restaurants often have very difficult familial circumstances, but for Xiaoyuan, Kuaishou fan interactions have been like a loving big sister that have helped her to shape a better idea of herself.

Positive and caring attention can make a person more confident. When we give our positive attention to more people, we can help them to improve continually in their interactions with others. Of course, such personal changes are not defined by Kuaishou. What we provide is a medium through which people can interact with one another and find out how they can change themselves. There are tens of thousands of women just like Xiaoyuan who would benefit from the attention Kuaishou is able to provide.

There are also many people with impressive academic credentials on Kuaishou—undergraduates and postdocs from top local universities, as well as graduates and teachers from top foreign universities—but they are not representative of the majority. Instead, it is those stories I have shared that are relevant to the majority of people in China today and that serve as representative examples from which society can draw lessons.

V. INCREASING EVERY PERSON'S UNIQUE SENSE OF HAPPINESS

I have put forward a mission for the Kuaishou team, and that is to increase every person's unique sense of happiness. Why do I say unique? This is because I believe every person has different sources of happiness. Put it another way: People have different pain points and reasons for their emotional problems. For some people, this is due to loneliness or poverty, while others long to be understood. So, how can Kuaishou accomplish this mission given these differences?

The underlying logic of a sense of happiness is the allocation of resources. However, in its allocation of resources, society is prone to the *Matthew effect*, that is, the people at the top are few but obtain abundant resources, while the people at the bottom are many but obtain scarce resources. As the Bible says, "For whosoever hath, to him shall be given, and he shall have abundance: but whosoever hath not, from him shall be taken away even that which he hath." Lao Tzu (an ancient Chinese philosopher, writer, and the founder of Taoism) put it a different way: "The way of nature is to take from the surplus to supplement the deficit. But the way of Man is to take from the deficit to supplement the surplus."

What Kuaishou seeks is to establish greater fairness in the allocation of resources by slightly reducing what the people at the top get and slightly increasing what the people at the bottom get. However, the cost of doing so is a decrease in overall efficiency. Figuring out how to prevent or minimize efficiency loss is also a test of our technical and executive abilities.

While allocating resources, we should try our best to preserve freedom. In essence, after we have established agreements and rules that are easy to understand and fair, we should minimize further changes and prevent others from meddling with the allocation of resources. If we feel that there is a problem, we should discuss it before making amendments, rather than intervene in a totalitarian way. I feel that the key source of happiness lies in prioritizing freedom and equality when allocating resources, provided that the efficiency or its loss is acceptable.

VI. WHERE DOES MY HAPPINESS COME FROM?

Let's return to the topic on my sense of happiness. As I mentioned previously, I have chosen altruism as my way of seeking happiness. I have found that the best form of altruism is to be able to help everyone in society and to find the greatest common denominators for increasing every person's sense of happiness. I believe that the allocation of attention is one of the methods for increasing happiness on a large scale.

Different factors affect people's sense of happiness in different societies and at different stages of economic development. The allocation of attention is one of the factors we have found today, and we will continue to look for other factors—this is how I define the source of my own sense of happiness.

Some people might ask me whether, as the Co-founder of Kuaishou, I am the person who knows the greatest number of internet celebrities. My answer is most simple: On the contrary, I am one of those who know the least number of internet celebrities, and I have never met in real life any of the internet celebrities I follow. This is because I am worried that, as the person who controls the resources and who formulated the rules of resource allocation, people would come and find me out of their own selfish interests, hoping that I can use my power to skew resources in their favor and subvert the system.

When a person first wields power, they tend to feel really great and enjoy the pleasure it brings. The plot in *The Lord of the Rings* comes to mind: When one first wears the Ring, one becomes very powerful and is able to manipulate many people and things. However, as time goes on, all of one's actions become defined by power—in reality, it is the Ring and the power it brings that manipulates and controls the wearer. This is what I am most afraid of, and so to prevent this from happening, I have set up a lot of mechanisms and put in place a lot of "firewalls."

I hope above all that the people of China can do more things together to make society better and people happier. We are living in a particularly interesting era today. The internet is able to transcend the limitations of distance so as to connect people faster and more conveniently than before. In China we have capabilities such as large-scale computing, AI, and machine learning, which many other countries do not have. What we should do is to tap into these capabilities so as to help those who do not possess the same capabilities and resources to improve in this era of rapid change.

This is the efficiency increase and the progress brought about by scientific and technological advancement. Returning the benefits of increased efficiency back to my fellow citizens is something I have always thought about, and I hope we can continue exploring and working on it in the future.

UNVEILING THE MYSTERY OF KUAISHOU

—ZHANG FEI
Associate at Morningside Venture Capital

THE LOGIC OF INVESTING IN KUAISHOU

I n 2011, we decided to focus only on projects related to *feeds* (data that automatically provides users with updated content) and began to systematically study all projects related to mobile social networking and mobile videos. It was based on this logic that we discovered Kuaishou.

In reality, the evolution of every generation of the internet is caused by tremendous changes to the internet ecosystem. (The term *internet ecosystem* implies that the organizations and communities overseeing the development and operation of the technologies and infrastructure of the global internet are guiding the progress and implementation of these internet technologies.) And each time the ecosystem is changed, many opportunities that you can choose from would be created. But if you pay attention to the things at the very source, you will discover that two factors—network structure and content—drive the ecosystem of the entire internet.

Factor One: Network Structure

There are fundamental differences in network structure between the PC web page era and the mobile internet era.

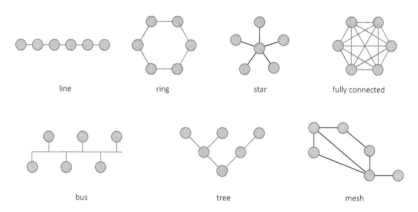

Figure 0.1. Basic Network Topologies (*iResearch*)

During the PC web page era, web pages served as the basic *nodes* (connection points for data transmission on a communications network) that were static and could not be privately owned. Therefore, as a typical tree index, search engines became a very powerful structure. Search engines such as Baidu and Google would recommend websites to users according to content relevance and link weight. The basic network topologies are shown in Figure 0.1.

Instead, during the mobile internet era, people have become the basic nodes through their mobile phones. The network structure is driven by semi-closed apps, and the node links have become more complex than before. Furthermore, the extent of network decentralization is very high. As a result, search engines have lost their core position in the mobile era.

Factor Two: Content

Content that cannot flow has very little value, just as a book placed in a quiet and desolate valley has no commercial value. During the PC internet era, the costs of content distribution and acquisition were very high. Back then, users had to enter accurate keywords and open many web pages on a search engine in order to acquire content that they were interested in.

The emergence of Really Simple Syndication (RSS) feeds in 2004 brought about great changes to content distribution, causing content delivery to shift from pull to push. Feeds can be pushed to users based on their personal characteristics and needs in an accurate and timely fashion, thereby greatly improving the user experience.

The value of water is reflected in the ecosystems that are only made possible by its flow. Just like water, internet content also needs to flow. Because feeds expedite the flow of content effectively, they form the very core of the entire internet ecosystem.

At the same time, social networks are a very good match with feeds. Facebook is a highly typical example. It started off as a way to help students increase their connections with other students on campus and distribute content, but has now become a way to help everyone on Earth increase their connections and distribute content. Today, Facebook has nearly two billion monthly active users and 1.3 billion daily active users; it has evolved into a very complex network structure. Ultimately, social network projects are all about building a network structure, which determines the path and efficiency of content distribution. Whether the links are one-to-one, one-to-many, or many-to-many, they are all for distributing content.

In social networks, content serves as a key element and also as the basic unit of distribution. It can take diverse forms, such as text, pictures, songs, videos, and, possibly, virtual reality in the future. As a new type of content carrier, videos are more intuitive in expression compared to text. Furthermore, thanks to the ever-decreasing costs and barriers to entry of video production, as well as the higher effectiveness of video distribution brought about through integration with feeds, video content will certainly see explosive growth in due course.

I have always been very interested in video and have invested in many related enterprises, such as PPS.tv (a Chinese streaming video platform) and Xunlei Limited (a Chinese multinational technology company in shared computing and blockchain technology) during the early stages. In 2004, I also invested in a company that did mobile livestreaming. Although the team had strong technical capabilities, they ultimately did not succeed. During that phase, there were already apps that were very well done, but the environment had not developed sufficiently.

It was only in 2011 that we could sense that "everything is ready." By then, Facebook and Weibo had developed considerably, while feeds had become relatively mainstream, closely integrated with mobile phones, and capable of achieving excellent communication effects. (The five types of apps with the highest growth rate in time used by mobile internet users worldwide in 2012 are shown in Figure 0.2.)

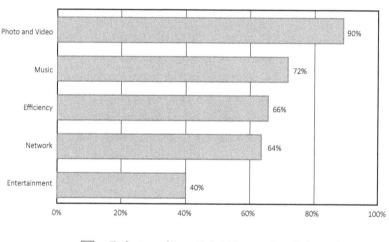

The five types of Apps with the highest growth rate in time used by mobile internet users worldwide in 2012 (%)

Figure 0.2.

In conclusion, it is only by changing the network structure and content in the new internet ecosystem that one can rise to the top in a certain domain.

Since 2011, we have been looking for such opportunities. Mobile social networks and videos, which are closely related to feeds, thus became our direction of aim. Kuaishou, Miaopai, and other companies I have invested in are all looking to seize the opportunities created by structural and content changes in the internet ecosystem in specific domains.

OUR FIRST MEETING WITH KUAISHOU

I had actually invested in Miaopai first. At that time, Han Kun (founder and CEO of Yixia Technology) was still at Ku6 Media. I convinced him to quit his job and start a business together, and then brought in Lei Liang and Zhang Hongyu from PPS.tv to serve as Han Kun's "angels" together with me. Later on, my colleague Elwin (an associate at Morningside Venture Capital) recommended Kuaishou to me. At that time, Kuaishou was still a GIF tool called GIF Kuaishou—it was only in November 2014 that it was renamed as Kuaishou.

Making a GIF animation tool at that time was rather difficult. It not only had to take up as little RAM as possible, but also had to be easy to learn and use. However, Cheng Yixiao (the founder of Kuaishou Technology) created a very simple tool that could be used by anyone with a little bit of creativity. As a result, interesting animations quickly became popular on Weibo. This is why the earliest users of Kuaishou can be aptly referred to as a group of creative animation enthusiasts.

Although Kuaishou's initial products were in the form of GIFs, they were derived from the same origin as videos; after all, pictures serve as the individual frames of GIFs and videos alike. However, Kuaishou and Miaopai differed in their starting points. As investors, we might know the general direction of the companies we invest in, but we are absolutely unable to assess what the starting point for a company should be.

Initially, I felt that Kuaishou's GIF-based starting point was pretty good, but after investing in them, I began to feel that they might as well have focused on videos from the onset. However, the companies that focused on video at that time were clueless. Han Kun's experience working on the app called Yixia Video was very painful at first—nobody used it or knew what videos to take.

When I first met Cheng Yixiao, Kuaishou was still a one-man software project. Later on, we helped him to set up a company and invested 2 million yuan for a 20 percent stake in the company. I prefer one-man software projects because most of the people who work on them are innate product managers—they will never stop thinking about and working on the things they do out of passion.

When we visited the United States for an exchange, we discovered that investors there followed the same logic as us—they preferred to invest in founders who had the traits of product managers. We also learned that the social networking products that make it big are usually created by first-time entrepreneurs.

People can generally be divided into two types. The first type is extroverted and socially competent people—they have no need to look for ways to express their emotions in the virtual world. The second type is people who are weak at communicating and expressing themselves in the real world—they have a strong motivation to express themselves in the virtual world. If the virtual world provides them with their only channel of communication, then they are likely to have a better understanding of how to express themselves in it as compared to other people.

Yixiao belongs to the second type. This type of people have a natural advantage when working on social networking products. In my view, Yixiao is an outstanding product manager who has a very unique understanding of many things.

My deepest impression of him was his insistence on not having a reposting feature on Kuaishou. At that time, Weibo's reposting feature was very popular and could be copied easily, but Kuaishou did not implement something similar. Yixiao's product thinking was to make sure that every piece of content published by a user was given maximum visibility. This was a logic that was based on equality.

If Kuashou enabled a reposting feature, the *head effect* (a phenomenon whereby the top posts get even more attention, similar to the idea that the rich get richer) would manifest, making it impossible to allow every person to be fairly seen. Besides, it is precisely because there is no reposting feature that users have to produce their own content and are encouraged to share their true lives. The value of user equality has played a very important role in Kuaishou's development.

THE BOTTLENECK IN KUAISHOU'S DEVELOPMENT

In 2013 there were three main categories of content on Kuaishou: beautiful women (selfie videos), children, and pets. That worked for a while, but users soon grew bored of such content. On top of that, the company had problems in management and team building then, and so it faced a series of bottlenecks in development after it had developed for some time.

First Bottleneck: Transition

GIF Kuaishou was an animation tool that allowed content dissemination only on Weibo. At the first board meeting after Morningside had invested in Kuaishou, we suggested to Yixiao to build an online community with its own traffic and user interaction. However, as if developing the tool was not exhausting enough, monetizing it also came with great challenges.

Things were difficult at first. After all, the process of cutting off the huge source of traffic that was Weibo—and then slowly reattracting traffic—was a very painful one. However, we knew that it would be even more painful to make the transition after the tool had reached a critical mass. User cognition is very difficult to change, and so the earlier the transition is made, the easier it will be. It did not take long for Yixiao to understand this; by November 2012 or thereabouts, the company began to transition its product to its own online community.

Second Bottleneck: Financing

Yixiao's attempts at transitioning were not quite successful at first, and the product's daily active users also stagnated. By then, the money from our first investment was also running out, and so the board meetings around that time were a painful affair.

I suggested to Yixiao to get more resources, including employees and money, but these were not easy for him to get. Investors did not have much confidence in him—he had met a bunch of investors and practically all of them ended up rejecting him.

Aside from being stood up by old-hand investors, we also met an investor who had wanted to invest in another project of mine, but because that project was nearly over, she asked me whether I had other projects worth investing in. I introduced Kuaishou to her, but after looking at it, she complained that I was always recommending bad projects to her.

Once, when the circumstances became really difficult, Yixiao even talked to Han Kun about selling Kuaishou to Yixia Technology. However, Han Kun was not interested then. Later on, when Su Hua joined Kuaishou, Morningside pumped in more investment to help Kuaishou pull through its difficulties.

Third Bottleneck: The Team

After analyzing Kuaishou's existing state of affairs, I suggested to Yixiao to look for a CEO who could complement him. Having gone from a one-man software project to a company, Yixiao might be a good product manager, but just like most product managers, managing and leading a team "to war" is very challenging for him. Therefore, being the CEO would be tough and unpleasant for him.

When Yixiao agreed to look for a CEO, I spent more than half a year interviewing many candidates, but most of them felt we were not reliable enough after talking to us.

I remember that we spent a lot of time negotiating with a woman who was doing well in the video field, but after we had worked everything out, she changed her mind at the last minute. Experiences like this were extremely agonizing for Yixiao and me; he was not very good at promoting himself or his company.

Later on, I got to know Su Hua through Zhang Dong (formerly an architect at Baidu's Phoenix Nest). At that time, he was working on a social e-commerce project called Quanquan. Su Hua is someone with extraordinary qualities. He had done research on the application of machine learning in search at Google China and was then invited by Li Yanhong to take charge of building the Phoenix Nest system. What was even more unique about him was that he also had several entrepreneurial experiences. His resumé proved that he was highly capable and ambitious. You could tell that he was someone with tremendous energy, passion, and the capability to do something great, albeit his path had not been smooth or successful up to that point.

Although I did not think highly of Quanquan, I regarded Su Hua highly as a person and so I was willing to invest some money to support him. Even if Quanquan failed, he could always try a new direction. However, Su Hua had money from the sale of his previous company, so he had no need for my financing. Three months later, he closed Quanquan and came to Shanghai at my invitation. I set aside a day to listen to him talk about more than 20 possible directions he thought he could go in, but I found none of them practical enough. At that point I suggested that he could consider joining Kuaishou.

Su Hua and Yixiao are a very good match; the former is talented in the technical and algorithm-driven side of things but badly needed a direction, while the latter is great at product design but badly needed the right person to complement him. I thus arranged for them to meet. After talking to each other a few times, they somehow clicked.

When reminiscing about that period of time with Su Hua one day, I asked him why he was able to understand Yixiao and Kuaishou back then. We came up with a conclusion: When things are going smoothly for a person, it is very difficult for him to perform deep introspection and understand himself deeply. Earlier on in his life, Su Hua had experienced many difficulties. This caused his mentality to change greatly—he became aware of his limitations and also the need for good workmates and partners.

Yixiao and I knew that Su Hua was talented and ambitious. It is usually very difficult to attract such a person to join a startup halfway, and so we had to make him an offer he could not refuse. At that time, Morningside held a 20 percent stake in Kuaishou, while Yixiao and two other people held the remaining 80 percent. Both of these parties offered up half of their stake to attract new teams to join. This amounted to a combined stake of 50 percent, of which the lion's share went to Su Hua and his team. I also proposed that Su Hua take on the role of CEO and run the company, while Yixiao would remain in charge of products.

Making these decisions was actually very difficult for us at that time. After all, it was uncertain whether Su Hua could really lead the company onto a new path, yet we would lose half of our stake immediately. This was particularly difficult for Yixiao, whose team lost a large part of their stake after setting up the option pool. However, I did not have to spend much time convincing him. As a person of great wisdom, he understood what he wanted and what was most important and knew how to make the necessary trade-offs. Su Hua, too, accepted our offer very quickly.

We wanted Su Hua to join us for two reasons: First, we hoped that he could recruit better personnel for Kuaishou, and second, we needed his engineering capabilities to strengthen Kuaishou's back end. We firmly believed in these two points. In actual fact, I had asked the opinions of many industry insiders at that time, and they were unimpressed by Su Hua's joining. Eventually, however, Su Hua surprised us all.

So, when you understand what we had gone through, you would realize that every startup that survives can be considered a miracle.

KUAISHOU'S EXPLOSIVE GROWTH

It took only six months for the cooperation between Su Hua and Yixiao to smooth out. Su Hua wasted little time in raising Kuaishou's engineering capabilities to very high standards, and also improved the performance stability and architecture of the system greatly.

At the same time, Su Hua applied a recommendation algorithm to content distribution, causing the user experience to improve immediately. This was possible thanks to his experience in the field of AI, which he gained as part of the team that built Baidu's business search engine Phoenix Nest. His methodology at that time was identical to Toutiao's (a Chinese news and information content platform) methodology today. However, Kuaishou started using algorithms earlier than Toutiao, and is also better at using them than the latter.

Shortly after their cooperation began, Kuaishou's users increased by more than 10 times, reaching over one million daily active users. This would later increase by another 100 times or more; the end result exceeded all of our imaginations.

The decision to apply a recommendation algorithm to content distribution was also a hunch. It was only after we had given it a try that we realized that this method was indeed very effective. At that time, the application of feeds remained on a fixed schedule; content was distributed in chronological order. To our surprise, Su Hua's combining of algorithms and user interests was able to improve the user experience greatly and achieve amazing distribution results. Looking at it from another perspective, this was also in line with our values—outstanding people are always able to find a better way to solve problems.

The explosive growth of Kuaishou is also owed to its satisfaction of its users' desire to create and share their own content. Leaving complex concepts aside, just think about human nature for a second—regardless of age, everyone has a need to express themselves and be recognized by others.

Kuaishou satisfies the need of young people to express themselves and expand their social circles. In 2013, we found that many young people liked to use Kuaishou—primary school students, secondary school students, and university students were all using it. In particular, secondary school students were the most fervent users. The world of young people is a vast grassland that they are seeking to expand; if your platform enables them to expand their world, it will certainly be very popular among them. While they have several creative and amusing forms of entertainment, such as somersaulting and finger dancing, they lack a platform that enables them to create and disseminate content easily and quickly.

Although Weibo is the stomping ground of celebrities and social media influencers, it is fairly disconnected from the actual lives of ordinary people. Thus, it is very difficult for ordinary people to form new horizontal relations on there. Qzone (another social networking website in China) is for connecting with people one is already familiar with, and it thus fails to satisfy people's needs to expand their social circles. Instead, Kuaishou not only makes it easier to film videos, but also allows user-created content to be seen and liked by more people. Moreover, it allows users to get to know more people with the same interests—for young people, this is a very powerful incentive.

The ability to meet new groups of people and form new relations on Kuaishou is what separates it from other platforms. In all new fields, the key to success is to gain the support of young users. This is because older people are prone to being fettered by old things. For practically all new applications, the breakthrough is driven by young people—and it is these new applications that represent greater efficiency and fuller self-expression.

There is another important reason why we did not give up on Kuaishou when it ran into bottlenecks initially: We discovered that users truly liked our product. A single video could garner thousands of comments, which was no mean feat for a new platform.

Online communities at that time did not have as many flamers as there are now. Among the comments, many were sincere words of praise and encouragement. Being respected by others is classified as the fourth level of Maslow's hierarchy of needs and is also a highly addictive need. For example, if a creator is accepted and respected by many people on Kuaishou, it would be unlikely for them to jump ship to a different platform. The growth of Kuaishou has all along been spurred by such a positive atmosphere in the community.

THE LOGIC BEHIND THE RISE OF KUAISHOU

We live in a very absurd world. As a popular song goes, "some people are on a diet while some are dying from hunger." In China, only a small minority of people live in prosperous first-tier cities, whereas the majority live in impoverished places.

In my opinion, Kuaishou is a very neutral platform. Many people find it fresh, surprising, or hard to accept. I think that this is a normal state of affairs. To put it in a different way, our world has become severely fragmented. The most special thing about the internet is that it grants you the ability and opportunity to see people who are completely different from you.

I follow a lot of people on Kuaishou. There are many people in China who dropped out of school because of poverty. On Kuaishou, there are many videos regarding children from poor families; they document the lives of left-behind children in China. Because I have met some of these children in real life, I can verify that their portrayal in most of these videos is very true.

Many left-behind children in China live in an environment where they are neglected by their parents and society. However, Kuaishou has given them a happy platform on which they can show themselves. This is actually a very respectable thing, as ordinary people are able to obtain emotional support and even some material incentives on Kuaishou.

Many people live in a relatively enclosed space and do not understand the world beyond their horizons. "Xiaowei the brick-mover" is a very typical example. I once showed the video of Xiaowei the brick-mover to a schoolmate at China Europe International Business School in Shanghai. She was dumbfounded by what she saw and could not understand how he had such a good physique. I told her in reply that it was actually not impossible for a brick-mover to build such a good physique.

Why was such a large group of people given no attention on the internet for so long? The main reason is that the network structure was not good enough. It was dominated by the elites because the costs of using it were very high; building a web page required capital, technical skills, and publicity. Today, the network structure of the mobile internet is highly optimized; everyone has the ability to spread their content, while the barriers to entry for content creation are low or practically null.

The reason why Kuaishou can penetrate into third- and fourth-tier cities is not as remarkable as many have said. The underlying reason is technological upgrade, which is the outcome of technological progress. Technology offers everyone the opportunity to express themselves. Thanks to Kuaishou's recommendation algorithm, everyone can distribute their own content in an equal playing field, while outstanding creators are more likely to be followed.

These people used to be out of sight, out of mind. For example, Zhao Benshan (a Chinese skit and sitcom actor) was unknown before his appearance in the Spring Festival Gala, which showcased his qualities and brought him fame. Today, thanks to Kuaishou's excellent algorithm, we are able to provide a stage for each and every ordinary person.

The three tabs on the homepage of the Kuaishou app have changed little over the years. The first tab is Following, the second tab is Discover (previously called Popular), and the third tab is Same City (which displays content created by users from the same city as the current user). The Same City tab provides everyone with an equal entry point. As soon as a piece of content is published, it becomes visible and imitable by users who find it interesting. Technology has given impetus to the creative aspirations of ordinary people, forming a virtuous cycle for content creation.

Many influential videos on Kuaishou are the outcomes of users' "votes." Our algorithm continually pushes content to the user groups who are interested in it. On their part, the pertinent user groups continually create content in these categories, thereby forming hotspots. However, this is not something that is deliberately fostered—the operation of Kuaishou is fundamentally technology-driven.

Although Kuaishou has gone from being a tool to a community to a social network, it is essentially still a network structure. We cannot simply define it as a community or social networking product to restrain its development; like a living organism, it will keep on changing and evolving.

Su Hua hopes to make Kuaishou a product with one billion users. That would require Kuaishou to be sufficiently open and not to set up too many fences for itself. Just like WeChat, Kuaishou must be accepting of all types of people.

In the future, Kuaishou will certainly influence the "elite" groups of people as well. The first step would of course be to change their stereotypes about Kuaishou—after all, diversity is the truth of this world.

––––––––

Zhang Fei is Kuaishou's first investor. He has more than 18 years of venture capital experience, focusing on communications, the internet, and media. This article was written by Li Zhao, founder of *iDoNews*, after his interview with Zhang Fei. It was first published on *iDoNews*.

WHAT IS KUAISHOU?

I n 1990, American futurist Alvin Toffler put forward the term *digital divide*, which refers to the gap between those who own and those who do not own the tools of the information age. The strategies of Broadband China, Internet Plus, Digital China, and even the upcoming "5G strategy"—all of which China is actively pursuing—are important strategic measures for bridging the digital divide.

The "attention gap," as brought up in this book, is an important component of the digital divide. On the internet, attention is a very precious resource—its distribution directly affects many people's sense of gain and happiness. Like many other resources, attention resources have a natural tendency toward the *Matthew effect*, that is, a minority of people get to enjoy the majority of the resources.

From an economic point of view, attention resources are very expensive. Most people are unable to enjoy such resources and thereby cannot express themselves or be taken note of by society. They are thus at a disadvantage.

If the attention gap can be leveled, more ordinary people would be paid attention to, thereby increasing people-to-people connections and bringing out the creativity and imagination of more people. Society would thus be more prosperous and people's sense of happiness would be stronger.

The core purpose of the internet is to connect everything. Coupled with Kuaishou's principle of inclusivity, the advent of the video age and the development of artificial intelligence technologies have made it possible to create more connections at a smaller granularity, enabling people who previously received little attention to receive more attention at the capillary level. Hence, the attention gap is currently being leveled.

CHINA'S LONG-TERM INVESTMENT HAS GIVEN BIRTH TO THE VIDEO AGE

In the past few years, because of China's long-term investment in the field of the internet, the basic conditions in the field of video have matured rapidly, thereby expediting the advent of the video age. Many of these conditions are naturally and uniquely endowed in China.

Today, we can see many interesting videos on Kuaishou, vividly showing the life of ordinary people.

The time-honored way of transporting timber from high mountains on bamboo rafts along the Yalu River used to be little known, but it has now received attention from millions of people.

Being a diver in urban construction sites is not a popular profession, but they are needed for every high-rise building in first- and second-tier cities. When laying the foundation for a high-rise building, it is necessary to dig deep pits with electric drills. When the drill bits drop, these divers have to dive tens of meters into the muddy water to restore the electric drills to their original positions.

A fruit seller who goes by the name "Luola Run" on Kuaishou conducts his livestreams in front of hanging persimmons in Fuping County, Shaanxi Province. There, he invites passersby to taste the persimmons on behalf of several hundred thousand viewers, who can immediately place orders online.

Five or six years back, the public had no access to such content and could not purchase such goods with a single tap on their phones. But in barely a few years, at least four conditions have been met.

The first is the prevalence of smartphones. Nowadays, it costs only 1,000 yuan—or even less than that—to purchase a smartphone with a built-in camera and comprehensive functions.

The second is the prevalence of 4G networks and the affordability of mobile networks. Even in very remote areas, the state has invested a lot of money to build telecommunications infrastructure.

Before the above two conditions were met, the internet could only be accessed through computers with plugged-in network cables, and thus the costs were much higher. Moreover, internet access could not easily move as the user moves about. On the other hand, mobile phones and 4G networks involve no movement costs.

The third is the convenience of payment. With smartphones, paying for things can be done anytime, anywhere.

The fourth is the robustness of the logistics network.

When all of these four conditions were met and could be enjoyed by all citizens, they paved the foundation for the arrival of the video age. Video, as the text of the new era, has its own characteristics as compared to text.

First, video is more authentic and richer in content than words. For example, there are many Chinese idioms for describing beautiful women, such as "one who would make wild geese alight and fish dive down for shame" and "a woman's beauty puts the flowers to shame and outshines the moon." As poetic as they are, they cannot compare to videos in showing and expressing beauty—a picture is worth a thousand words after all.

Second, video recording and viewing have relatively lower barriers to entry, and so all citizens can participate in them. The receptivity of humans to video information is most natural. A two-year-old child might not be able to speak or understand what you say, but he can see and understand the general meaning expressed in a video. While humans require a long period of training in order to learn to write, they can learn to record videos with their mobile phones in barely a few seconds.

Just as words have changed every aspect of society, video will also change everything in society. Such changes are not just simple supplements or increments but radical changes instead.

In the future, if our personal devices evolve from mobile phones to eyeglasses and then to virtual reality (VR) or augmented reality (AR), then imaging products would change the world much more and all existing applications would need to be redesigned.

From this point of view, Kuaishou is not simply a short video company, as many people think it is. Video or short video is not an industry but a new type of information carrier instead. This is much the same as the fact that text is a way of carrying information, but no one regards text as an industry.

AI TECHNOLOGY RUNS DEEP IN KUAISHOU'S VEINS

Phones with built-in cameras have made it convenient for everyone to record videos, causing the number of videos out there to skyrocket. As a result, the precise matching of videos to people has become a core issue.

The core of the matching mechanism involves three aspects: to understand content, to understand people, and to link content and people so that they match. The barriers to entry lie in data because modeling can only be done when there is data on people-content interactions.

The first aspect is to understand content. The technology for understanding text was already very mature 10 years ago. Various forms of text analysis such as word segmentation, part-of-speech tagging, heading extraction, keywords extraction, entity extraction, weighting, and affective analysis are already in use.

In the past 10 years, the academic world has developed a complete set of tools for image analysis, text analysis, and speech content analysis. The scene in any given image can be analyzed to tell whether it was taken in a school or a bar, whether there are any people or animals in it, and whether they are happy. Be it textual or image content, computers can build an understanding of it.

The second aspect is to understand users. First, we need to understand a person's long-term static attributes, which are called user portraits, such as age, gender, height, birthplace, and so on. Second, we need to understand this person's interests and preferences, such as their preferred taste, whether they prefer ball games or running, or whether they prefer to travel or stay at home. Finally, we need to understand their intentions in using an app, such as whether they are looking to purchase an iPhone or a Samsung phone, or whether they are hungry for food.

If we can build a rich understanding of a user at these three levels, we would be able to establish a good match between this person and content. This matching relationship is not established by rules, but instead by a deep learning model that uses data from user-content interactions in a given software. This model only has to do one thing, and that is to predict the matching probability between a new piece of content and a new user. With such predictive power, the matching of content and users would become a very simple problem to solve. Yet, this problem needs to be broken down into those three aspects for people competent in each aspect to solve.

Kuaishou is such a technology company with artificial intelligence (AI) as its core technology. AI technology runs deep in the veins of its products, pervading the entire business process of content production, auditing, distribution, and consumption.

Besides the distribution segment, Kuaishou also widely applies AI technology in the segment of video creation. We hope that everyone can become the director of their own lives—in other words, that they can record their lives and generate high-quality videos by using even the most ordinary of mobile phones.

The application of AI technology in the segment of user video recording and the addition of several virtual elements to real-life images have served to enhance reality, by enabling the virtual world and the real world to interact better with each other and provide people with more novel experiences when recording their lives. Previously, Kuaishou launched a "magical" emoji called the Kuaishou Time Machine—it allowed users to see their own faces growing old within a minute or so. Filming videos of oneself becomes boring over time, and we hoped that users would gain a better sense of how precious time is after seeing themselves growing old.

We also use image-related algorithms to help users rectify problems in video recording, such as blurred videos caused by dirty lenses, dim pictures caused by lighting problems, and color biases.

Behind these fun methods and functions is Kuaishou's cutting-edge development of AI technology, which involves many technical modules such as human pose estimation, gesture recognition, and background segmentation. These are all new experiments by Kuaishou to make recording formats more interesting.

This process involves a challenge—all of these technologies have to be computed and rendered locally and in real time, but Kuaishou has hundreds of millions of users whose mobile phone models vary greatly. Therefore, our algorithm must be able to run smoothly on all models, which demands very high AI capabilities and consumes a lot of computing resources. In order to solve this problem, Kuaishou independently developed the YCNN deep reasoning and learning engine, which solves the issue of AI technology operation being limited by the computing capability of user equipment.

We have also done a lot of work as far as audio is concerned. For example, in the past, professionals felt that subtitle editing was a very tedious task. However, thanks to speech recognition technology today, we can help video producers to automatically add and edit subtitles, and also to display subtitles in various forms. With the help of AI technology, we have greatly reduced the cost of generating subtitles.

Music plays a very important role in short video scenes. According to statistics, 60 to 80 percent of Kuaishou videos use background music to set the atmosphere. It is actually not easy to choose the right music to express one's mood. Asking users to keep their movements in line with the rhythm of the music is very demanding on them; besides, very few people actually possess a strong sense of music.

In order to reduce the barriers to entry for users to select music when creating videos, we have developed the technologies of intelligent dubbing and AI music generation. Intelligent dubbing can recommend suitable background music for users according to their video frames and user portraits. As for AI music generation, it can perceive the human actions in video frames through AI analysis algorithms, and then match the generated musical rhythm with these human actions. This greatly reduces the barriers to entry for users to select music when creating videos, thereby increasing people's willingness to create their own videos.

THE APPLICATION OF THE PRINCIPLE OF INCLUSIVITY IN OUR ALGORITHMS

Kuaishou is in service of the recording and sharing of ordinary people. Equality and inclusiveness are our core values; we believe that everyone deserves to be recorded. Be it famous celebrities or ordinary city and village dwellers, everyone has equal rights to share and to be paid attention to. Kuaishou does not provide special treatment and publicity to celebrities and does not tilt traffic in favor of anyone.

We protect every ordinary video producer and give every video a chance to be distributed. This is a fair starting point; regardless of whether you have a million fans, 10,000 fans, or 1,000 fans, there is a possibility for your video to become instantly popular.

By protecting ordinary video producers, we have brought about a diversity of filmed content. After all, when the number of video producers increases, the diversity of content naturally becomes richer.

We have matched the diversity of viewing needs with the diversity of filmed content. Because the video recorders have filmed many fresh and interesting things for people to see, and because viewers have seen a lot of content that they usually do not see, we eventually returned to the most basic values of fairness and inclusivity.

Today, the total number of videos on Kuaishou exceeds 10 billion, almost all of which are non-repetitive life records. This is unprecedented in history, but at the same time, it poses a huge challenge in terms of figuring out how to match these 10 billion videos with viewers.

In the past, a common practice in the industry was to simply focus on the popular videos at the head of the distribution curve. However, Kuaishou hopes that the videos at the long tail of the distribution curve can similarly be seen by those who are interested, thereby truly enabling everyone to receive attention.

In terms of video distribution, we do not want the videos at the head of the distribution curve to take up too much exposure. Therefore, we use the Gini coefficient to control the rich-poor gulf among users on the platform.

CROSSING THE ATTENTION GAP

Kuaishou's efforts in leveling the attention gap reflects its principle of inclusivity. These might seem like nothing more than abstract words, but in reality, there have been many inclusive technologies in history that have leveled all kinds of gaps.

This is also the logic behind technological and economic evolution: When a certain product is expensive at first, only a few people are eligible to enjoy it, whereas most people cannot afford it. But thanks to a certain kind of technological improvement, its price will fall, thereby allowing the average person to enjoy it as well. As a result, people become more equal in a certain regard, while their lives improve and the whole of society becomes more advanced.

Once upon a time, the price of text was very high. Only a few people could write and read. In medieval Europe, most of those who could write and read were monks. The invention of printing greatly increased the literate population and allowed the free exchange and production of ideas. At that time, this was an extremely important technology of inclusivity.

Due to the lack of preservation technology, pepper was expensive in medieval Europe and only a few rich people could afford it. But after Portuguese navigators discovered the route to India during the great voyage period, large amounts of peppers from Southeast Asia began to be transported to Europe by sea. This caused the price of pepper to fall, and soon pepper became a condiment available to every household.

Prior to the 19th century, pigments were expensive and so most Europeans wore black clothes. In 1856, an 18-year-old chemist called William Perkin synthesized an aniline violet dye. As pigments became cheaper, every piece of clothing could be made in different colors and every house could be painted in different colors, and thus, the world became a more colorful place than before.

Motorcycles and cars are also tools of inclusivity. In the past, only a few people could afford these vehicles, but these days ordinary people can afford them, too. For people who live in mountainous areas, motorcycles are indispensable tools of life and production.

Postal offices, telephones, and mobile phones are all important technologies of inclusivity—they enable ordinary people to write and send letters and to express themselves.

Kuaishou is an extension on this basis and a tool for everyone to record and share their life. It uses AI technology to match content and users accurately so that everyone has the chance to showcase their life. What it achieves is actually to reduce the cost of attention, to cross the attention gap, and to provide everyone with the ability to express themselves.

THE SEEN WORLD IS WONDERFUL

If the information channel is not thick enough and attention is expensive, then self-expressions would need to be prioritized and, as a result, not every life can be seen. Lives are naturally differentiated and discriminated—excellent lives are deemed worthy of being seen, whereas "mediocre" lives are deemed unworthy of being recorded and shared.

Handy Geng's creations are considered useless, while Uncle Benliang's singing skills are unprofessional. Were they judged by the original standards, they would find it difficult to be seen.

Kuaishou allows every life to express itself, to be seen, and to be appreciated. Every being is unique, and life is no longer discriminated. This is a reflection of a more genuine world and a realm in which "every flower is a world of its own." On this basis, because people can see one another, several communities have formed on the platform.

There are 30 million truck drivers in China. They spend all year long on the roads, have little time with their families, and might even run into road bandits and robbers. They have their own joys and pains, just like everyone else, but are seldom noticed and often find it difficult to communicate with others. This also goes for the urban drivers who transport the bodies of deceased people to and from funeral parlors, and ship crew members who spend most of the year braving the world's oceans.

On Kuaishou one day, when a truck driver inadvertently filmed his life and the scenes in the cab of his rig, it was seen by another truck driver, causing the two of them to find resonance and gain self-confidence through seeing each other's joys, pains, and pressures. This is the formative process and the power of a community.

Perhaps, many videos are of little worth to outsiders, but they are an inseparable part of the filmer's own life. Such social functions can partly be brought about via an artist's creations, but the creativity of an artist is ultimately limited. Instead, communities enable many people to acquire new knowledge, to gain recognition, to support one another, and to improve their sense of happiness.

When we enter different variables into the formula of being seen, we can derive still different answers.

When the talents of every person could be seen, what we got was the Kuaishou education ecosystem. For example, Lan Ruiyuan lives in an ordinary city in Jiangxi Province and only attended school up to technical secondary school, yet she can teach users all over China how to use Excel properly, earning more than 400,000 yuan a year for herself in the process.

When every good commodity could be seen, what we got was Kuaishou e-commerce. For example, when videotaping kiwifruit, Luola Run discovered a business opportunity and has since established his own brand called "Junshan Agriculture."

When intangible cultural heritage could be seen, what we got was a Kuaishou showcase of intangible cultural heritage that nobody paid attention to originally.

When a poverty-stricken village could be seen, the beautiful scenery that cannot be found in cities suddenly unfolded in front of all Chinese people. The village thus gained visitors and saw an increase in the incomes of the local people, providing the work of poverty alleviation with a natural foothold.

Such examples are endlessly emerging in large numbers.

Everyone has a longing in their heart for their living conditions, emotions, and inspirations to be seen and understood by more people. By recording these things through short videos, people are able to connect with others and the world. Building such connections is a very meaningful task indeed.

KUAISHOU'S MILESTONES

2011

- "GIF Kuaishou" was launched for users to create and share animated images known as GIFs, in essence the earliest form of short videos.

2012

- Kuaishou became the first mover in China's short video industry that enabled users to create, upload and view short videos on mobile devices.

2013

- Kuaishou launched the short video social platform.

2016

- Kuaishou launched a livestreaming function as the natural extension to our platform.

2017

- Kuaishou Flagship became the world's largest single livestreaming platform in terms of revenue generated from virtual gifting in the 4th quarter of 2017.

2018

- Kuaishou Flagship's average DAUs (daily active users) exceeded 100 million in January 2018.

- Kuaishou commenced its e-commerce business.

2019

- Kuaishou Express was launched in August 2019.

- Kuaishou became the world's second largest livestreaming e-commerce platform in terms of GMV.

2020

- The average DAUs of Kuaishou's apps and mini programs in China exceeded 302 million in the first half-year of 2020.

- Kuaishou Express's average DAUs exceeded 100 million in August 2020.

2021

- Kuaishou listed on the Main Board of The Stock Exchange of Hong Kong Limited on February 5, 2021, stock code 1024.HK.

CHAPTER ONE

ENABLING EVERY LIFE
TO BE SEEN

CHAPTER OVERVIEW

Kuaishou allows every life to express itself, to be seen, and to be appreciated. Every existence is unique and every life should be treated equally. Thus, Kuaishou is a reflection of a more genuine world, and a realm in which "every flower is a world of its own."

Being is perfection.

But if the information channel is narrow and attention is expensive, then self-expression would have to be discriminated and prioritized, and the outcome would be that not every life can be seen. If a life is deemed to be "not perfect enough," it would not have the "right" to be widely shared and disseminated.

Kuaishou is purely a video community. Our principle of inclusivity encourages everyone to freely record their lives. As long as a video does not violate law and public decency, Kuaishou treats it equally and provides it with traffic. Thanks to Kuaishou, the ideal of nationwide recording and sharing has been realized for the first time. Connections on Kuaishou have led to the creation of a large number of communities that transmit love and improve every person's unique sense of happiness.

SUCCESS STORIES

Handy Geng: The Imaginative and World-Famous "Thomas Edison of Waste Materials"

Professor David from Oxford: An Expert Who Reminds Us of Santa Claus Shows You How to Perform Experiments

Farmer -Turned-Airplane-Maker Mr. Zhu: I'm Not Edison, but I Love Invention, Too

Mr. Bao the Truck Driver: I Filmed My Journeys on the Road and Unexpectedly Entered the Spotlight

ENABLING EVERY LIFE TO BE SEEN

He Huafeng, president of The Kuaishou Research Institute

It took us a few rounds of discussion before deciding on this motto. Why not phrase it as "Seeing Every Life" or something that rolls off the tongue? Why "every life" and not "every kind of life"?

In the end, we still settled on this slightly tongue-twisting version. The idea it conveys is that every person can record and share their own unique lives and be followed by others, thereby achieving the goals of self-expression and attention. Kuaishou enables these goals to be achieved by providing the technical tools for recording and sharing videos and upholding the principle of inclusivity.

It is on the aforementioned basis that seeing every life becomes possible.

As for "every" versus "every kind," it was not about being pedantic. "Every" is smaller in granularity than "every kind." In Kuaishou's communities, everyone can show every aspect of their unique life, and so "every" is more accurate.

Part 1

I used to work for newspapers and magazines. Because periodicals have limited page space, journalists have to compete for space whenever they want to publish an article. Rejection of journalistic works that are deemed not good enough is common; only articles that meet the requirements are published.

To look at this from a different perspective, this happens because the information channel is not wide enough, causing attention to become more expensive. As a result, only a small proportion of people in society can receive attention.

Television is another type of information channel. Because there are a limited number of television channels, reporters also have to compete for airtime. However, video offers greater space than text. Some news cannot be conveniently transmitted over newspapers and magazines but can be transmitted over television.

On September 26, 1960, the United States held the first televised presidential debate in history. Thanks in part to the influence of television, John F. Kennedy was unexpectedly elected as president.

In the run-up to the election, Richard Nixon was considered more politically experienced and would probably have won had newspapers remained as the only information channel. However, when television became mainstream, the vigor displayed by the candidates began to play a part in deciding the election. If a haggard-looking Nixon and a spirited Kennedy appeared on screen at the same time, who would you support?

Television can also showcase the brilliance of dialects. During the 80s and 90s, the Spring Festival Gala featured many skits that produced humor through dialects. This created a new phenomenon of dialect programs that could not be reproduced in text.

When internet blogging became popular in the mid-aughts, the monopoly on mass communication held by professional journalists was broken. Ordinary people could write blogs to express their ideas and showcase their personalities—content production began to flourish.

When Weibo (which had a 140-character limit just like Twitter) emerged in 2009, the barriers to entry for recording and sharing content were lowered even further. With it, even people who were not good at writing long articles could become content creators.

WeChat came into being in 2011, and in May that year, WeChat 2.0 introduced voice messages, allowing people to express themselves without having to type. Self-expression thus entered an era of natural interaction. Subsequently, WeChat introduced video features—particularly the video call feature—that greatly lowered the barriers to entry for recording and sharing content.

Today, the era of video has quietly arrived. Internet users no longer have to learn new technical skills in order to express themselves. Compared to the abstract encoding system that is text, the barriers to entry have been lowered even further.

Kuaishou is purely a video community. Our principle of inclusivity encourages everyone to freely record their lives. As long as a video does not violate law and public decency, Kuaishou would treat it equally and provide it with traffic. Thanks to Kuaishou, the ideal of "nationwide recording and sharing" has been realized for the first time.

Part 2

If information channels are narrow and attention is expensive, then self-expressions would have to be discriminated and prioritized, and the outcome would be that not every life can be seen. If a life is deemed to be "not perfect enough," it would not have the "right" to be widely shared and disseminated.

Handy Geng makes "useless gimmicks," while Uncle Benliang's (a very popular singer on Kuaishou) singing skills are unprofessional. Were they judged by the usual standards, they would find it hard to be seen.

However, both of them have amassed tens of millions of fans on Kuaishou because people have found resonance with them.

In July 2019, a production team called "Zhao Mingming's Stall of Limited Edition Groceries" created a compilation of 160 Kuaishou videos that they liked, with the background music set to "Being Is Perfection" (a popular Chinese song that is also called "Celebrate"). It was well-received on the internet and moved many people to tears.

The video featured more than 100 diverse people, including a girl who runs with prosthetic legs, an old woman who plays with marbles, and a plump woman who loves dancing. None of the people in their videos are superstars, but each has their own brilliance and together they form a genuine world that is full of fireworks.

According to Zhao Mingming's Stall of Limited Edition Groceries:

> I didn't expect Kuaishou to be such an enchanting place until I tuned in.
>
> Kuaishou is one of the most dynamic and lively places I've ever seen.
>
> Everyone tries their hardest to show themselves on it—to show their work, their skills, their family, the interesting or uninteresting things that they have seen, and the lucky or unlucky things that life has given them. And after that, they go back to living their life courageously.
>
> Life is not perfect at all, but hard work and courage are the only means of making it perfect.
>
> China is a vast land of mountains, seas, and diverse lives. With a territory of 3.7 million square miles and a population of 1.39 billion people, every place and every person is wonderful in their own way.

When only a portion of people have the opportunity to express themselves, that would mean that life stories can be classified as superior or inferior. Lives deemed superior are considered worthy to be seen, while the rest are considered mediocre and unworthy to be recorded and shared.

Kuaishou allows every life to express itself, to be seen, and to be appreciated. Every existence is unique and every life should be treated equally. Thus, Kuaishou is a reflection of a more genuine world, and a realm in which "every flower is a world of its own."

Being is perfection.

Part 3

What is the role of an artist? Recently, I read an article written by a famous female author regarding this question. Her father is a veteran who left home at 16 and never saw his mother again thereafter. When the author took her 85-year-old father to watch the opera *Silang Visits His Mother*, he could not stop weeping as he watched. Subsequently, the author brought her father to watch the same opera many more times, and each time he would be mentally jolted, with tears in his eyes.

She wrote:

> Culture and art enable isolated individuals to walk out from behind deeply locked doors and find others like themselves. My father discovered that his experience was not an isolated case and that he could share his pains and joys with others. Through culture and art, isolated individuals can develop a sense of belonging, while small groups of scattered and alienated people can find connections and transform into spiritually linked and sorrow-sharing communities

Life is full of unspoken or even indescribable pains. An outstanding artist is able to capture some of these pains and write about or enact them in a way that soothes hearts and souls.

After all, art comes from life. However, there are a limited number of artists, a limited number of pains that can be uncovered, and an even more limited number of types of people that can be given attention to. Many people, especially those at the bottom of society, often do not get artistic attention or sufficient public attention. For example, there are 30 million truck drivers in China. They spend all year long on the roads, have little time with their families, and might even run into road bandits and robbers. They have their own joys and pains just like everyone else but are seldom noticed and often find it difficult to communicate with others. This also goes for urban drivers who transport the bodies of deceased people to and from funeral parlors, and ship crew members who spend most of the year braving the world's oceans.

On Kuaishou one day, when a truck driver inadvertently filmed his life and the scenes in the cab of his rig, it was seen by another truck driver, causing the two of them to find resonance and gain self-confidence through seeing each other's joys, pains, and pressures. Perhaps, many videos are of little worth to outsiders, but they are an inseparable part of the filmer's own life.

Recently I read a sentence stating that "Life is the best play; the joy and sorrows in the human world can be interlinked." Such interlinking can be achieved through the artworks created by professionals, including the many dramatic works we have today. Kuaishou offers another way to achieve such interlinking; there are countless communities on Kuaishou that are similar to that of the truck drivers.

Psychologists say that seeing is love. Thanks to Kuaishou, the life of truck drivers can be seen by other truck drivers and many interested others. This allows them to be nourished by love and soothed of their pains, thereby gaining in self-confidence and happiness.

These communities transmit love and improve every member's unique sense of happiness.

Part 4

We live in a three-dimensional space that involves the concept of distance, but distance does not exist in the online world.

Although Kuaishou's several hundred million users are scattered across China and separated by mountains and rivers, everyone is next-door neighbors with everyone else on the platform. With a simple click, users can enter other people's homes and see their lives. If you meet someone congenial, you can tour their home to your heart's content and interact with them through livestreaming, but if you find someone disagreeable, you can leave anytime you want.

In the 1960s, a Canadian scholar called Marshall McLuhan opined that, with the emergence of electronic media, human beings would eventually return to a tribalized "global village." Just like in a real-world village, visiting a neighbor's house would be just a matter of a few steps, and communication would be mostly be done through face-to-face conversations rather than text.

Kuaishou communities are one of the best ways to realize such a global village.

HANDY GENG: THE IMAGINATIVE AND WORLD-FAMOUS "THOMAS EDISON OF WASTE MATERIALS"

Handy Geng (a popular handcrafter on platforms such as Kuaishou and YouTube) is known online as "the Louis Fan of Baoding City" (in reference to the actor who starred in *Ip Man*) for his good looks and as "the Thomas Edison of waste materials" for his brilliant talents. Any video he publishes can quickly attract tens of millions of hits. Through his various craftworks and gizmos, he has gained millions of followers online. Two of the popular phrases used to describe him are "Whatever Handy Geng creates is junk" and "He does everything except proper things."

His creations include a comb made out of a kitchen knife, a fan made out of several kitchen knives, a gadget for giving one's friends a painful flick on the head, and a tool for eating noodles during an earthquake. Thanks to these creations, he has appeared on China Central Television (CCTV) and also became popular overseas.

Since he became active on Kuaishou, Handy Geng has published more than 200 videos and attracted nearly 3.5 million followers. At first, he thought his followers were young people from third- or fourth-tier cities, if not craftsmen like himself. But one day, he discovered to his surprise that his followers were from all across the board, including real estate owners and overseas students.

His real name is Geng Shuai and he comes from a family of three generations of welders, yet he seems to have changed the trajectory of his family. He says that his life before 30 was full of lows and extremely dreary. It was only one day when he logged on to Kuaishou that he discovered what he wanted to do, allowing his life to enter a peak at 30.

Kuaishou name: V 手工 ~ 耿 (V Handy ~ Geng)

Kuaishou ID: Vshougong

Hometown: Baoding City, Hebei Province

Age: 32

Education: junior middle school

Production style: turning his wild, unconstrained ideas into "useless gimmicks" but inadvertently arousing the audience's imaginations regarding daily life

Message to his loyal fans: I will continue to present good design content on Kuaishou

Business model: create interesting inventions to attract many fans and sell replicas of these inventions through the Kuaishou platform

Narrator: Geng Shuai

My First 30 Years Were Full of Lows and This Only Changed When I Unexpectedly Became Popular on Kuaishou

I dropped out of school at 16. At that time, I quite disliked studying and was a little conceited. I believed that knowledge such as quadratic equations was useless and learning was just a waste of time. So, to enter society and gain experience earlier, I left school and went to work in Beijing with my uncle. I was excited—even ecstatic—to finally make money for myself.

I was dumbfounded when I first entered a construction site. The workers in helmets all looked listless and I just couldn't understand why.

My first task was to smash a wall. That sounded fun to me. I said to my workmates "look at me" and then I picked up the sledgehammer and began to swing.

However, I never expected this seemingly exciting job to be so tiring. After one whole day of work, my hands got swollen and I struggled to sleep. Then when I did sleep, I continued to work in my dreams.

I came to realize that the life of a school dropout was not so great.

I migrated to different places to do odd jobs, and eventually returned home when I did not find any more jobs. I've tried various kinds of jobs: waiter, cell phone salesman, and gas stove installer. Such boring experiences had almost worn away all my longing for a better life.

It can be said that my life was full of lows before I chanced upon Kuaishou.

In 2017, I was 30. The Chinese sage Confucius said: "At 30, I was self-established; at 40, I could no longer be confused or tempted." At that time, I had only 25,000 yuan in savings and decided I had to try something else. Otherwise, I might not become self-established even at 40.

By chance, my childhood friend mentioned to me that there were a lot of welders on Kuaishou and I could use some old parts to weld small ornaments for sale online at an attractive price.

I became enlightened at once. This was exactly what suited me!

As someone born in Yang Village, Dingxing County, Baoding City, Hebei Province, I am your standard "small town guy." My grandfather and my father were both welders. I grew up listening to the welding noises when my father was working, and I have also inherited good welding skills.

I saw that someone had made a stainless steel weapon and was selling it for 2,000 yuan on Kuaishou. I thought to myself that any welder can make that—no biggie.

However, I never like to just mimic what others have done. Instead, I always want to create things that are new. What's more, I have really strict demands on my own creations and spend a long time deliberating on every aspect.

I did my first video on Kuaishou as a test, showing the procedure of making an electric-welded mechanical grasshopper. In just three days, the video was viewed more than 700,000 times! I was too excited to sleep and thought about the video into the wee hours. I kept refreshing the video page to check for any new likes or comments.

It was the success of this video that made me resolve to continue making more videos.

I experimented with more videos online for a month—some failed and some succeeded. Gradually, people began to follow me.

My creativity is usually drawn from life, while the materials I use are also commonly seen things. Soon after I started making videos, I spent thousands of yuan buying raw materials to make key chains, ornaments, and other trinkets. An ornament that I used 600 ordinary machine nuts to build took me more than a month from design to production. That video attracted more than 1,000,000 viewings in just 24 hours and I gained 100,000 followers. Please realize: there are only 5,000 people in my village, so 100,000 fans was quite a lot to me!

The First Praise I Received on Kuaishou Was "Whatever Handy Geng Creates Is Junk"

As my followers grew in numbers, I started to make money. Surprisingly, most of the useful things I tried such as slippers, wallets, and small benches did not sell at all. Instead, it was those things that I deemed impractical that sold very well, such as a comb made out of a kitchen knife, a fan made out of several kitchen knives, a gadget for giving one's friends a painful flick on the head, and a tool for eating noodles during an earthquake.

My first best-seller was a bracelet made out of machine nuts. At first, I made it only for myself, but after I uploaded its video on Kuaishou, the video quickly garnered 400,000 views and hundreds of people added me on WeChat asking how they could buy the bracelet.

I selected seven people out of the many interested buyers and sold them the bracelet for 45 yuan each with free delivery included. That day, I began working on the bracelets at 8:30 in the morning, finished packing them at 1:00 the next morning, and shipped them when day broke. I made more than 100 yuan in total and felt extremely happy.

In November 2018, I received my first good review. One of the bracelet buyers commented that "Whatever Handy Geng creates is junk." I posted a screenshot of this sarcastic comment on Weibo—the next day, the number of orders soared and I sold 70 more bracelets!

Among the many things I have made, the most popular is the "Brain Damage Aid Kit," which is a gadget for giving one's friends a painful flick on the head. I jokingly said it could enhance friendships. To my surprise, it turned out to be one of the best sellers in my store, and I sold about 100 pieces a month. For artisans, this was a significant number!

I even appeared on the list of most searched people on Weibo because of this gadget. It also went popular abroad, so much that the *Washington Post* had an exclusive interview with me.

My Followers Have Found a Kind of Resonance and Hope in Me

Why do people like my videos? Through the private messages and comments I received, I discovered that many people, too, enjoy handcrafting a lot, but do not have the time, place, or energy to pursue this hobby. I happened to be doing things that seemed very useless but still interesting to them. So, they may be paying attention to me to find a kind of resonance and hope.

Some people call me an inventor, but I don't think I deserve that title. An inventor is someone who designs something that is great and benefits mankind. I see myself more as a comical inventor.

Kuaishou is not only my window but also my stage; it has increased my income, raised my standard of living, and enabled me to maintain my hobbies. Through this window, I can also get to know about the wider world and more interesting people.

My monthly salary as a welder was about 6,000 to 7,000 yuan. Now, in addition to the income from handicraft sale, I can also make money from livestreaming.

What's more, I thought at first that most people who watched my videos were young people from third- and fourth-tier cities, but I later found that this was not the case. Real estate investors and cultural workers have interacted with me, too. Not long ago, I had the honor to participate in a craftsmanship competition organized by Kuaishou and was up against a real estate tycoon named Pan Shiyi. I didn't win the contest but was still very happy to have partaken.

I had never thought I would become someone influential. On September 22, 2018, Kuaishou invited me to sell my gadgets at an in-person event and I was nicely surprised that many people came over from Shanxi, and other places to take photos with me and buy my works. That event gave me the great feeling of being really popular.

Netizens have given me many nicknames such as "the Thomas Edison of waste materials" and "the Louis Fan of Baoding City." Foreign journalists have also come to interview me. There was also a person who "@" me on Weibo after watching a *CNN* interview of me on a screen in Seattle-Tacoma International Airport—I joked that the director of the airport must like me.

I have also made a lot of friends online and they have given me a lot of ideas and suggestions. The "Foosball Grill" (a grill for playing foosball while cooking the food, with the food serving as the figures) I made was an idea from one such friend. He had sent me a picture of the idea and I found it very interesting. It took me two or three days to create it and the result was very good.

I Hope to Mass Produce My "Useless Gimmicks" in the Future

After I became famous, some people asked me to livestream more so as to earn more money. Some people have also asked me to do advertisements for them, such as by promoting their products in my WeChat Moments. However, I declined because I didn't know about the quality of those products. I believe that it's irresponsible to introduce a product I don't know about. After all, I gained so many followers because people trust me.

In my opinion, the only way to be followed in the long-term is to keep on producing good-quality video content. Let me share a few tips from my own experiences. Good videos must have an interesting cover—if possible, make it an animation so as to pique the audience's curiosity. In addition, your first few videos should be short—the shorter your videos, the more compact the content and thus the higher the number of views and completed views.

How can you make your videos more interesting? Take my own works for example: In the video of myself making a sword out of machine nuts, I used the sword to poke a chicken in the rear at the end of the video. I discovered that many people enjoyed videos with this kind of comedic effect.

In the future, I hope to form a small team and mass produce my gimmicks so that anyone who likes them will be able to get them.

I am very satisfied with my current life as compared to the earlier low points I went through. I can do what I like, participate in various activities, and even be interviewed. These things have enriched my life greatly, and they are all thanks to Kuaishou.

PROFESSOR DAVID FROM OXFORD: AN EXPERT WHO REMINDS US OF SANTA CLAUS SHOWS YOU HOW TO PERFORM EXPERIMENTS

"Professor David's Lab" on Kuaishou has released more than 200 videos of interesting chemical experiments and attracted more than three million fans in the year and a half since its launch. The Lab is run by David G. Evans, a 61-year-old British man who is as kind and lovely as Santa Claus and speaks fluent Chinese.

David G. Evans is the president of the Beijing Branch of the Royal Society of Chemistry, a distinguished foreign professor at Beijing University of Chemical Technology, and an Officer of the Order of the British Empire. He is a famous chemist who holds a doctorate from Oxford University. With his solid academic background and his humorous experiments and explanations, he has become an "internet celebrity teacher" who is well-liked by many Chinese primary and middle school students on Kuaishou.

For now, Professor David's main focus in China is to popularize the science of chemistry. Wherever he goes he wears a tie with the full periodic table printed on it. He hopes that through his presentations and explanations on Kuaishou, more Chinese primary and middle school students will understand the charm of chemistry and cultivate the scientific spirit of hands-on verification.

PROFILE

Kuaishou name: 戴博士实验室 (Professor David's Lab)

Kuaishou ID: ukdaiwei

Nationality: United Kingdom

Age: 61

Education: doctorate

Production style: conducting chemical experiments personally and presenting the charm of chemistry through simple and humorous explanations of profound knowledge so as to cultivate children's scientific thinking

Message to his loyal fans: with the help of the Kuaishou platform, I hope to enable the charm of chemistry to transcend the limitations of time and space and be transmitted to more primary and middle school students

Narrator: David G. Evans

Chemistry and China Are My Two Major Interests

My name is David and my loyal fans on Kuaishou call me "Professor David." I never expected that my chemical experiments on Kuaishou could help so many Chinese children to fall in love with chemistry and, in turn, science. Fans often leave me messages saying, "if you were my chemistry teacher, I wouldn't have hated chemistry so much." These messages have helped me to recognize the influence of Kuaishou and given me impetus in my efforts to popularize science in China.

Let me share my story about China and Kuaishou.

I have been highly interested in chemistry since I was an elementary student. I enjoyed studying various compounds and their changes after undergoing chemical reactions. I am grateful to my parents for always supporting me in my pursuits. At the age of 11, I started doing all kinds of chemical experiments that, in retrospect, were more dangerous than I realized.

If chemistry is the natural science that I am most interested in, then China is the social science that I am most interested in. What they have in common is change.

I was born in Europe, and when I was a student, there was no real news about China. Then in the 1970s, when China and the United States established diplomatic ties, the journalists accompanying President Nixon on his visit to China released a lot of news about China. I began to understand China from that time, but the news about China soon dried up. Yet, by then, I had developed a deeper interest in China and wanted to know what was happening there. So, at the beginning of China's reform and opening up, I took the opportunity to go to China myself.

The first Chinese sentence I learned when I visited China was neither "hello" nor "goodbye" but instead "we don't have this." I heard it on many occasions, such as when I went out for dinner at 5 p.m., when I went to a store to buy something, and when I wanted to book a hotel. From 1987 to 1996, I visited China once or twice a year and observed that the changes every year were greater than the last.

In 1996, I officially began to work at Beijing University of Chemical Technology as a chemistry teacher for undergraduate and graduate students. At the time, my European friends thought I was crazy, but my thinking was that they saw only the problems in China while I saw the great potential in China. And so I stayed in China for more than 20 years.

China has undergone tremendous changes over these two decades, from "we don't have this" to "we have everything you want." From smartphones to high-speed trains to the internet to sharing products, China's changes have been like chemical reactions and I feel fortunate to have witnessed this process.

Thankfully, I have also attained a few professional achievements in China. Together with Chinese researchers, I designed a new additive for plastic greenhouse film that can improve the insulation of greenhouses. The improvement helps crops inside greenhouses to grow better and yield more output, and also makes the process more environmentally friendly. I have also participated in the development of a new type of flame-retardant material for cables. With it, the concentration of smoke can be reduced when a cable catches fire, thereby ensuring safety.

Kuaishou Offers New Possibilities for My Popularization of Science

Many people still misunderstand chemistry to be dangerous, pollution-causing, explosion-prone, and so on.

People who don't understand chemistry are also susceptible to scams and false rumors. For example, some people think that drinking alkaline water can prevent cancer. The truth is that an ordinary bottle of purified water costing 1 yuan has the same health benefits as a bottle of alkaline water costing 25 yuan. Don't waste your money.

Cosmetics have similar problems. Nowadays, both women and men are conscious of their looks. Many people prefer to use chemical-free skin cleansing masks. But think about it—how could they possibly be chemical free? For example, they contain water, and we all know water is made up of H_2O molecules. Aside from water, there are also many other chemicals. So, don't waste your money on expensive chemical-free cosmetics and just buy the regular ones.

These myths all stem from a lack of understanding of chemistry.

Therefore, since 2011, I have shifted my focus from scientific research to the popularization of science.

In 2011, which was the international year of chemistry, the non-profit Royal Society of Chemistry granted 1,000 British pounds to each of its branches around the world, including its China branch, to fund their efforts in promoting the development of chemistry. At the same time, a friend of mine in Beijing organized a charity activity that gathered volunteer teachers to teach English and art in a school for migrant children, and she asked me if I could join in to teach chemistry. I readily agreed.

From then on, I began to work on popularizing science. Every day at the school, I demonstrated experiments to the children or brought my graduate students from Beijing University of Chemical Technology to help guide the children in their experiments.

In October 2014, I officially became a member of the lecture group on science popularization reports by famous scholars of Beijing University of Chemical Technology, and thus began to travel to more places to teach science to primary and middle school students. To date, there are only three regions of China I have not taught in: Tibet, Jiangxi, and Guangxi. In total, approximately 30,000 primary and middle school students have attended my classes and hands-on labs.

In-person teaching is necessary, but I don't think it's enough. With so many children in China, only a limited fraction of children can attend class, and there are only a limited number of teachers to conduct class.

During the 2018 Spring Festival break, my assistant heard about Kuaishou from a friend and suggested that we try uploading videos of chemistry experiments for a while. He said that if nobody watched our videos, then we could just give up on it at any time.

Contrary to his pessimistic prediction, however, our videos were heavily viewed and we gained more and more followers. Many people also asked very interesting questions in the comments. We thus decided to continue.

The interaction among our followers was very active. At times, they would even discuss among themselves in the comments section, with some followers answering the questions posed by other followers. The atmosphere of exchange was most pleasant.

I also noticed that many of our followers wanted an even more systematic training in chemistry, and so I recorded a series of longer videos called "Magical Experiments" and uploaded them to Kuaishou for users with heightened interest to learn more.

I now have 2.89 million fans on Kuaishou. Through the Kuaishou platform, my influence has continually grown. Many teachers and parents have told me that their children want to perform experiments themselves rather than simply watch me doing so. Thus, they requested that I send them the equipment and materials that I use. In response, my team developed the "Experiment Pack." It can be said that Kuaishou has helped me to widen my thinking and go deeper into the work of popularizing science.

Using Kuaishou to Popularize Science in a More Inclusive Manner

It isn't that Chinese children hate studying science, but rather that they lack the opportunity to feel its charm.

Having taught chemistry experiments in China and the United Kingdom, I can say that my feeling in class is completely different between the two countries. For example, both British and Chinese junior high school students would react with "wow, that's awesome" when observing a chemistry experiment. However, this situation changes in senior high school.

For British senior high school students, you would need to perform even more exciting experiments in order to elicit surprise from them. But for Chinese senior high school students, you only need to perform a few simple experiments for them to go "wow." This is also the case in university.

The reason for that difference is due to differences in the ways that children learn science between the two countries. British children learn chemistry starting at an early age, and hands-on chemistry experimentation is taught in a chemistry laboratory early on. Teachers and students can do experiments anytime and anywhere. With class sizes of no more than 20 each, students have more opportunities to use instruments such as bottles and canisters, and thus they quickly become familiar with various experiments.

Meanwhile, Chinese students are relatively unfamiliar with the materials and experiments of chemistry. They usually have high levels of theoretical knowledge but are weak in hands-on ability.

I later learned that classes in China often comprise of more than 60 students each, and so the teachers do not have sufficient time and energy to let their students conduct too many experiments. Furthermore, the experimental instruments are limited in numbers.

That is why my videos on Kuaishou have attracted so much interest and attention. Through my experiments, I hope to enable the children to receive on-site learning and on a deeper level to learn how to think.

To give an example, I always wear goggles while conducting chemistry experiments. This is a basic formality when performing lab work in the West. But in China, I found that students have not been trained in this habit.

Often, they would ask during class, "Why do you need to wear goggles? It's not like you would drip hydrochloric acid into your eyes." My reply to them would be that sometimes a careless mistake can have tragic outcomes, and I would then perform a small experiment to show them the dangers.

Using eggs to represent human eyeballs (because both egg white and human eyeballs contain a lot of protein), I would drop a little hydrochloric acid on the eggs, causing them to quickly shrink and blanch. I would then say to my students, "See that? Chemicals will damage our eyes, and irreversibly so. That's why we must always wear goggles to protect our eyes when performing experiments." Having seen my experiment, they would gain a more intuitive understanding of the importance of wearing goggles. This is the benefit of in-person learning.

The most important thing to have when performing chemical experiments is a spirit of questioning. All scientists like to ask "why?" and then perform experiments to verify their ideas. In life, scientific thinking means that everything we observe can be verified using experiments. This is what true learning is, and it promises endless fun.

At present, Kuaishou is the main platform I use in my work of popularizing science. The three aspects I admire most about Kuaishou are:

1. Kuaishou brings huge viewer traffic. There are more than 200 million daily active users on Kuaishou. I have uploaded various chemical experiments on Kuaishou, and each video has gotten

over a million hits. To my astonishment, some videos even have as many as 15 million hits.

2. Kuaishou is a new company that is very flexible in its ideas and is always thinking about how to innovate. When I have a new idea and reach a consensus with Kuaishou on it, they can start implementing it immediately. That gives me a lot of confidence and support.

    For example, in August 2018, there was a new event jointly organized by Kuaishou and the Royal Society of Chemistry. We invited 20 senior high school students and 10 teachers from remote areas of Yunnan and Hubei provinces to participate in our summer camp.

    That summer camp had two purposes: to heighten the students' interest in chemistry, and to train the teachers in new experimental methods and ways of thinking. Traditional methods of performing experiments require large spaces and lots of instruments and materials. Now, however, some experiments can be miniaturized. For example, an experiment that required 50 milliliters of a certain chemical previously might now require only two milliliters of said chemical.

    Aside from teaching, we also provide mentoring. For instance, we hope to help children in poor areas to build up their self-confidence. I want to imbue in them the idea that they can change their lives as long as they work hard. This is also a belief that Kuaishou has brought to many ordinary people.

3. I appreciate Kuaishou's value of inclusivity. Kuaishou has a diverse range of users, including people who live in remote areas, yet everyone can watch my videos equally. When we did offline science popularization previously, we generally went to high schools that had relatively good conditions. On Kuaishou, however, my lessons can transcend geographical limitations.

    In Europe, there are many university teachers who are engaged in science popularization education, which has become a tradition. They believe that science popularization is just as important as scientific research. Instead, university teachers in China are usually very busy writing theses and working on projects, and thus do not have time to do science popularization. I believe that the only way to train more scientists is to do the right thing for our disciplines and for our children.

Nowadays, there are more and more foreigners working and living in China, including foreign teachers. Someone asked me, "Performing chemical experiments is such a tiring job. Wouldn't it be easier on yourself to teach English instead?" I replied that there are many people in China who can teach English, but few who can popularize chemistry, and therefore I am willing to give full energy to my expertise and continue to work on the popularization of chemistry.

Half a century has passed since I did my first chemical experiment at home. My hope is for more Chinese children to enjoy the rich and exciting world of chemistry just as I have done.

FARMER-TURNED-AIRPLANE-MAKER MR. ZHU: I'M NO EDISON, BUT I LOVE INVENTION, TOO

Owning a plane may be the dream of many people, but very few people can actually build their own plane. Mr. Zhu is one of the rare few; he has built an A320 with his own hands and received official recognition from Airbus.

From making plans for an airplane-themed barbecue restaurant to building a life-sized replica of an airplane model to now running an airplane-themed amusement park, the entire process of Mr. Zhu's success has been witnessed by Kuaishou.

Mr. Zhu knows he's no Thomas Edison, but he loves inventing, too, and likes to make things by hand. "Life is full of inadvertent moments, but dreams will never waver," he says. It was in one such inadvertent moment that he fulfilled his childhood dream of building an airplane.

Kuaishou name: 农民工造飞机（开原）(A Migrant Worker Builds an Airplane) (Kaiyuan City)

Kuaishou ID: zhuofeiji8888

Hometown: Tieling City, Liaoning Province

Age: 40

Education: primary school

Topic: airplane building

Production style: filming the entire process of building an airplane, with airplane-themed comic sketches added

Message to his loyal fans: as long as you have a dream, it's never too late to start

Narrator: Zhu Yue

My Dream of Building an Airplane Began 33 Years Ago

I am Zhu Yue, the builder and owner of a handmade Airbus A320. I'm from Kaiyuan City, Liaoning Province. My dream of building an airplane began 33 years ago.

When I was seven years old, I watched on TV as two Americans completed a round-the-world journey in their homemade airplane. I was so moved that I wanted to do the same and make my own airplane. However, my life didn't go the way I wanted. I had poor academic performance and dropped out of middle school. I helped with my family's farming for a year but then realized I couldn't sustain my family or find a wife by farming, and so I set out to learn a skill.

My family sent me to a technical school in the county to learn home appliance maintenance. But after a year of study, the school closed down and so I went to look for a job. I have taken up many different jobs: repairing motorcycles, repairing electrical machinery, welding, riveting, and lathe operating. Later on, I opened my own motorcycle repair shop. I neither drink nor waste time in karaoke or cards. I don't have any hobbies other than fiddling with my mechanical gadgets and sometimes doing a little inventing.

My name on WeChat is "I Love Inventing"—it's a summary of my daily life. But I'm no Edison, and I don't know if my "inventions" can contribute to the advancement of science and technology. Most of the time, I simply handcraft things that I want.

I Created an "Automatic Paper Ingot Folding Machine" That Became Popular All over Northeast China

I often see foreigners on the internet making all kinds of strange and interesting musical instruments and toys and filming these production processes into videos. I find that interesting and so I would often make the same things that they had made by copying what they do in the videos. I once built a mini popcorn machine that popped one kernel at a time, and I have also turned an abandoned car into an electrical transformer. I keep many of such gadgets at home, all made using my own hands

A few years ago, I saw my family making paper ingots during the Tomb-Sweeping Festival. The burning of joss paper in the shape of money is a Chinese custom as a sacrificial provision for deceased ancestors. Shaping paper to resemble silver or gold ingots for burning is not complicated but quite time-consuming. While watching the paper folding, I wondered if I could build a machine that automates this process. I assembled the machine materials and spent a few days building the first Automatic Paper Ingot Folding Machine. It turned out to be more useful than I had thought initially. After many people inquired about buying it, I made a few more improvements and sold many sets of it. Today, this machine is used all over Northeast China.

Many inadvertent moments will take place throughout one's life, but dreams will never waver. Inadvertently, my small inventions created convenience for many people, and I built up several hundred thousand yuan in savings. It was then that I decided to pursue my childhood dream of building an airplane.

It Was by Using Kuaishou That I Solved the Problems I Faced in Building an Airplane

To be honest, I am a pragmatist. I believe all beautiful ideals require practical support if they are to be fulfilled. Many people have built airplanes before me—some succeeded and some failed. But my original intention was simple. From the beginning, I never thought about getting my airplane to fly—I merely wanted to run an airplane-themed barbecue restaurant, which was something popular at that time.

What's more, I'm already 40 years old. Beside my house is a military airfield. I would watch as planes take off and land every day, and that made me more anxious to have my own airplane. Some people advised me to earn more money so that I can buy one, but how can an old peasant like me afford an airplane? As I possessed some building skills, I told myself I would build an airplane if I could not afford one. It being my childhood dream, I knew I had to get started on it or otherwise I would soon be too old to do it.

I called over five of my best friends, bought 50 tons of steel, and started on our airplane project in an abandoned factory near my home.

My relationship with Kuaishou had an interesting start. I used to be a very conservative person, and I was not very skilled in the use of the internet. When I saw people in the factory playing on their mobile phones, I would stop them as I consider fiddling with the phone a way of loafing at work.

This only changed when, one day, a young man in an accessories factory filmed the process of me transforming a water pipe into a musical instrument and uploaded it to Kuaishou. It quickly became popular and many people came to ask me about the instrument. That was when I realized that Kuaishou is actually an interesting place where I can get to know and be known by many people. Kuaishou is like a larger version of WeChat Moments: it is oriented toward the entire world and people from various backgrounds.

It took a longer time for me to build the airplane. We recorded the progress we made every day on Kuaishou. On this "larger version of WeChat Moments," what was seemingly a boring video about steel bar welding turned out instead to be a huge hit with people who shared the same interest as me. Among them are aviation enthusiasts from Beijing, professional aerial photographers, flight attendants, camera makers, decorators, vehicle painters, sellers of insulation materials, and even technical experts on aviation fittings—a real cross section of society.

In my opinion, Kuaishou is a window for getting to know the world and a platform for following many people. The life situations of different people are all presented on Kuaishou, as if allowing us to experience their lives for a little while.

Of course, it isn't easy to build an airplane. Due to our lack of experience initially, we repeatedly failed to build the nose even after making five major changes and countless small ones. Every part of the airplane was cut out from iron plate, butted, and welded.

We also had blueprints. When designing the wings of the airplane, I heard that the wings are based on the principles of leaves. I asked a workmate to pluck two elm leaves from a tree for analysis. We scanned the leaves on to a computer and then used CAD software to scan their shapes for modeling the wings after. Using this method, we made so many blueprints that they weighed more than 20 pounds in paper.

Having started on this journey, we realized that it wasn't as difficult as we had imagined. Often, we would record a video of our progress and upload it to Kuaishou. Sometimes, we would also discuss questions with our viewers in the comments section. This is an amazing place where I have learned a lot from our followers. Many of the problems we faced while building the airplane were solved over Kuaishou.

One day, I saw one of my teammates squatting in a corner crying. He is a big man who usually would not even groan in pain when accidentally struck by a hammer. I asked him what was the matter but he said it was nothing. When I pressed further, he told me that he was moved to tears after seeing the photos and videos of our airplane-making process—and listening to the background music—on Kuaishou.

Kuaishou Made Me the "Second Most Popular Person from Kaiyuan"

I had never expected our videos to be so popular on Kuaishou. At the peak of our popularity, even videos of us building the airplane taken by people who passed by our factory could become popular. And due to the high viewership of our videos, many people approached us to do advertisements. At the beginning of 2018, I received an ad request on Kuaishou that offered 6,000 yuan for putting up a few words on the airplane. This gave me great delight. A professional decorator also contacted me on Kuaishou and offered free decoration services to me as long as I helped to advertise his company. Back then, I had no idea what traffic monetization and ad exchange were, but I knew that these practices could help me to achieve my dream of building an airplane. In any case, I exercised discretion in accepting advertisements, and would think twice about accepting those that might be harmful to my followers.

Through Kuaishou, I became known to more people. This, of course, had the side effect of making me busier. Nowadays, I receive requests for media interviews on a daily basis. This gives me the feeling of fame.

The most famous person from my hometown is Zhao Benshan (a Chinese skit and sitcom actor). People now say that I am the second most popular person from Kaiyuan. I don't mind it as long as they are happy. However, when various newspapers, TV stations, internet media platforms, and even foreign TV stations came to interview me, I began to reconsider whether to continue with my original plan. After all, it might be a letdown to all my followers if I merely opened a barbecue restaurant in the airplane that cost 800,000 yuan to build.

I'm A Peasant Who Built a "Peasant-Class" Airplane

I began to visit factories across China that made model airplanes to become acquainted with people who had experience in this field. I also went to a fire department to look at model airplanes used for fire drills.

I also established connections with a number of other professionals. For example, when building the cockpit, I was assisted by a large number of industry insiders, including aviation enthusiasts from Tsinghua University. Now, even professional pilots who have visited the cockpit cannot find any fault with it.

It took us more than two years and more than 2 million yuan to complete the airplane. I poured my heart and soul into this project, which began with me buying a small model airplane on Taobao and ended with Airbus officially recognizing my 1:1 scale replica airplane. Airbus even invited me to a delivery ceremony for the new airplane—this was a huge inspiration to me.

I am a peasant who has made a "peasant-class" airplane. A great moment was when a 90-year-old woman came from out of town to visit our construction site. Though confined to a wheelchair, she requested to go onboard to have a look and fulfill her dream of boarding an airplane. At that time, the airplane was not yet complete, but I was so touched that I agreed without hesitation. I brought her around the airplane and introduced its features to her one-by-one. We even simulated the experience of flying an airplane in the cockpit.

It was at that moment when I felt I had done something absolutely right, and my estimation of my own life's value increased.

MR. BAO THE TRUCK DRIVER: I FILMED MY JOURNEYS ON THE ROAD AND UNEXPECTEDLY ENTERED THE SPOTLIGHT

Before he turned 32, Mr. Bao was a typical member of the silent majority in China.

He grew up in a poor family in the countryside. With little farmland and just a few years of schooling, he seemed to have a bleak future. He works in the high-risk business of long-distance trucking, and travels alone on the road every day. For a long time, his life seemed to have little to do with the outside world.

Before 2017, the only online content he knew about was WeChat Moments. He had never watched livestreams or short videos, and never interacted online with anyone except his family, friends, and cargo owners.

Mr. Bao began his work in the line of long-distance transportation shortly after getting his truck-driving license and getting married. His mundane life only became more exciting in 2017 after he started using Kuaishou, which has now become his most important social networking tool. It has not only increased his income but also made him and his fellow truck drivers visible to more people.

PROFILE

Kuaishou name: 河北沧州开卡车的宝哥 (Mr. Bao Who Drives a Truck in Cangzhou City, Hebei Province)

Kuaishou ID: wang376612192

Hometown: Cangzhou City, Hebei Province

Age: 34

Education: primary school

Topic: Daily life of a truck driver

Production style: presenting his work and life candidly

Message to his loyal fans: wishing all my fellow truck drivers safe journeys and higher freight fees

Narrator: Mr. Bao

A Video That Changed My Life

I began using Kuaishou in the second half of 2017. Back then, a friend suggested I download Kuaishou. He said that there are many users on Kuaishou and I could make many new friends. Though he started using the app earlier than me, he has never uploaded a video even up to this date. But I was different; it didn't take long for me to begin filming and uploading short videos. I figured out how to upload videos and interact with other users all on my own—it wasn't difficult.

I felt good when I began using Kuaishou. Everyone called each other "loyal fans" and gained more and more friends. Most of my videos were filmed by my wife when she accompanied me in the truck, and I would then upload them on Kuaishou. The production was always unstaged—we would film whatever goods we were transporting, whatever food we ate, and whatever was interesting along the way. In truth, it did not take much energy to film these simple videos.

At first, our followers increased at a slow rate. However, there were already a few followers who had grown accustomed to watching our videos and would question us whenever we skipped a day.

We uploaded our first video on November 26, 2017.

It showed me opening the side rail of my truck and waiting to unload. I washed my face with soap and water in a red basin on the concrete floor beside the truck. The video has received more than 690,000 views, 7,000 thumbs up, and 3,000 comments. Up to this day, people are still leaving comments. One of them said, "Your destiny began to change with this video." He was right.

I uploaded two videos that day, with the second one taken by me. I specially wrote in the description: "My wife was afraid that I would get sleepy while driving, so she bought me a bag of big apples." That video was shot in the cab of my truck. When my wife got into the truck with a bag of apples, I took a picture of the ground in front of the truck and then a selfie of my face. Hoping to gain more followers, I also stated in the description that I would livestream every day if I hit a certain number of followers.

I also added the popular Chinese song "Kindred Spirits Join Hands" by Yang Yuying to that video because of the lyrics: "We are forever in love. As we hold each other's hands, our hearts feel warmth. As we hold each other's hands, the loess ground turns golden." I like that song a lot. Most of the background songs in my videos are of a similar sweet-loving style.

That video has garnered more than 900,000 views.

My Loyal Fans Love to Watch Me Cook

I have filmed videos of myself loading and unloading goods, and also of my truck running into traffic jams and accidents. When stuck in traffic, I would cook meals on the spot. At night, I dare not sleep in order to prevent diesel theft. During my breaks, I would do a dance of my own style, and my fans are very fond of it. In addition to driving scenes, I have also filmed videos of my family's daily life.

Many of my videos are of myself cooking on the road. As the food sold at the rest areas is too expensive, I save money by cooking my own meals. Many fans have dubbed me the "cooking god," and because it is always me—and never my wife—doing the cooking, some also call me the "most loving truck-driving husband." I have also shared my cooking techniques and recipes with my fans. To be honest, I am not sure why so many people like to watch me cook, but they certainly make up a large part of my followers.

It was my own idea to film all of these things. I find it fun and my wife is very supportive, too.

The comments left by my loyal fans are very touching. "We like the down-to-earth personality of Mr. Bao and his wife." "Watching Mr. Bao's videos has helped me to understand what life is." "Jiayou, this is the real trucking life." "Life is not easy, cherish what you have." They show that my fans place great value on seeing my authentic daily life. I had never thought I would ever come to possess a stage like this.

My hometown is in the countryside where I don't have much land. I used to run a small business selling things such as ballpoint pens and liquefied gas. Although the income was okay, it was less than what I make as a truck driver. Of course, there was less personal risk involved in that business.

I got my truck driver's license in 2004, but didn't start driving full-time until 2008. The round-trip time for a trucking order may take anywhere from 5 to 15 days.

I used to have a monotonous social life. Aside from my classmates from school, the only people I socialized with were my fellow villagers. But now, I have loyal fans from all over China, and I have also added more than 3,000 of them on WeChat after getting to know them on Kuaishou. We often meet up to eat and chat. Certainly, my life has become much more vibrant than before.

Nowadays, I come across loyal fans almost every time I'm on the road transporting goods. They consist of not just other truck drivers, but also people from all walks of life. A few days ago, I recorded and uploaded yet another video of myself cooking a meal roadside. When a nearby waistcoat seller saw the video, she drove to me by electric bike and gave me a waistcoat as a gift.

My most unforgettable memory was an encounter with a Shijiazhuangese woman who drove a Land Rover and owned a shoe market in Beijing. I ran into her at a rest area in March 2019. Being a fan of mine, she asked if she could record a video of me and I agreed. She then gifted me a pair of leather shoes and I added her and her husband on WeChat. We are still in contact to this day and have become as close as relatives. She knows my home address and often sends us slippers, sandals, and cotton shoes, such that we no longer have to buy our own footwear.

Once, when I transported a truck full of watermelons back home, she offered to come over from Beijing to help me sell them.

My Wife Was Worried That I Had Female Fans

There are 30 million truck drivers in China, and driving trucks is a high-risk industry. Few people paid attention to us in the past, but Kuaishou has made us visible to tens of millions of people. We used to be thought of as a strange species; when people saw a truck on the road, they would become nervous and keep away. But now, they have seen that we are just as human as they are.

Over my one year or so of uploading videos to Kuaishou, the upload that left the deepest impression on me was a video that garnered more than 20 million hits. It was a video of me making shredded potatoes cooked in chili oil. People often eat shredded potatoes, but not many have eaten shredded potatoes cooked in chili oil. In the video, the flames rose more than three feet high after the oil was heated. I also added a few peppercorns in the oil to make it more delicious. I uploaded the video and got back on the road immediately after. The next day, I was astonished to see that I had gained 100,000 new followers.

But my biggest surge in followers took place in 2019. I had bought a second-hand, 9.6-meter truck for 200,000 yuan to replace my 3.9-meter rig. The truck is so long that backing up is difficult. A lot of my fans wondered whether I could actually handle such a long truck. Well, of course I can—my driving skills are top-notch. After buying the truck, I gained up to 400,000 new followers per freight transportation journey. I generally upload two or three videos a day, and since a transportation journey usually lasts a week or so, I would upload more than a dozen videos per journey. I had approximately 600,000 followers before buying the bigger truck, but the number has now grown to more than 3.18 million.

As my followers kept increasing, there came a point in time when my wife wanted me to stop filming videos. This was because many of my female followers left messages saying that they wanted to marry me. At first, my wife thought that they were serious, but after she realized that they were just joking, she allowed me to resume filming.

In less than two years, I have uploaded more than 1,000 videos. I also follow hundreds of my loyal fans, many of whom are truck drivers as well. We often meet up offline. On Kuaishou's Same City page, I am able to see which of my loyal fans are nearby.

My loyal fans often contact me to transport goods. Online communication has helped me to save on information costs. Prior to joining Kuaishou, I had to pay 500 yuan each time I picked up goods. Now, I not only save on that cost but also receive more pickups every month.

When I am in an unfamiliar place, I often ask my loyal fans for help. For example, when transporting saplings to Yunnan once, I could not make out from the mobile map whether certain mountain roads were big enough for a truck. Thus, using WeChat, I asked for directions from my fellow truck drivers whom I got to know on Kuaishou. We constantly exchange information such as which roads are unsuitable for a big truck, which places to avoid picking up goods, and which places have the heaviest fines. Whenever I encounter difficulty on the road, I can also broadcast it live on Kuaishou and nearby loyal fans come to help me. Once, when I needed some help making a temporary pass, it was a fan who constantly flamed me in my livestreams who came over to help.

I Have Become a Center of Attention in This Big World

In June 2019 I helped a seller to transport a batch of purple onions to Beijing. I thought he would be able to sell them out and pay me quickly. Instead, he sold less than half of the onions in two days. Purple onions spoil quickly, so I bought the remaining onions at a low price and created a 57-second video about it on Kuaishou:

> My loyal fans, I want to announce something: I have bought a truck of onions from an onion seller who couldn't pay me, and I'm paying out of my own pocket. Nothing is easy. So this is an advertisement: if anyone wants to buy onions tomorrow, please come to Xigaoji Bridge and I will sell them to you at a low price. Thank you for your support.

I had thought it would take another two days get rid of those onions. To my surprise, I sold all 16 tons of onions that morning. After hearing my plea, nearby truck drivers who were my loyal fans came over and each of them took away a bunch of onions to sell elsewhere. Some followers who could not make it also offered to transfer me money as a show of support. In addition, there were a few truck drivers who drove more than 200 kilometers from Shenyang or Shijiazhuang to Beijing just to meet me.

After that onion-selling experience, I became smarter in business. Nowadays, whenever I transport goods to a place where there are cheap specialty local products, I won't transport a further batch of goods from the sellers there. Instead, I would buy a few specialty local products and bring them back to my hometown to sell. Once, I bought a truck of watermelons and sold them in my hometown. They sold out within two days, netting me about 6,000 yuan more than transporting goods. I had never done such business prior to using Kuaishou; it is only now that I have fans and followers that I dare to do something like that.

Although I have a certain marketability, I don't do advertisements. This is because I don't understand products and am afraid of being scolded by my fans for endorsing a poor product. I also don't do livestreams often; being talentless, not many people would watch my livestreams. Most of the time, I simply film and upload short videos.

ENABLING EVERY LIFE TO BE SEEN   47

I once spent two days transporting a Rolls Royce from Shijiazhuang to Cangzhou for He Erdan (a popular livestreamer on Kuaishou), who is from the same village as me in Cangzhou. In my circle of truck drivers, everyone knows about him. I got to know him through Kuaishou. He has sent me gifts, treated me to meals, and provided me with transportation jobs.

I don't have much creative talents; the only thing I know how to do is to use my mobile phone to film my life, my work, and the wonderful world around me. I never expected to become a center of attention. For now, I intend to continue along this path.

Nowadays, I am very much focused on uploading short videos to Kuaishou, and I do so nearly every day. Whenever I close the app, I feel like there's something missing. I can never quite figure out why Kuaishou is so magical.

CHAPTER TWO

KUAISHOU E-COMMERCE: A WAY FOR FANS TO BUY GOOD PRODUCTS DIRECTLY FROM THE MANUFACTURER

CHAPTER OVERVIEW

Kuaishou E-commerce has a user base of more than 100 million today, and this number is growing rapidly. In June 2019, "Queen of the Internet" Mary Meeker cited Kuaishou Livestream Shopping and Kuaishou Store as examples of online retail innovation in her annual Internet Trends report.

An analysis of the success story of Luola Run (see below) would help one to understand the driving forces behind Kuaishou E-commerce's development. The first driving force is China's long-term and foundational investment in the internet field. The second driving force is the power of short videos as a content carrier. The last driving force is the real-time interactions that livestreams offer, thereby further reducing the distance between buyers and sellers as compared to videos.

Short video e-commerce is a part of e-commerce 4.0. The development of e-commerce goes like this: e-commerce 1.0 (textual communication) evolved into e-commerce 2.0 (textual and pictorial communication), then into e-commerce 3.0 (radio and television communication), and finally into e-commerce 4.0 (interactive and real-time communication, as represented by Kuaishou).

SUCCESS STORIES

Wawa and Xiaoliang: How We Received 110,000 Orders in One Hour of Livestreaming

Luola Run: Selling "Tree-Ripened" Fruits to the Whole of China Through Kuaishou

Shancun Erge: After Cutting an Orange on Kuaishou I Inadvertently Became a "Fruit Hunter"

Xianyang Erqiao: From "Kitchen God" on Kuaishou to King of Red Chili Oil E-Commerce

Hao Dong: Kuaishou Fulfilled My Performance Dream and My Hot Pot Dream

KUAISHOU E-COMMERCE: A WAY FOR FANS TO BUY GOOD PRODUCTS DIRECTLY FROM THE MANUFACTURER

Bai Jiale, head of Kuaishou E-Commerce

Shen Junshan used to sell ceramic tiles. One day in 2017 he uploaded a video of a kiwifruit orchard to his Kuaishou account named Luola Run (now changed to Junshan Agriculture) and garnered more than 400,000 hits and hundreds of orders.

With that, he stopped selling tiles and concentrated solely on his fruit business on Kuaishou. Today, he makes millions of yuan a year and owns several fruit farms throughout China. He has also established his own brand called Junshan Agriculture.

Luola Run is one of the success stories of Kuaishou E-commerce, which is developing rapidly today. In June 2019, "Queen of the Internet" Mary Meeker cited Kuaishou Livestream Shopping and Kuaishou Store as examples of online retail innovation in her annual Internet Trends Report.

E-Commerce 4.0

By analyzing the success story of Luola Run, we can see the driving forces behind Kuaishou E-commerce's development.

The first driving force is China's long-term and foundational investment in the internet field. Luola Run was able to engage in e-commerce because of at least four conditions: The prevalence of smart phones, the prevalence and affordability of 4G, convenient electronic payment, and a robust logistics network. China is possibly the only country in the world to have all four of these conditions at present. It was also under these conditions that Kuaishou E-commerce came into being and developed.

The second is the power of short videos as a content carrier. In the past, product information was communicated through text, pictures, and sound. However, videos have greatly improved the communication of product information and the effectiveness of consumers' purchase decisions. For example, Luola Run has a video in which fresh persimmons are opened and eaten right in a persimmon orchard. The intuitive feeling conveyed by such a video cannot be done through text, pictures, and sound.

The third is the real-time interactions that livestreams offer, thereby further reducing the distance between buyers and sellers as compared to videos. Luola Run livestreams every day. During a livestream, buyers can raise questions at any time and the seller will answer immediately to reassure the buyers. Livestreams also serve as a form of supervision; if an item sold by the seller is poor, buyers can bring up the matter in front of all other viewers.

This puts a lot of pressure on the seller.

Short video e-commerce is a part of "E-commerce 4.0." The development of e-commerce goes like this: "E-commerce 1.0" (textual communication) evolved into "E-commerce 2.0" (textual and pictorial communication), then into "E-commerce 3.0" (radio and television communication), and finally into "E-commerce 4.0" (interactive and real-time communication, as represented by Kuaishou).

The Beginnings of Kuaishou E-Commerce

Near the end of 2018, we discovered that there were more than 1.9 million comments related to business demands posted on Kuaishou every day. After repeated deliberation, we decided to broaden the scope of Kuaishou E-commerce slowly and carefully. After half a year of hard work, Kuaishou E-commerce was greatly improved.

Our efforts were focused on the following aspects:

The first was to simplify the tools of content creation. By enabling sellers to create better product displays and distributing content to interested people more accurately, what we were doing was actually to match and connect information from different aspects of business, thereby reducing information asymmetry. In line with our principle of inclusivity, we offered every user the opportunity to be discovered, and lowered the barriers to entry for individuals to take part in various aspects of business.

Second, we made the various aspects of a transaction more convenient. Merchants could list their products on their personal home pages and enable the "Yellow Cart" function on their video pages and livestream frames. By clicking on Yellow Cart, users would be brought to the product display page and would be able to complete a purchase directly on our platform.

Third, we provided users with purchase assurance. In cooperation with many e-commerce platforms such as Taobao, JD.com, Pinduoduo, and Mockuai, we introduced the feature of buying good products directly from the manufacturer.

A Community of Loyal Fans

E-commerce is a test of a company's overall operational capabilities. Sellers have to pay attention not only to the exposure and conversion of their products, but also to the phases of delivery, after-sales, repurchase, and so on. Small merchants on Kuaishou often have limited funds and need to improve their e-commerce capabilities, while their control over their own goods also requires official support. As for big brand merchants, they might lack traffic and a sound understanding of Kuaishou's ecosystem, and thus find it difficult to gain followers and increase sales. In order to meet the business needs of merchants of different sizes and industries, Kuaishou E-commerce has to develop a comprehensive and diverse range of e-commerce functions and services.

The first thing that Kuaishou did was to bring in brand businesses. Since 2018, we have brought in many high-quality brands. Today, more than 3,000 top brands distribute their products through video advertisements on Kuaishou. In 2018, Kuaishou cooperated with various merchants to organize special events such as "Kuaishou Sales King" and "Kuaishou Spring Festival Sale." More than 100,000 sellers and livestreamers participated in these events, generating hundreds of millions of yuan in sales and more than 10 million clicks or taps. Merchants and livestreamers on our platform have established close partnerships and creatively developed a new mode of using online celebrities to sell goods.

The second thing was to develop the Kuaishou Store, which is a new e-commerce transaction feature under Kuaishou E-commerce.

It allows users to edit and manage their product information directly on the client, thereby achieving closed-loop transactions. And thanks to its comprehensive ordering system that supports various payment methods, it is able to support the payment scenarios of users from third- and fourth-tier cities and effectively increase conversion. At the same time, its simple process of listing and delisting products lowers the barriers to entry for small merchants to engage in e-commerce. In terms of obtaining traffic, Kuaishou has replaced the traditional method of "buying traffic" with a new method that allows users with content creation capabilities to increase their followers and sales through short videos. This has lowered the costs of customer acquisition, achieved monetization of followers and traffic, and given greater impetus to creativity.

The third was to develop a market for e-commerce services. Kuaishou E-commerce brought in a number of high-quality e-commerce service providers to provide e-commerce knowledge and training to users. This also achieved a two-way connection between upstream suppliers and influencers. By equipping our users with supply chain capabilities and e-commerce sales techniques, we helped to solve their pain points of having no goods to sell or having no means to sell goods. The first batch of service providers we brought in included Ruhnn, Jindi Interactive, and Kmeila. They offer reliable supply chain resources, e-commerce sales training and services, and even agency-based store operation.

The Road Ahead

It is short-sighted and unhealthy for a platform to focus only on maximizing its own business interests. Instead, the ecosystem can only gain longevity and vitality by allowing more users to benefit from the platform. In line with this belief, Kuaishou E-commerce has proposed a development strategy of ecosystem security, ecosystem prosperity, and ecosystem co-prosperity. It is committed to achieving win-win-win outcomes among users, merchants, and the platform, and realizing the long-term development of its e-commerce ecosystem.

First of all, ecosystem security. While seeking to develop our services rapidly, we cannot neglect the user experience. Kuaishou has always given top priority to its users' interests and placed utmost importance on consumer protection while improving its service capabilities. The introduction of "Thunder Plan" was aimed at improving the Net Promoter Score (NPS) of the Kuaishou E-commerce platform, specifically to increase the Detail Seller Rating (DSR) score to 4.6 or above and maintain it at that level. By cracking down on typical cases of unethical business, strengthening management and control, improving our services, and so on, we seek to improve Kuaishou E-commerce's product capabilities and operational capabilities. Since the Thunder Plan started, 1,038 businesses have been closed down, more than 1,500 livestreamers have been subjected to disciplinary action, and more than 30,000 types of products have been delisted. As a result, the overall DSR score of the platform has risen greatly and user satisfaction has increased by 50 percent.

Second, ecosystem prosperity. Kuaishou E-commerce hopes to generate user following through *grass-growing* (a metaphor in China for growing product awareness by highlighting and sharing its good qualities and arousing purchase desire in others) content, and then use that generated user following to achieve conversion, enrich video creativity, and display a wider range of life scenarios. At the end of 2018, Kuaishou E-commerce launched the "Wheat Field Plan" driven by "content + social interaction," it serves to integrate Kuaishou E-commerce with Kuaishou's other ecosystems so as to better empower users in e-commerce aspects such as "people, goods, and place." In addition, by taking New National Products, New Agricultural Businesses, New Public Welfare, New Entertainment, New Craftsmen, and New Classrooms as its six major directions of development, it will establish exploration and cultivation of vertical industries and in-demand content, thereby building up the unique competitiveness of Kuaishou E-commerce.

Finally, ecosystem co-prosperity. Kuaishou E-commerce hopes to achieve co-prosperity between the top influencers and the medium- and long-tail merchants, between online transaction and offline consumption, and between affluent regions and poor regions in China. To do so, Kuaishou E-commerce will stimulate an increase in the number of medium- and long-tail e-commerce merchants and provide content creators with more valuable support. At the same time, it will cooperate with commercial departments to create *LingShouBao*, which would map offline transactions to the online platform, thereby reducing the impact of e-commerce on brick-and-mortar merchants and enabling these merchants to better achieve digital transformation. Meanwhile in poor regions, Kuaishou E-commerce will leverage its traffic and technological advantages to discover and promote the specialty products of these regions. By systematically supporting the *new farmers* (farmers who have technical and digital knowledge and expertise) who produce these specialty products and repaying poor regions, we hope to achieve precise poverty alleviation and rural revitalization.

WAWA AND XIAOLIANG: HOW WE RECEIVED 110,000 ORDERS IN ONE HOUR OF LIVESTREAMING

Having transformed from being simple street vendors into e-commerce merchants on Kuaishou and increased their daily income from 200 yuan to over 200,000 yuan, Wawa and her husband Xiaoliang can be regarded as models of successful e-commerce entrepreneurship. Though they once hit the bottom, they eventually bounced back and achieved success. It was during the economic downturn of 2017 when the couple started using Kuaishou. By accumulating followers and using livestreams to promote their products, they have ultimately returned to the peak of their careers and even gone one better than before—all thanks to Kuaishou.

They regard Kuaishou as a place full of joy and positive energy. Compared with other platforms, the biggest difference in Kuaishou lies in its sincerity toward its users. Every step of Kuaishou's growth bears the mark of its users advancing together with the platform.

Today, Wawa and Xiaoliang have more than 11 million followers on Kuaishou, and by selling their products through Kuaishou livestreams, they can attain a conversion rate of up to 10 percent. They love this platform and their fans on it and are willing to grow together with Kuaishou into the future.

PROFILE

Kuaishou name: 娃娃（每周一 6 点) (Wawa [6 p.m. on Mondays])

Kuaishou ID: wawawawa

Hometown: Xuzhou City, Jiangsu Province

Age: 33

Education: junior high school

Topic: running e-commerce through livestreaming

Production style: Wawa livestreams and interacts with fans while wearing clothes and accessories from the store

Message to their loyal fans: after the rain comes a sunny day; every cloud has a silver lining

Business model: selling products through livestreaming on Kuaishou and guiding people from their hometown to start a business together

Narrator: Wawa and Xiaoliang

Kuaishou Brought Our Store out of Its Slump

I am Xiaoliang and Wawa is my wife. Before we started livestreaming on Kuaishou, our business and life were at a low ebb. It was Kuaishou that gave us the opportunity to start a new business and the hope of rebirth.

My wife and I worked somewhere outside our hometown for many years. We initially made a living by running a street stall that sold bags, accessories, clothes, and suchlike. Because we were young, we could accept new things quickly and understood the aesthetic sense of consumers. This, together with our strategy of selling a high volume of goods at a low margin, enabled us to make up to 200 yuan a day in 2008. Later on, we moved to a store in a shopping mall. Because we had long acquired internet know-how, we began to purchase inventory online. Our daily turnover was 4,000 yuan, and this increased to 10,000 yuan in 2009.

Later on, we sold the house we bought when we married, and moved to Guangzhou City with the 120,000 yuan from the sale plus our savings. We started an online shop that sold suitcases at first but shifted to clothing in 2011. During that period, we slept only three to five hours a day—after all, highly popular apparel could fetch up to 2 million yuan in less than two months.

Our business subsequently experienced rapid growth. At our peak from the end of 2010 to the end of 2014, we earned a total of approximately 100 million yuan. But then a downturn ensued. Coupled with the death of a family member, we were unable to recover for a while. Feeling disheartened, we moved our business from Guangzhou back to our hometown of Xuzhou City, Jiangsu Province, and it was around this time when we discovered Kuaishou.

At first, we thought of it as just a fun app and so we only used it as any ordinary user would. Because Wawa likes to take photos of herself in nice clothes, we would often upload these photos to Kuaishou. However, many people began to follow us, hence we started to upload displays and matching combinations of certain products. By 2017, we had accumulated 5 million fans.

Fans would ask via private messages where they could purchase what they saw on our Kuaishou page and in reply we would give them the web address of our online store. It was in this manner that Kuaishou saved our online business and brought it back to its peak. During the Singles' Day promotions (the largest e-commerce selling day in China, akin to Black Friday in the United States) in 2017, we realized sales of more than 5 million yuan in just half an hour, all thanks to the traffic brought in through Kuaishou.

At first, we did not intentionally use Kuaishou as a way to improve our business. We simply displayed our products on Kuaishou, but this led to more and more people liking our products and becoming our followers. This is completely different from traditional e-commerce sales—and the conversion rate of Kuaishou followers is unexpectedly high.

The Sincerity of the Platform and the Enthusiasm of Our Followers Led to a High Conversion Rate

An analysis of our orders reveals that, before 2019, our Kuaishou followers mainly came from small towns and villages. But after 2019, the geographical distribution of our Kuaishou followers became similar to that of our Taobao followers. Compared with other platforms, Kuaishou followers have high spending power and loyalty. The Kuaishou official team also provides us with a lot of support. On one hand, they support our spreading of positive energy, and on the other hand, they often invite us to test out e-commerce features. In 2017, they helped us to set up a "Purchase Now" test. That same day, we sold 30,000 pieces of a particular waistcoat, breaking the previous record.

The total sales for the previous month did not even reach 30,000, yet we managed this number in just one or two hours on Kuaishou. We thus began to wonder: why is the purchase enthusiasm of Kuaishou followers so high?

Our intuitive feeling is that our relations with our Kuaishou followers are not just buyer-seller relations but more so friendships. Our business philosophy is to deal honestly with our customers and to sell a high volume at a low margin. The key is not about selling cheap, but about honoring the trust that our followers have in us. We believe that by doing business with empathy and constantly putting ourselves in the consumers' shoes, we would definitely be able to achieve success in our business.

There are two further things we know which have enabled us to stand out among so many sellers. First, a livestreamer must have an affinity with their followers, and must not transmit negative energy. Most people come to Kuaishou for entertainment, and so a livestreamer should not spread any negative emotions to the audience. At the same time, a livestreamer must mind their words and deeds; uncouth language must not be spoken during a livestream, otherwise the audience's favorability will greatly diminish. Second, a livestreamer must find common ground with their audience. For example, in terms of image, temperament, and fashion, the audience must know that what they see is what they get. In other words, they trust that if they buy a certain piece of clothing that the livestreamer wears on stream, they will look just as good in it as the livestreamer.

On Kuaishou, the trust and loyalty of followers are extremely valuable.

Today, we have accumulated more than 11 million followers on Kuaishou. We can sell 700,000 to 800,000 yuan's worth of goods in one livestream session, or even 2,000,000 yuan on a good day. If the number of viewers is 100,000 or more, the conversion rate can reach 10 percent or more. At the same time, thanks to traffic brought in from Kuaishou, the repurchase rate on our online store has reached 75 to 80 percent.

Through a comparative analysis we did, we found out that Kuaishou's conversion rate is the most competitive among all platforms. For example, my sister runs a store on another platform where she has 12 million followers. She employs six models who each work three hours a day for a total of 18 hours of livestreaming every day. However, her daily revenue is only around 150,000 yuan.

Kuaishou Has Witnessed Our Comeback and We Hope to Continue Growing with Kuaishou

The era of e-commerce has given grassroots people like us the opportunity to bounce back from downturns. Kuaishou has witnessed our process of getting out of the slump and returning to the peak, and has made us even more grateful for this era.

Both my wife and I came from poor families and dropped out of junior high school. When we started our business, we moved from our hometown of Xuzhou to Guangzhou. To save money while looking for a home, we roamed the city on bike for three days until we rented an apartment. Subsequently, we slept only three to five hours a day and wrote all orders by hand. As we could not afford to hire models and photographers, Wawa served as the model while I served as the photographer.

When business got better, we began to hire employees. Their strength grew from 3 to 10 to 50 and then to 100, reaching 180 at one point in time. We also brought our parents to live with us in Guangzhou, where they contributed greatly to the management of our store. My father used to work in freight transport while my mother once ran a pedicure shop. After arriving in Guangzhou, they began to help me to collect and arrange our goods. Later on, my second and third aunts, my mother's friends, and some other relatives all came over to Guangzhou to help in our enterprise. We could be said to have settled down in Guangzhou.

But then the unexpected happened. In our seventh year in Guangzhou our life suddenly suffered a series of setbacks. First, our business became very bleak: daily sales orders tumbled from 10,000 to 1,000 to finally less than 600. Falling finances forced us to cut the number of employees by more than 40 percent.

On top of that, my father died of a sudden cerebral hemorrhage that same year, and my mother also had some health issues. At that time, I fell into confusion and felt very tired. As a son, I was at a loss: I had done my utmost yet was unable to even take care of my own family, and, in that case, what was the point of trying to earn more money? I thus decided to return to my hometown.

I remember very clearly that while carrying my father's ashes onto the train, I lost all desire to work anywhere but my hometown.

But I also knew many people who were successful in Guangzhou but failed after returning to their hometowns—I was worried about that, too. During that time, my wife Wawa gave me plenty of encouragement. She told me she was certain that we would make it in our hometown. Subsequently, we began making arrangements for our move back to Xuzhou.

On June 1, 2018, we officially moved our company back to Xuzhou and started our second venture on Kuaishou. At first, due to the uncertainties ahead, we felt a bit worried.

But soon, Kuaishou gave us great confidence. We are proud to say that after we officially started business on Kuaishou in 2018, our sales results within the first three months were equivalent to the sales of the past three years. Recently, in a livestream with approximately 10,000 viewers, we completed 1.47 million yuan's worth of sales from nearly 110,000 orders after just one hour—that could never have been imagined before.

Today, after a year and a half of returning home, our business has become better than it ever was in Guangzhou. Our company employs more than 200 people, and last year's gross revenue reached up to 500 million yuan. To achieve such results is all down to the magical place that is Kuaishou—it is here that I regained my self-confidence and found a direction in life.

Our next step, if possible, is to pass on our successful experience through Kuaishou and guide people from my hometown to start businesses together. We will provide them with free training on running online stores so that they can sell local specialties such as potatoes, cucumbers, and mandarins to the whole country through Kuaishou.

LUOLA RUN: SELLING "TREE-RIPENED" FRUITS TO THE WHOLE OF CHINA THROUGH KUAISHOU

The Kuaishou account named Luola Run (now renamed Junshan Agriculture) has more than 500,000 followers and receives hundreds of fruit orders a day, while the repurchase rate of their customers is more than 80 percent. Shen Junshan, the owner of this account, calls himself the "first seller of Fuping dried persimmons on Kuaishou" and claims he can sell more than 300 tons of dried persimmons a year.

Before he started using Kuaishou in 2015, Shen Junshan was doing alright with his business that sold building materials. However, selling fruits on Kuaishou has enabled him to not only transform from a bicycle rider into a BMW driver, but also to help many poor local households to improve their living conditions.

Shen Junshan has established four fruit-producing centers across China, founded a company, and built up his own brand which is called Junshan Agriculture. His wish is to expand his company to Beijing so that more of his followers can have high-quality fruits to eat.

PROFILE

Kuaishou name: 俊山农业 (Junshan Agriculture)

Kuaishou ID: v4444444

Hometown: Anyang City, Henan Province

Age: 40

Education: junior high school

Topic(s): orchards and fruits

Production style: personally showing the seasonal fruits in the orchard and interacting with viewers on the livestream

Message to his loyal fans: To do Kuaishou E-commerce, you must have your own uniqueness and positioning. If selling fruits,

> you must perform supervision and be present at the production centers
>
> Business model: establish a company and sign cooperative contracts with orchards in fruit producing areas, then sell high-quality fruits and fruit products through Kuaishou while also providing fruits wholesale to downstream distributors
>
> Narrator: Shen Junshan

A Fruit Business That Was Inspired by a Video

It was quite fortuitous that I became popular on Kuaishou, but perhaps it was also destined.

I had innocently uploaded a kiwifruit video on Kuaishou—an action that changed my life. I became popular almost at once; I remember clearly that the video astonishingly garnered more than 400,000 hits in just one day.

Actually, the kiwifruits in the uploaded video were my landlord's. Because they had ripened at that time, my landlord suggested that we go pick some to eat together. I casually uploaded my first video on Kuaishou after the fact.

Unexpectedly, many people began to send me private messages asking if these kiwifruits were for sale. I answered offhandedly in the affirmative. Someone then asked me for the price and I said 40 yuan per kilogram without much thought. Back then, the market price of kiwifruits was not quite so high at 4.6 to 5.4 yuan per kilogram. My offhand quote, however, led to further events.

I was in the ceramic tile business at that time and took home hundreds of thousands of yuan a year, and thus had never thought about selling fruits. However, the enquirer asked me for my contact information and so I gave him my WeChat ID. He was quite an old stager—together with his name, phone number, and address, he also sent me a red envelope on WeChat. I opened the red envelope and was dumbfounded to find that he had transferred 200 yuan to me on what turned out to be my first order. I wondered if he was crazy to transfer such a sum to someone he only knew through a video, but over the next few days, I received many more kiwifruit orders.

Because of the reaction to the initial kiwi video, I produced another video and uploaded it to Kuaishou. Since I had gained a little fame, my wife suggested putting my WeChat ID in the video.

Once again, as soon as the second video was uploaded, my cell phone began to ring with messages from people wanting to buy kiwis. On the first day of that second video, I received more than 20 orders, and this was followed by hundreds of orders a day on the subsequent days. I started to panic because I didn't how to ship so many fruits at once. I asked around and found out that SF Express was considered the best courier available. Their delivery cost was 36 to 38 yuan for every 5 kilograms. After calculating all costs involved, I worked out that I could earn more than 100 yuan per order. I told my landlord to supply me with his pitayas and kiwis; I had come up with a strategy—or you could say an advertising tactic—of including a free pitaya with every kiwifruit order for the buyer to taste.

It was a very exciting time. I stopped selling ceramic tiles and instructed my workers to pack fruits instead. They would do the packing in the day and ship the fruits at night. On the first day, we shipped more than 300 orders. When calculating my earnings for that day, I was astonished to find that I had earned more money than I did in a few days of selling tiles.

My association with Kuaishou was even more fortuitous. I have a nephew who is a die-hard user of Kuaishou. One day, when his eyes were glued to his phone, as usual, I asked him what exactly he was looking at. He told me, "Uncle, you are so 'out.' Let me download it for you." He then took my phone and installed Kuaishou on it.

From that day on, I would watch Kuaishou videos every night before bed. There were many weird, funny, and thought-provoking short videos. At that time, I had not thought that this could be a business opportunity; it was purely entertainment to me.

I registered an account with the name "罗拉快跑" (Luola Run). Some people thus think that my surname is "罗" (Luo). I explained to them that my surname is not "Luo" and nor am I called "Luola." My surname is actually Shen and my full name is Shen Junshan. I am from a county seat in Anyang City, Henan Province, and I am 40 years old.

It was only because I had registered this account that the aforementioned kiwifruit story and the subsequent story of selling tree-ripened fruits to the whole of China took place.

Hard Work in the Pursuit of Freshness

In the first month I sold a lot of kiwifruits, such that I don't even remember how many orders there were in total. Having realized that I could use Kuaishou to earn money, I picked and shipped kiwifruits every day. During this period of time, many people trusted me and felt that my kiwifruits were tasty. Later on, they asked me whether I had durians for sale.

I replied that we do not grow durians in our area. In fact, I didn't know what a durian was and had never even seen one before. I searched on the web and found out that durians were produced in Malaysia and Thailand. I sillily decided to book a plane ticket to Thailand, but after I had done so, many people asked me whether I had a visa to go there. I didn't know what a visa was for and didn't have a passport either.

I thus applied for an expedited passport and received it within eight days. My nephew then helped me to apply for an expedited visa. With my passport and visa in hand, I got on the plane to Thailand. However, I didn't understand the local language. Thankfully, there were a few taxi drivers by the airport who could speak Chinese. I asked them how much it would cost to hire a taxi for a day, and they replied in Chinese that it would cost 5,000 baht. I then asked them to get me an interpreter and they told me that it would cost 4,000 baht.

I felt like I was being cheated as my plane ticket did not even cost 5,000 baht. However, being in such an unfamiliar place, I had little choice but to pay up.

After they provided me with a car and an interpreter, I told them to take me to a place with durians. They okayed my instruction and told me that I would certainly be satisfied. And so, we went to a durian production base where the durians grew like corns, causing me great bewilderment. I filmed many videos there and uploaded them to Kuaishou. Many people promptly asked me how much the durians cost. I told them I would reply to them at a later time, as I still had to go to the market to see the local price of durians before I could negotiate a price with the suppliers.

I walked around the market and talked to local fruit growers. Later, I called my friend and asked him what the market price of durians in China was. He answered that the price was about 26 yuan per half kilogram in China. In comparison, the market price in Thailand was the equivalent of 12 to 16 yuan. At first, I thought that the price was not okay, because after factoring in transport fees and import duties I would not make a profit at that price. However, it was soon clarified to me that the market price in Thailand was for a whole kilogram and not half. With that information, I came up with a plan.

There were many trucks on the market that were meant for hire by Chinese merchants. I negotiated a price with these "agents"—as they were called locally—who could collect durians on behalf of buyers. The cost at that time was hundreds of thousands of yuan for a truck that carried up to 26 tons. I then found a factory that could supply me with containers. In all, it took me several days to collect a whole truck of durians bound for China.

I had the durians shipped to a fruit wholesale market in Nanning City, Guangxi autonomous region (which is just over the border from Vietnam), and then advertised the durians on Kuaishou. Of course, I was able to set a price that was lower than the market price. I wholesaled durians to many durian sellers in the market while also selling durians directly over Kuaishou. In total, I made 150,000 yuan from this first truck of durians—it could be considered the first bucket of gold I had earned.

I was absolutely buzzing at that time. It would have taken me several months to earn 20,000 yuan from a truckload of ceramic tiles. Instead, I earned 150,000 yuan in 10 days by shipping a truckload of durians from Thailand and selling them in China.

After gaining the trust of my clients, they asked me whether I sold mangoes and persimmons as well.

I went on the internet and searched for mango-producing areas. The first variety I found was called Xinshiji, which is produced in

Panzhihua City, Sichuan Province. I would subsequently visit three mango-producing areas that were located in Hainan Province, Guangxi Autonomous Region, and Panzhihua City respectively, and went to different markets and tasted many local mango varieties in these places. Having previously been in the ceramic business, where I had to visit different manufacturers to ask the price of each tile pattern, I was familiar with the ins and outs of doing business. Selling fruits is not much different from selling ceramics—what you have to do is check the price in the local markets and then check the wholesale price in fruit supermarkets. You should also note that the prices of fruits produced in North China are different from those produced in South China. Regardless of whether you are doing a wholesale or retail business, there would definitely be a profit point somewhere in the middle.

I also began selling snake fruits. Some people may not like its taste; it is grimacingly sour, while its sweet aftertaste only lasts for a moment. However, women and particularly pregnant women generally like its taste. It is produced in Thailand, but not in China as of yet.

Another fruit I began selling is pitayas, which are commonly found in China. The variety that I sell is a special variety called Jingdu No. 1. Its exterior is different from other varieties; its skin is thin and can be either red or green, while its pulp is sweet. In addition, it does not go bad even if exposed to the sun for a week—this is its advantage.

Running a fruit business is also a lot of hard work. We have many things to do every day, and because of transportation reasons, we cannot guarantee that the fruits will arrive in perfect condition. Unlike clothes and shoes, fruits cannot be returned or replaced if they are not of the desired quality. By the time they are received by customers, some of them might have gone bad already. We have received messages from our customers on Kuaishou asking us why we shipped damaged fruits to them. In actual fact, we would never intend to ship damaged fruits, but we have no control over the handling of the fruits by the courier during the transportation process. I believe that people who have bought fruits online before might have had similar experiences. If a customer informs us that they have received damaged fruits, we compensate them proportionally—all they have to do is to take a photo of the damaged fruits and send it to us.

We ship mangoes in boxes of 9 to 10. If there are one or two damaged mangoes, we compensate the customer proportionally. If more than half of them have gone bad, we send the customer a new box of mangoes. Slowly but surely, we will continue to improve our after-sales services and packaging.

The First Seller of Fuping Dried Persimmons on Kuaishou

I am probably the first person to sell Fuping dried persimmons on the internet. Thanks to the trust that many of my loyal followers have in me, Fuping dried persimmons have become popular online. These fruits can be stored in the freezer for up to two years without going bad.

We produce dried persimmons on sticks. Many people wonder if the white powder on the skin is flour. In actual fact, that is not flour but instead a naturally forming "persimmon frost" that contains glucose, fructonic acid, and fructose. It does a lot of good for people with oral ulcers and stomach problems.

I was very lucky to find an exceptionally smart e-commerce business partner who is an expert in the deep processing of fruits. I found her contact information online and contacted her directly. Dried persimmons are produced not only in Fuping City, Shaanxi Province, but also in Shandong Province and Guilin City, Guangxi Autonomous Region. I have been to all of these places personally to find out about the different varieties—the taste of dried persimmons from Guilin is particularly unique.

However, I ultimately decided to sell Fuping dried persimmons because of its unique processing procedures. After a persimmon is picked, it is washed with water and peeled. Then, it is dried under mild sunlight rather than intense sunlight. This is the key to a good dried persimmon.

The drying generally takes three to five days, during which time the persimmons are "massaged" to soften them. Just like massaging a child or milking a cow, the pressure applied must neither be too soft nor too hard.

If the pressure is too hard, the persimmons develop two layers of skin, while if the pressure is too soft, the center becomes hard. Therefore, the massage must be done well in order for the persimmon to taste good.

Dried persimmons were packaged manually in the past, but now that they have become an industry of their own, they are machine-packaged instead.

Before I started selling dried persimmons, they were mostly exported to Japan and South Korea, where there are relatively strict product requirements in place, and product quality takes precedence over a low price. Nowadays, however, dried persimmons are no longer exported because of the high demand in China. This newfound demand is not because I have made dried persimmons suddenly taste a lot better, but because of Kuaishou's ability to promote them widely and let many people know of their great taste.

I have filmed and published a few videos that show how dried persimmons are processed, dried, cleaned, stocked, sold, and so on.

To be clear, it was Kuaishou that helped me to change my life and increase my income to a highly substantial figure. When I was selling ceramic tiles, I made approximately 300,000 to 500,000 yuan a year. However, ever since I started doing business on Kuaishou, I have been making millions of yuan a year.

Leading Poor Families to Change Our Fates Together

There is an elderly Fuping woman whose surname is Chou. Though she is from a poor family, she has an especially kind heart and is highly skilled in making dried persimmons even in her old age.

In the past, she would make dried persimmons mainly for her own consumption, and only the excess would be sold. Because of a lack of scale, she did not earn much from this unique skill and her living conditions were poor. When our dried persimmons began selling very well on Kuaishou, we started to buy dried persimmons from local merchants, including Madam Chou. Of course, the 1,000 kilograms of dried persimmons that Madam Chou was able to produce per year were far from enough for us.

Madam Chou does not use a mobile phone and does not even know what Kuaishou is. Nevertheless, Kuaishou has served as a channel for the sale of her products. There is no denying that Kuaishou is changing real lives.

In the past, the sale volume of Fuping dried persimmons was mediocre, and many of the goods were backlogged by sellers who could not move them. But ever since Kuaishou started being used to sell them, the demand has exceeded the supply. Some poor families that earned a few thousand yuan a year from selling dried persimmons in the past now earn more than 80,000 yuan a year, showing a 15-fold increase. I bought dried persimmons from them at 10 to 12 yuan per kilogram in the first year. But after their dried persimmons became popular on Kuaishou, the purchase price soared to 30 yuan a kilogram. I have signed more than just cooperation agreements with them. In fact, their income is pegged to our company's, meaning the higher our company's earnings, the higher their returns and vice versa. We have also invested human, material, and financial resources in them so that they need only put their full efforts in producing dried persimmons.

Ms. Chou is skilled and dexterous even in her advanced age. When we start processing dried persimmons again in October (as we do every year), I will film and upload a series of videos on Kuaishou to show everyone her skill in making dried persimmons.

Naturally ripened mangoes are hard to come by during winter. However, my company is indeed able to provide naturally ripened mangoes all year round. The mangoes that we deliver during winter are fully ripe; they are delivered as soon as they ripen on the tree. As for other seasons, the mangoes that we deliver are 80 percent ripe. Thus, regardless of the season, our customers can enjoy fresh mangoes right after receiving them.

Because our loyal followers on Kuaishou have trust in us, we get many repurchase orders. Our busiest times of the year are the Mid-Autumn Festival and the Spring Festival, when we receive more orders than we can manage. As China is a country of ceremony, it is natural to bring gifts when visiting our seniors and relatives during the Spring Festival. In the old days it was drinks and snacks, but now it has changed to fruits. Eighty percent of my loyal followers have repurchased fruits from us to serve as gifts.

I'm Not Handsome, but I Want to Show That I Am Present

When our fruits started selling well, my friends often asked me what my secret formula for business success was. The truth is that I don't have a secret; all I do is keep my feet on the ground. For those of you who might want to do Kuaishou E-commerce one day, just remember to decide whether your business is intended to make people laugh or to sell things.

If you are in it to sell things, then you must go down to the factories to check if the quality of the products is good. For selling fruits, you must perform supervision and must be present at the production centers. In most of my videos, I am present at the pertinent production center—for example, when I am promoting mangoes, I am next to a mango tree.

Many people have asked, "Why do you have to put yourself in your videos? Do you think you are very handsome?" Actually, I know I am not handsome, but by putting myself in my videos, I am showing that I am present at the production center.

I Want to Expand My Company to Beijing

As of now, I have four fruit-growing bases and they are located in Panzhihua City, Sichuan Province, Xishuangbanna Dai autonomous prefecture, Hainan Province, and Zhangzhou City, Fujian Province respectively. All of them are contracted orchards. While my business has grown and I have many people supporting me, my true supporters are my loyal followers on Kuaishou.

I now have my own brand, namely Junshan Agriculture. All of the shipment boxes have my brand printed on them, unlike in the past when the boxes did not have any sort of logo on them. I have also begun trying to deep-process fruits, such as dried mangoes and loquat pastes. Perhaps in the future, you will be able to taste our self-made preserved fruits and jams.

Because there was no Yellow Cart (a direct link to Kuaishou Store) on Kuaishou in the past, purchases used to be done through WeChat. I had 16 WeChat accounts, each of which had 5,000 friends. From the moment I woke up in the morning until 4 a.m. the next day, I would be taking orders together with three customer service employees. But ever since Kuaishou added Yellow Cart, customers can place orders directly and thus things have become much more convenient for e-commerce merchants like myself.

My next goal is to open brick-and-mortar stores in first- and second-tier cities. Although the rental and labor costs in Beijing are considerably expensive, such that my business might not even be profitable there, I still want to open a brick-and-mortar fruit store that I can call my own over there. After all, expanding my company to the capital of China has always been my goal.

SHANCUN ERGE: AFTER CUTTING AN ORANGE ON KUAISHOU I INADVERTENTLY BECAME A "FRUIT HUNTER"

Shancun Erge was originally the owner of a hairdressing salon. His business on Kuaishou began from an "accident": he casually uploaded to Kuaishou a video of the oranges in his friend's orchard. The video became popular on the Discover page, and this would change his life forever.

When a business opportunity arose, Erge decisively made the switch to become a full-time "fruit hunter." Every year, after the season for Nanxi Blood Oranges passes, he goes to Yunnan or Hainan to look for mangoes. At the end of June, he returns to Sichuan to sell plums. In this way, he is busy throughout the four seasons of a year. He says that doing business on Kuaishou is not just about buyer-seller relations but more so about friendships with loyal followers, and he "cannot let friends down." This is the secret as to why his business keeps on getting bigger.

PROFILE

Kuaishou name: 山村二哥 – 汇奉源 (Shancun Erge – Huifengyuan)

Kuaishou ID: miaosi11

Hometown: Yibin City, Sichuan Province

Age: 32

Education: junior high school

Topic: display of blood oranges and other fruits

Production style: displaying the freshness, sweetness, and juiciness of the fruits from his production center

Message to his loyal fans: Word-of-mouth has the most value for sellers on Kuaishou. It is really difficult to keep hold of a customer, and besides many of our customers regard us as friends, and so we must have high standards on quality

Business model: buy high-quality specialty fruits (such as Nanxi Blood Oranges) from various places and sell them to our loyal followers all over the country through Kuaishou Store

Narrator: Miao Li

The First Box of Oranges We Sold on Kuaishou

Just as Newton discovered gravity when an apple fell on his head, I became a full-time "fruit hunter" after cutting an orange on Kuaishou.

My name is Miao Li, and my nickname on Kuaishou is "Shancun Erge." I was born in 1987 in Yibin City, Sichuan Province. I began to learn hairdressing after graduating from junior high school, and then later on I opened a hairdressing salon.

I have a friend named Yi Song—we got to know each other over Kuaishou. We both enjoy outdoor activities. Once, when I was back in my hometown, I visited Yi Song's orchard to pick some oranges for myself. While there I casually shot a video and uploaded it to Kuaishou. There was nothing special about that video: all I did was cut an orange into two. However, it quickly became popular and attracted many comments.

The orange I picked is called a "blood orange" in my hometown. The orchards here are situated along the Yangtze River. The summer temperature is high during the day, but when the wind blows over the river at night, the temperature immediately drops. The big temperature difference between day and night is conducive to the buildup of sugar in blood oranges, which explains why they are so sweet. Although we had never actually measured the sweetness of the oranges at that time, we could taste that they were sweeter than sugar. And when using a knife to cut an orange, the knife would often stick on to my hand. Later on, when we bought a tool to measure the sweetness, we found that the sweetness rating of the blood oranges could reach up to 16. In comparison, oranges on the market today with a sweetness rating of 14 or 15 are considered sweeter than average already.

After seeing the video, a Kuaishou user asked us if the oranges were for sale. My friend answered in the affirmative, because he had more than enough for his family. This thus became our first order from Kuaishou: five kilograms of blood oranges for 48 yuan.

We didn't have a packing box, so we bought a box with netting for 4.5 yuan from the express post office. The delivery fee at that time was 15 yuan per parcel, while the cost of growing the oranges was approximately 13 yuan. In total, we calculated that we could earn a profit of about 10 yuan from that first order.

We had been using Kuaishou for a long time but did not realize that it could be a business opportunity, and neither did we notice that people were doing business on Kuaishou. That first order enlightened me to the fact that Kuaishou could be used not just for entertainment, but also for making money.

Later on, our buyers and sales kept on increasing, and there were also a lot of repurchasers. Some people would even upload videos that helped us to advertise our products and brought many customers to us. Because of that first video I uploaded, we ended up selling several hundred kilograms' worth of oranges.

Due to the success of selling blood oranges, I decided to focus on a business of helping my followers to find high-quality fruits.

Aside from blood oranges, I have also sold plums from my hometown over Kuaishou, but by the end of August 2018, all of the plums were sold out. As luck would have it, however, the plums grown in Wenchuan

County were not yet in season, and so I went over there to purchase plums for resale. I met up with a Kuaishou acquaintance called Chen Rong and we cooperated to sell plums directly from Wenchuan through express delivery. The sales went on until October; in total, we sold more than 10,000 kilograms of plums.

After returning from Wenchuan, I began to build a team. My hometown did not have fruits for every season of the year; the only marketable fruits we grew were plums and oranges, and so we had no fruits when these two fruits were out of season. It was therefore necessary for me to venture out and find more types of fruits, and that was how I became a true fruit hunter.

There are many people on Kuaishou who also have good hometown products for sale. Through Kuaishou, I got to know the group of people who were the first to run fruit businesses on the platform. By chatting on Kuaishou, we became familiar with one another and soon established cooperations. Later on, I joined several hometown groups and got to know even more people. They are mainly located in places such as Yunnan Province, Hainan Province, and Fuping City, which are all places where fruits are grown in abundance.

In 2018, I registered a company. The shareholders are my friend Yi Song and me. Yi Song used to work in a security company and his responsibility was installing cameras. His brother, who had just returned home from working in Wuhan City, also joined us. When the company was founded, the three of us were the only employees. Now, the team has grown to seven people.

The seven of us are distributors, employees, and partners, and we all got to know one another through Kuaishou. I don't assign responsibilities—instead, we discuss and do everything together, regardless of whether it's purchasing, packing, or shipping. For example, when we receive orders, we would pool together all of the orders we individually received, and then we would pack and ship the orders together.

Each of us can keep the profit from a sale we made. For example, if the selling cost is 50 yuan per box, I would only need to turn in 50 yuan to the company for each box of fruits I sold. This is fine as long as the company does not lose money on an order and can cover its expenses;

together, we work to ensure that the company can keep on operating normally.

Using Kuaishou Store to Accelerate Business Development

In 2012, I opened an online store that helped people to sell electronic products. And when I started selling plums in 2018, I also opened an online store—its user rating was considerably high.

However, running an online store has become more complicated than before. For example, there are things such as click farming, keywords, and weight ranking, which I do not know about. Furthermore, negative reviews would give me sleepless nights. Eventually, I decided to give up.

Another issue was our pricing. For example, our price for four kilograms of Aiyuan oranges was 68 yuan, but users told us that they could find many online stores that offered the same product for a much cheaper price. Those vendors had paid money for through train promotion. I personally saw that there were Aiyuan oranges being sold at 29 yuan for four kilograms. For us, that price would not even be enough to cover our costs. Some buyers do not understand this and only care about getting the cheapest deal. These through train products have very a high display weight and enjoy a high transaction volume.

I feel that Kuaishou Store is still the quickest way of doing business. The simplest method of all is to accumulate followers on Kuaishou and allow them to place orders directly on Kuaishou Store. When a user sees something that is good, they would want to buy it directly, and so the conversion rate on Kuaishou Store is very high. After an order has been placed, I export the data from the back end platform and then pack and ship the goods. Livestreams on Kuaishou yield even higher order rates as they can directly display fruits that are delicious.

Starting a livestream immediately after your video becomes popular on the Discover page would also make it more effective. After watching the video, followers would enter the livestream. If, during the livestream, they see you picking fruits or sealing a box that is about to be shipped, the effect would be even more direct and the conversion rate would be phenomenally high.

My videos have appeared on the Popular page several times. One of my videos received more than 800,000 hits and brought nearly 1,000 people to my livestream. I received a lot of orders in no time. Once, at 3 a.m., someone ordered two boxes of fruits through a voice message. It took me a while to find out that this person was living in the United States.

Word-of-mouth ranks first for driving the sale of goods. Our quality control standards are very high. It's really not easy to keep hold of customers, so we don't want to lose a single one of them. If a customer reports that a few of the received fruits have gone bad, we compensate them proportionally. And if the number of gone-bad fruits is significant, we would quickly send them a new box of fruits.

Our followers also have a high degree of trust in us. On other e-commerce platforms, our relations with users are purely buyer-seller relations, whereas on Kuaishou our followers feel like friends.

I once did a livestream with only a few dozen viewers, but many of them were my regular customers who had bought our blood oranges before. Suddenly, an unfamiliar person came in and said that blood oranges are only red because food coloring is injected in them. Some of my followers retorted, "You don't understand. Do you know what a real blood orange is like? What you bought were fake blood oranges. Of course, you wouldn't know what a real blood orange is like." Denounced by so many people, the troublemaker promptly left the livestream.

Sharing Hometown Specialties with the Rest of China

My focus has now shifted to finding ways to increase sales. Without a doubt, sales have to be the top priority. We intend to use blood oranges, which are a very special type of fruit, to showcase our business. After the season for blood oranges is over, I will go to Yunnan or Hainan to find good mangoes for everyone.

After selling mangoes until the end of June, it will be the season for plums from my hometown in Sichuan. Now that we are selling fruits to make a living, we cannot have any gap period during the year, otherwise we won't earn any income.

I have hired professionals to run my hairdressing salon so that I can focus fully on running my fruit business on Kuaishou. When every aspect of our fruit sources has stabilized completely, we will be able to supply fruits to other teams, thereby doing wholesale sales along with retail.

In my opinion people like us are the "sharers" of good stuff from our respective hometowns. By using Kuaishou, we are able to share hometown specialties with the rest of China. This is beneficial to us, to farmers, and to the buyers of such good stuff. Everybody wins.

XIANYANG ERQIAO: FROM "KITCHEN GOD" ON KUAISHOU TO KING OF RED CHILI OIL E-COMMERCE

Old Qiao is a retired brickyard worker while his son Little Qiao is a computer science graduate. Together, the two of them made short videos depicting Shaanxi cuisine on Kuaishou. Old Qiao prepares the cuisine while Little Qiao records the videos. Through their 30-second cooking tutorials that never fail to include the line "one more clove of garlic" spoken in Shaanxi dialect, they have received countless "little hearts" from their loyal followers on Kuaishou who come from all over China. Rather than producing exquisite documentaries, what they did was to capture a "kingdom of cuisine" and a "life of smoke and fire" at home on a mobile phone.

With more than 4.12 million fans, they have set up two companies and sold more than 30,000 bottles of red chili oil in less than a year, with monthly revenue exceeding 300,000 yuan. They have also been interviewed by and reported on by national television and other media. Traveling by high-speed rail and airplane to various parts of China to participate in various short-video related activities has become a part of their lives, often meeting people who recognize them.

From a retired father and an ordinary tech worker to short video creators and then to e-commerce businessmen, Old Qiao and Little Qiao have thoroughly transformed their lives with the help of Kuaishou. In doing so, they have also bridged the communication gap between father and son.

PROFILE

Kuaishou name: 陕西老乔小乔父子档 (Old Qiao and Little Qiao, Father and Son From Shaanxi)

Kuaishou ID: shanxilaoqiao

Hometown: Xianyang City, Shaanxi Province

Age: 63 and 33 respectively

Education: high School and undergraduate respectively

Topic: Shaanxi cuisine

Production style: creating tutorials on homemade cuisine, with the father Old Qiao appearing in the videos

Message to their loyal fans: if you want to succeed on Kuaishou, you need to persist, persist, and persist!

Business model: set up companies and register trademarks, then produce Shaanxi cuisine such as red chili oil and sell them through Kuaishou E-commerce

Narrator: Qiao Fei

We Foresaw a Future of Mobile Internet and Decided to Join Kuaishou

Choosing to start our business on Kuaishou might very well be one of the most correct decisions I ever make in my life.

I am Little Qiao and I graduated from Xi'an Jiaotong University with a major in computer science. My father worked in a brick factory all his life. If it wasn't for Kuaishou, my father and I could not possibly have become cuisine livestreamers and then started an e-commerce business that sells Shaanxi cuisine to various parts of China.

As a person, I prefer to live close to my hometown and thus, did not want to leave home after graduation. However, there were not many internet-related work opportunities in Shaanxi and so I did gardening work instead.

In 2015, I heard on the news that the era of the mobile internet was coming. I was stirred up by these words and thus began to do some research. I was bullish on Kuaishou, as I felt it was more grounded and closer to its users as compared to its "we-media" rival in Weibo. I therefore decided to give it a try.

At first, I wanted to make comedy videos to upload to Kuaishou and thus invited many friends to join in the fun. However, I was disappointed to find that none of my friends were quite as bullish on this as I was. When I returned home, my father asked me about it and offered to have a go of it with me. And so that was how it all started.

My father is generally supportive of whatever I do. In the past, my mother wanted me to go down the path of a civil servant, but my father disagreed. He felt that the salary of a civil servant was too low at 3,000 to 4,000 yuan a month, and besides he felt that a young man should go out and find his own kind of life. When it comes to my career, my father certainly has a more liberal view than other parents would have for their children.

Shaanxi is famous for its history, its culture, and its snacks. The dissemination and promotion of history and culture require time and a buildup of knowledge. In comparison, food is an easier way to attract viewers, and so we decided to start with cuisine videos.

In October 2016, I registered a Kuaishou account. At first, we merely showed all kinds of Shaanxi cuisine and snacks in our videos and did not provide tutorials on how to prepare them.

Later on, many fans asked us how the food in our videos was prepared and commented that they really wanted to taste it for themselves.

I could not find any cooking tutorial videos on the internet at that time. Instead, all I found were pictures that could be pieced together to explain how a certain dish was prepared. In comparison, I felt that videos would be more vivid and direct. I thus came up with the idea whereby I would film my father preparing food and then add voice-over to the video. That would certainly be more vivid and attractive to viewers.

Besides, Kuaishou was mainly based on videos from the onset, and so pictures were rarely recommended to users. We thus began to film cooking tutorial videos from that time on and might even have been the first to do so on Kuaishou.

My father began cooking for himself from a young age and is highly skilled in cooking as a result. He is also very interested in cuisine. Whenever he has a free day, he will be tinkering about in the kitchen. He is able to learn how to cook almost anything just by watching the preparation once. Therefore, preparing food on camera is a walk in the park to him.

We hit an impasse when our followers reached 40,000. For that half a month, seeing the stagnated follower count rendered me unable to eat or sleep. However, I never once thought about giving up because I knew the key to success was persistence, persistence, and persistence. I began to do some research on presentation, such as what kind of cover was more attractive to viewers and what topics were more interesting.

Subsequently, we released a video about how to make cold rice noodles; it was an instant hit and we gained 100,000 fans overnight. This was our breakout moment—many newspapers and TV stations came to interview us.

In actual fact, the video was no different in content from our earlier videos. The main difference was the attractive timing of the video. Many people all around China know about Shaanxi cold rice noodles and enjoy eating them, but do not know how to prepare them. We were the first to share the preparation method online. On top of that, it was summer at that time, and so cold rice noodles were all the more desired.

The other videos that I have a deep impression of are the ones on lamb paomo and rolled noodles. For the video on lamb paomo, the ingredients alone cost me more than 300 yuan. I also paid a considerable sum to learn the recipe from a good chef. As for the video on rolled noodles, the noodles were entirely handmade, and so the filming of the video alone took 36 hours.

Most of our cuisine videos were completed in one take and failures were rare. However, my father and I occasionally disagreed during production—he wanted to do things his own way while I also wanted to do things my own way.

For example, there was once when the camera was close-up to the food and so I told my father to use less salt or else the food would not look so good on camera. However, my father disagreed and felt that it was necessary to add the normal amount of salt. We ended up quarreling over that matter. However, in the big picture of things, he is generally very supportive of my ideas.

Red Chili Oils Opened the Way to E-Commerce for Me

When I first started filming Kuaishou videos, I did not do livestreams and did not earn any money from it. My idea at that time was very simple: as long as I build up a base of followers, I would be able to sell things in the future, and so earning money was not important for now.

Half a year later, when I had accumulated more than 700,000 followers, I began to sell handmade red chili oils. The red chili oils were first fried by my parents at home. We would then disinfect the bottles to be used for packing the oils before pouring the cooled-down oils into each bottle. The filled bottles would then be sealed with plastic and placed into boxes.

I still vividly remember that we had to take orders on WeChat back then. It was very tedious and tiring work placing delivery orders and filling in the tracking numbers by myself. We worked nonstop from morning till night for half a year—my mother's back began to hurt from exhaustion.

I later made some adjustments to our production process as I felt that we could not just keep slogging away. My idea was to refocus my efforts on accumulating followers and then do something big. After I had spent a year building my own production team, I applied for a trademark and completed all of the formalities for officially entering the e-commerce industry.

I also looked at how other people on Kuaishou were doing e-commerce. However, I felt that their methods were not viable in the long term. This was because they were all recommending products produced by other people, which is as good as giving their followers to those people. If a follower buys one of these recommended products and likes it, they will not repurchase it from the recommender in the future, but if they dislike the product, they will blame the recommender for recommending it to them, often causing the recommender to lose followers.

This is why I invested a lot of time on my products. By the time I entered e-commerce, I had built my own team, founded my own company, developed my own products, and established my own brand.

I now have sales of more than 300,000 yuan a month, with a net profit of more than 10 percent.

We mainly sell red chili oil, beef, dried persimmons, millet, and chili powder, and remain in the midst of launching other products, most of which are Shaanxi specialties.

Our main products such as red chili oil are produced by an engaged manufacturer using our own recipe. Our new red chili oils are all factory-produced. It took nearly a full year of work for my professional team to straighten out the entire manufacturing process. After we stopped producing the old handmade red chili oils, I have been visiting markets and doing surveys and research on the recipe and taste for the new red chili oil.

We finally settled on our product after getting more than 1,000 people to serve as tasters.

Nowadays, China is very strict on food safety. All products must carry a clearly stated production date, a valid quality certificate, and a clearly stated manufacturer in order to be sold. Furthermore, a production license or a food circulation license is required to sell products on Kuaishou.

We produced 2,000 bottles of the new red chili oil in the first batch and they sold out in no time. Red chili oil is a highly representative Shaanxi specialty and is thus very well-liked among our followers. Often, when it is out of stock, our livestream will be full of comments asking when it will be available again.

There was a follower who bought two bottles of red chili oil and greatly enjoyed the taste after trying it. Because we were out of stock, he messaged me every day for more than half a month asking about the re-stock time. And whenever I started a livestream, he would send me gifts hoping that it would make me hasten the production of the red chili oil. When the next batch was ready, he bought 10 bottles at once.

The price for two bottles of red chili oil is 38.8 yuan. By the end of 2018, more than 5,000 bottles of the new red chili oil had been sold. For our major products such as this, we pace the release of the product so as to generate hype.

In 2018, I also sold melons, sweet potatoes, kiwifruits, and pome-granates. As I have all along been involved in poverty alleviation activi-ties, we also have tie-ins with the government to sell agricultural products from impoverished areas.

We try to choose the best sources of goods. My dad and I value our followers very much, so we strive to sell good-quality products even if the price is not the cheapest.

Being responsible to my fans is one of my principles. This applies to the red chili oils we are selling now as well. If a follower tells us that the red chili oil does not taste good, we will fully refund them their money.

Initially, Kuaishou did not support monetization on their platform. It is only in the first half of 2018 that Kuaishou officially began to help cre-ators to monetize with the launch of Kuaishou Store. Followers can enter a merchant's store to purchase items after coming in through a video or livestream.

In the past, sales were done over WeChat. Customers had to add a seller on WeChat in order for the seller to make a sale to them. I feel that this was quite inconvenient because, as a seller, I did not have enough en-ergy to reply to every single customer, get each customer's address, and fill in each order number.

Now that I have opened an online store, sales are done directly through the platform. The platform provides third-party insurance and third-party control of product quality. If the food I want to sell can be up-loaded to the platform and displayed on the Sales page, that would mean it has been reviewed and so I don't have to worry. We also no longer have to take care of things such as after-sales ourselves.

Two months after the launch of Kuaishou Store, our total number of received orders increased to more than 20,000 orders.

Kuaishou is a shopping platform in itself. I believe that in the near future, many people will be directly buying things on Kuaishou. As for some regular users, I'm certain that they would go back to watching Kuaishou even if they had gone to other platforms to buy what they saw on Kuaishou.

My Future Plan Is to "Brandify" Our Business and Establish a Cuisine MCN

I now have two companies, and my business partners are two ex-classmates of mine. They had asked me on their own initiative if they could join my ventures.

Before that, when my Kuaishou followers reached approximately 1 million, many of my ex-classmates wanted to become my business partners, and so I began to screen them.

The first criterion that I have is good character. The two ex-classmates that I chose are both very serious in their work. One of them also has a very good grip on many detailed aspects; he would personally check on everything even if it just packing or shipping. Hence, this saved me a lot of trouble and I no longer had to worry about all of the details.

Because my father is over 60 years old, he isn't concerned about the daily operations of the company. Now, all of the video content on the platform is produced by me alone. My business partners are instead responsible for e-commerce, product management, corporate management, before-sales, after-sales, and so on.

My business partners would also make suggestions about my video content. For example, they once suggested engaging a professional team with professional equipment and professional production to film a "Hollywood-like" video.

We did try it but did not continue with it in the end. The reason was that many people felt that this wasn't our style after watching the video.

Our initial style was all about staying grounded, and so to suddenly change our style was not acceptable to our followers.

There are at least tens of thousands of people—if not hundreds of thousands of people—teaching people how to cook on "we-media." So, why are we able to stand out? It is precisely because our style is more sincere and down-to-earth, which is a very good selling point in itself. Every person has his own attributes and intellectual property that cannot and must not be changed.

In January 2019, I also entertained a Suzhou-based multi-channel network (MCN). They had more than 200 food writers who were separately responsible for food appraisal, store visiting, and production, as well as work related to "emotional cuisine." I wanted to glean experience from them so that I can set up my own MCN organization in the future.

We have already grown attached to Kuaishou. After all, Shaanxi people like ourselves tend to be loyal and honest. Kuaishou was the first platform to bring me popularity and success; having started my business on Kuaishou, I will continue to use it as the core of my business.

In terms of monetization, Kuaishou is probably the best platform on the internet. To give an example, I receive at least 10,000 orders of red chili oil on Kuaishou over any two-month period. The other platforms, however, can only provide me with up to a combined 4,700 orders over a two-month period. According to a professional analysis that I heard regarding other video platforms, there is a platform on which a video that garnered 10 million hits only yielded four orders. In comparison, the sales volume and conversion rate on Kuaishou is much higher.

My father and I have become very well known. Whenever we are on the streets or even when taking a train or airplane, there are people who recognize us.

My father is an outgoing person, whereas I am a bit shy. When we are asked to participate in an activity or to go on television, I am unwilling to go and more so to show my face. My father, however, is more communicative on these programs.

When I was a child, my father worked outside our hometown in order to earn money. We thus had little time together throughout the year. Now, however, our relationship has grown very close. This is in part thanks to Kuaishou for giving us a business in common and conversation topics in common, ensuring that there is no longer a generational gap between us.

HAO DONG: KUAISHOU FULFILLED MY PERFORMANCE DREAM AND MY HOT POT DREAM

Hao Dong is a young man from Chongqing, a municipality near Sichuan Province, who likes performing. On Kuaishou he is called a cross of Hu Ge and Lü Ziqiao (two famous actors in China) by his fans. His videos on Kuaishou have similar emotional and comedic effects to the Chinese sitcom *iPartment* and are deeply enjoyed by many netizens.

Hao Dong, who has worked as a snack stall vendor and a salesman, now has more than 4.2 million fans on Kuaishou. Together with his wife, he has created his own brand of cosmetics and self-heating hot pot cookers. Thanks to Kuaishou and his Kuaishou followers, his and his wife's lives have continually improved. His cosmetics brand has made more than 30 million yuan in sales, while his self-heating hot pot cookers have managed around 2 million yuan in sales just four months after launch. It can be said that both the "dreams in his head" and the "life beneath his feet" are becoming more and more promising.

PROFILE

Kuaishou name: 浩东大大 (Haodong Dada)

Kuaishou ID: AAAA9999

Hometown: Chongqing Municipality

Age: 24

Education: technical secondary school

Topic: funny sitcoms

Production style: daily dribs and drabs of him and his wife

Message to his loyal fans: enjoyment and application will brew the soul of a work

Business model: sell his own brand of cosmetics and self-heating hot pots

Narrator: Hao Dong

Kuaishou Unleashed My Passion for Performing

Who wouldn't want to be a star in the spotlight if given the stage? I was once an ordinary boy in Chongqing, but now I have my own stage in Kuaishou and my own followers—all of these are like a dream to me.

My name is Hao Dong and I'm from Chongqing. I graduated from vocational school with a specialization in online crowd analysis under website operation. After graduation in 2012 I had a hard time finding a job. So, to earn a living I set up roadside stalls and sold fried potatoes. Later on, I worked as a salesman for big companies. It was during that time that I discovered Kuaishou.

I first filmed a video and released it on Kuaishou in March 2014. Unexpectedly, it made it on to the Popular page. At that time the image quality of my production was not so great and the editing was also very basic, but I put a lot of application into my creativity and performance. I thus learned a truth firsthand: as long as you perform conscientiously, everyone would be able to see you. From then on, I decided to grow myself on Kuaishou. The content of my videos is similar to that of sitcoms. My wife and I wrote, directed, and acted out the productions ourselves. Sometimes, we would spend 15 to 18 hours a day planning and designing our videos.

Actually, I have had a dream of performing since I was a child. I especially wanted to enroll in an arts school. However, be it singing or performing, my family was quite opposed to the idea. They thought it was unrealistic and believed that ordinary folk like us should stick to doing honest work. Nevertheless, this dream I had remained buried in my heart. After I discovered Kuaishou, I knew that this was an opportunity I could not afford to miss. I thought to myself that even if I don't become a huge star, I would be able to create a name for myself by working hard and might even get to perform on the same stage as the stars.

Finding the Right Positioning Is Halfway to Success

After deciding to pursue the filming of Kuaishou videos seriously, we begin studying how to use Kuaishou, what content to film, what style to use, and so on. I discovered that there were very few husband-and-wife pairings on Kuaishou at that time. Besides, the few that there were merely talked about household affairs and lacked eye-catchiness.

In Chongqing, we use the phrase *soft ears* to refer to a henpecked husband. Using this as inspiration, we blended Mandarin and Chongqing dialect to perform various stories of a native Chongqing man who is very afraid of his wife.

We also made many adjustments along the way. For example, we started by filming landscape videos, but then changed to portrait videos as it was more in line with the viewing habit of mobile users. We also gradually began to use Kuaishou's editing and dubbing features. After making such adjustments, one of our videos garnered six million hits. Nearly a month later, our followers exceeded one million.

I believe that finding the right positioning for ourselves is the key to our success during this stage. For instance, in acting, a handsome and charming man usually does not play the role of a fool, while an honest-looking man usually does not play the role of an ideal man. It is very important for the image that we portray in our performance to be in line with our natural image. Only by finding the right positioning and establishing a persona would the audience remember what kind of person you are and be willing to watch your other productions.

Infusing Our Souls into Our Productions

We have grown considerably thus far. We now have a team of 14 people who are respectively responsible for editing, data analysis, post-production, and so on. Previously, we invited more than 20 directors to try editing our videos, but none of them could get it just right. My wife and I thus decided to remain in charge of the creative side of things. No matter how busy we are, we spend five or six hours a day thinking and writing the script, and sometimes this will take until the early morning.

In my opinion, the theme and plot of our productions should ideally be close to real life, because we are most familiar with the people and things around us, and it also allows the viewers to find resonance with the video. Only we know what we want to express most and what suits the tastes of our audience. At the same time, it is my hope that viewers can alleviate the pileup of negative emotions from work by watching my productions.

To a creator, it is important not only to have fresh ideas but also to enjoy performing. Productions that are done simply to earn money are lifeless. For example, some companies operate accounts that upload dozens of videos per day. Although they change their style every day, very few of their videos feel like a breath of fresh air or have memorable characters. Only creators who enjoy what they are doing can infuse their souls into their work. And when a production is full of creativity and soul, it is highly memorable even if only watched once.

A "Hot Pot Hero" with a Dream of Performing.

When I first started uploading videos on Kuaishou, I was thinking less about how to make money through the platform and more about just wanting to fulfill my long-cherished dream. At that time, I had neither income nor savings, and even had to ask my parents for money on occasion in order to get by. Later on, we were part of the first batch of users for the closed beta of Kuaishou's livestreaming feature and were also part of the first batch of people to promote and sell goods on Kuaishou. Subsequently, in order for my wife to have good cosmetics to put on, we researched and developed our own brand of cosmetics. And because Chongqing is the birthplace of hot pot, we also launched our own self-heating hot pots—it has since become a product with a very high repurchase rate.

I realized that it was especially suitable for me to sell self-heating hot pots because my image on Kuaishou was that of a wife-loving yet wife-fearing man from Chongqing. On the other hand, there was always going to be a little disconnect for a man to sell cosmetics. When trying to do business, choosing products that match one's image yields better results.

I came to understand a truth during this process: You don't necessarily need to have a lot of followers, but you can improve the retention and conversion of your followers by creating focused and precise productions. While followers like or even worship the creators they follow, I believe what is more important is that they trust these creators. If they have watched as a creator grew from a "nobody" into an influential online celebrity, they would feel a sense of achievement themselves and would be willing to buy products from said creator. In 2018, our cosmetics web page received 30 million hits through Kuaishou, while our self-heating hot pots garnered 2 million yuan in sales just four months after launch. These are all due to our followers' approval of us.

In the future, I want to make our self-heating hot pots into a brand through Kuaishou. Nevertheless, my focus will remain on video production. Performing has always been a seed deeply buried in my heart, and thanks to Kuaishou, this seed has now blossomed and borne fruit. We hope to keep on improving in the production of our future videos. For now, I hope to film a good series of videos so as to offer my followers even more, even better, and even more satisfying productions. My wife and I have never deviated from this original aspiration of ours.

CHAPTER **THREE**

KUAISHOU EDUCATION: REDEFINING *KNOWLEDGE*

CHAPTER OVERVIEW

W e launched the Kuaishou Education ecosystem so that more creators can come to Kuaishou to provide free video content and social educational services, thereby maximizing the positive social benefits. Kuaishou Classroom hopes above all that more education professionals will feel moved to get involved after seeing these success stories.

It is on this basis that Kuaishou Education has formed a very friendly environment, where every kind of talent can be seen and brought out. As Confucius said, "In a party of three or more people, there must be at least one from whom I can learn." To get closer to finding happiness, each user simply needs to give full play to their own strengths and join courses that are relevant to their circumstances.

Kuaishou Education's ultimate vision is for the Kuaishou platform to bring out every kind of talent and to make the pursuit of happiness easier with the help of its inclusive values, technologies, and products.

KUAISHOU EDUCATION: REDEFINING *KNOWLEDGE*

Tu Zhijun, head of Kuaishou Education
Li Zhuo, operations director of Kuaishou Classroom

From her home in the countryside, Lan Ruiyuan offers lectures to people across the world.

With the aid of an interconnected mobile phone and computer, she answers questions regarding Microsoft Excel for 860,000 students while speaking in a southern Mandarin accent. In doing so, she earns 400,000 yuan a year more than she used to. At just 30 years old, she has not only created value for her students but also improved her own life through this accumulative process of teaching.

Stories such as Lan Ruiyuan's take place on Kuaishou every day—they all share a common identity as a lecturer on Kuaishou Classroom.

Through its "short videos + livestreaming" form, Kuaishou has greatly expanded the connotations of education and knowledge and real-ized a friendly educational ecosystem where anyone can teach, learn, and change their destiny through knowledge.

Kuaishou Has Greatly Expanded the Connotations of Knowledge and Education

In the past, subjects such as how to paint walls, how to install cement tiles, how to make dumplings, and how to provide aftercare for goats were taught through mentorship and word-of-mouth and shared within a small range as experience or skill—they had not been internetized, structured, or knowledgized.

Through short videos and livestreams, Kuaishou has served to build up interpersonal connections and form a rich social ecosystem. At the same time, it has generated a powerful force—experience or skill have become knowledge that can be reproduced, taught, disseminated, and even converted into offline use.

In the old times, the transmission of knowledge was seen as the outcome of education. For example, topping the imperial examinations granted entry into the Hanlin Academy. Fast forward to today, and many people continue to regard the purpose of education to be to lead to a bright future.

However, knowledge is not actually like that. For example, if the owner of a steamed bun shop learns how to make a new type of bun on Kuaishou, they can make and sell said type of bun the very next day. Seeing such a unique type of bun, customers might buy a few more buns or offer words of compliment. This would comfort the owner psychologically and raise their sense of happiness.

Unlike traditional educational resources, this kind of knowledge is not very academic, yet highly practical. Such practicality does not necessarily equate to obtaining certain resources using the academic degrees and social identity gained from taking tests on teacher-taught knowledge.

Today, tens of thousands of courses are available in the Kuaishou Education ecosystem, while users from more than 360 different professions have recorded and shared their life experiences on Kuaishou.

The Kuaishou Education ecosystem allows for several modes of teaching and learning. The first mode is about practical technology, as mentioned earlier. The second mode is about interest-based teaching and learning. When a person has satisfied their need for warmth and food, they have higher-order spiritual needs. For example, interests in comics and handicraft might not be convertible into actual income, but they can enrich a person's spiritual world. The third mode is about pure knowledge, such as historical storytelling—this serves to cultivate a person's mind.

There are certainly a lot of knowledge lessons in the traditional sense on Kuaishou. A philosophy professor from Tsinghua University has shared the ideas of philosophers such as Socrates, Plato, and Aristotle on Kuaishou. He has hundreds of thousands of followers and his courses sell very well.

Although more than 70 percent of content in the Kuaishou Education ecosystem is about practical knowledge, this traditional form of teaching and learning is still evolving, and we look forward to the possibilities that lie ahead.

It can be said that a new community ecosystem like Kuaishou has greatly expanded the connotations of traditional knowledge and education.

"Short Videos + Livestreaming": A Rich Medium of Knowledge Transmission

Back when I was in school, I read the short story *My Uncle Jules* by Guy de Maupassant for literature class. It mentioned eating oysters by the sea. As someone from an inland region of China, I did not know for many years what an oyster looks like, not to mention that I could not imagine such a fancy way of eating at all.

My teacher also taught us a Chinese idiom that takes the blooming of a broad-leaved epiphyllum as a metaphor for something that is a flash in the pan. What is a broad-leaved epiphyllum? And why does it only bloom for such a short time? No matter how lifelike it is drawn, or how detailed a photograph of it is taken, it is very hard for children to gain a complete understanding of it from just drawings or photographs. And while textual information certainly has its unique logic and value, it also has its own limitations.

Kuaishou is able to provide corresponding videos for every language lesson. This would enable students to gain a more vivid comprehension of the things that they are being taught. If you are interested, you can watch the blooming of broad-leaved epiphyllums or find out a hundred different ways to eat oysters, anytime and anywhere.

Short videos are a combination of various communication symbols. They certainly come with text, but images rather than text serve as their main body. They are also associated with music, synchronous sound, temporal relations, and suchlike. In particular, Kuaishou Live offers face-to-face, real-time communication and interaction. Its form of "short videos + livestreaming" has become a rich medium of knowledge transmission and is the most perfect combination of communication symbols available today, paving the way for more knowledge-diverse and immersive modes of transmission.

My feeling is that a video encyclopedia will definitely arise in the future. With the nearing of the 5G era and the improvements in interactive hardware, the ways of acquiring knowledge will increase in number and become more convenient as time goes on. What kinds of changes will it bring to society? Will it engender a great transformation in the structure and organization of society? And will it bring about new social relations? Judging from this perspective, the Kuaishou Education ecosystem offers plenty of room for imagining the future.

Kuaishou Classroom Has Realized the Greatest Ideal of an Educator

Education today is high in cost. This does not imply that the resources invested by the state or schools are great in amount, but rather that the exclusion rate of education is too high. There are many reasons for this, such as disparities in the teaching resources, educational infrastructure, or average school proximity among different regions. As a result, many children are unable to enjoy a truly complete education. In a traditional education-centric society, failure to receive education would mean that a person's social identity has already been decided to a certain extent.

The Kuaishou Education ecosystem actually serves to improve this reality, even if only ever so slightly. Kuaishou's ever-evolving education program is not only becoming more and more fun, but more importantly, Kuaishou Classroom, which is built upon a social ecosystem of short videos and livestreaming, has achieved a few of its own breakthroughs.

Since Kuaishou Classroom's official launch in June 2018, more than 10,000 producers have steadily gained knowledge on it. And over the past year, more than 1.5 million users have purchased courses on Kuaishou and spent an average of over 30 minutes a day on these courses. As a result, people who had been excluded from the education system have been brought back in once again.

Kuaishou conveys the idea that users take the initiative to learn when it can help them to change their lives. In a sense, Kuaishou Classroom has realized the greatest ideal of an educator: anyone can teach, learn, and change their destiny through knowledge. In the past, access to education was limited by the high costs of information transmission; for example, a portion of people would never come into contact with certain classical readings or academic speeches. Today, however, Kuaishou has provided the possibility to access these learning opportunities.

Kuaishou Education Has Formed a Very Friendly Ecosystem

When a user is learning a skill on Kuaishou, they can ask their teacher for guidance whenever they have a problem—such as if they forgot the ingredients for making steamed buns or if they have trouble repairing a car—and in turn their teacher can provide real-time guidance online. In short, Kuaishou emphasizes the possibilities created by the interpersonal connections brought about by the pursuit of knowledge.

If the core idea of the Kuaishou Education ecosystem can be summed up in one sentence, it would be: "Enabling every kind of talent to be seen." No matter what kind of talent a user has, they are indiscriminately afforded the opportunity to showcase said talent.

The Kuaishou Education ecosystem has fundamental differences from traditional online paid education. The latter is mostly just a reproduction of offline lessons; knowledge transmission is one-way and linear. Moreover, emphasis was placed on a market-oriented logic that is centered upon enticing users to purchase courses, and thus it became nothing but a profit-making tool. In a traditional transmission of knowledge from Person A to Person B, the mindset of Person B certainly plays an important role, or otherwise a highly market-oriented logic has to be applied. As a result, its innovation is essentially unrelated to the education ecosystem. Instead, the Kuaishou Education ecosystem is truly built on the basis of people's interests and is therefore more in keeping with people's inner and genuine needs.

There are a few platforms that often publicize myths about wealth creation, such as that "so-and-so made tens of millions of yuan by using our platform." Of course, there are many similar cases on Kuaishou, too. However, we need to think carefully about the purpose of each platform in doing so—for example, whether the purpose is to get more people to purchase certain courses or to attract more producers to learn on the platform.

We launched the Kuaishou Education ecosystem so that more creators can come to Kuaishou to provide free video content and social educational services, thereby maximizing the positive social benefits. Kuaishou Classroom hopes above all that more education professionals would feel moved to get involved after seeing these success stories. However, we do not hope to make use of this to create certain effects that would entice more people to buy courses.

It is on this basis that Kuaishou Education has formed a very friendly environment where every kind of talent can be seen and brought out. As Confucius said, "In a party of three or more people, there must be at least one from whom I can learn." To get closer to finding happiness, each user simply needs to give full play to their own strengths and join courses that are relevant to their circumstances.

Kuaishou Education's ultimate vision is for the Kuaishou platform to bring out every kind of talent and to make the pursuit of happiness easier with the help of its inclusive values, technologies, and products.

LAN RUIYUAN THE EXCEL TEACHER: I LECTURE TO THE WORLD FROM THE COUNTRYSIDE

On one side: Kuaishou Classroom. On the other side: a remote, rural village in Jiangxi Province. With the aid of a computer and a microphone, Lan

Ruiyuan delivers lectures on Excel skills and knowledge while speaking in a southern Mandarin accent. When watching her livestream, one can occasionally hear the clucking of chickens outside.

At 30 years old, Lan Ruiyuan has not only created value for her students—who come from all over China and include many overseas Chinese students as well—but also quietly changed the trajectory of her own life. Since she transformed from a self-learned Excel customer service representative to an Excel trainer, and transitioned from offline lectures to online lectures just over a year ago, she has made more than 800,000 yuan in income through Kuaishou Classroom.

PROFILE

Kuaishou name: 兰瑞员 Excel 办公教学 (Excel teacher Lan Ruiyuan)

Kuaishou ID: lanruiyuan

Hometown: Fuzhou City, Jiangxi Province

Age: 30

Education: technical secondary school

Topic: Excel skills

Production style: screen recording on a computer and sharing tips and tricks

Message to her loyal fans: on Kuaishou, you would have a chance to earn income as long as your content is good

Business model: make tips-and-tricks videos to accumulate followers, and sell paid courses through Kuaishou Classroom to earn profits

Narrator: Lan Ruiyuan

My Original Aspiration: To Become an Accomplished Individual and Help Others

You might not imagine that a 30-year-old person who only graduated from a technical secondary school would be teaching Excel skills to the world from a village in Jiangxi Province. Perhaps such an amazing story is not considered rare on Kuaishou, yet it is a miracle in life to me.

I graduated from a technical secondary school with a major in computer studies in 2008. Subsequently, work was very tough as a bottom-tier employee. I have worked as a customer service representative and an operations assistant for e-commerce platforms—every day I would spend more than 10 hours facing a computer at work. After bearing with it for five years, I began to feel that this kind of work was not suitable for me. I thus conceived an idea to give lecturing a try. It did not occur to me at the time that I would have my own "classroom" on Kuaishou a few years later.

At first, I would provide answers to questions asked by people regarding how to use Excel in a few messaging groups. This led me to be invited by two tutorial websites to serve as a lecturer, because they felt that I was very knowledgeable about Excel. My Excel skills and knowledge are all self-taught by searching the internet for bits and pieces of information. For example, whenever I find something I do not know how to do, I look it up on a search engine and learn it quickly. However, I also found that some of the methods suggested online were flawed, such as by having more complicated steps than necessary, and so I would work out a simpler method and write it down.

Later on, I signed on as an online lecturer for many different tutorial platforms. Having gained niche popularity, I was invited by some local enterprises to provide in-house training for their employees—my price for each lesson was 20,000 to 30,000 yuan.

In March 2018, I registered an account on Kuaishou. I was still a lecturer at that time and had not thought about making money through Kuaishou—all I wanted was to help others using my expertise. Hence, I started by uploading a few videos on Excel tips and tricks so as to teach my audience how to improve their work efficiency.

The theme of all my videos was Excel tips and tricks. The tools I used were very simple: a microphone and a computer with screen recording software.

When I first started, I was unable to control the duration of my videos very well. My earlier lectures tended to be relatively slow-paced and verbose, but because Kuaishou sets a duration limit on videos, there is not enough time for a traditional lecture. I thus spoke more quickly in my videos. This led many students to complain that I spoke too fast to be understood.

Upon doing some reflection on my initial experience, I decided that I would only talk about one tip or trick per video, while more complicated tips and tricks might even be explained in several videos.

Every time after recording a video, I would play it back and watch it myself. Sometimes, I would also send it to my friends and then make revisions based on their suggestions. It is common for a video to take four or five takes before I am satisfied with it, and there was even once when a video took more than 20 takes—it was less than a minute long, yet I had to spend an entire afternoon on it. The reason for this was not that I was unfamiliar with the particular Excel operation, but rather that I did not know how to explain it well.

All of my video productions are my own original ideas. Every night before I go to bed, I think about what I am going to record the next day for uploading to Kuaishou.

When I first started recording Kuaishou videos, I noticed that a couple of people were already teaching Excel skills on Kuaishou and were doing pretty well. However, my advantage was that I had been a lecturer for many years and thus had a little more teaching experience than them. In fact, some of them even added me on WeChat and consulted me on a few questions.

I remember that one day in 2018, one of my videos made it on to the Trending page and garnered more than two million views. That brought me a lot of new followers. In less than a year after I started using Kuaishou, I had already accumulated more than 800,000 followers.

I was among the first batch of people to teach on Kuaishou Classroom. In July 2018, Kuaishou began to allow paid courses. I thus contacted

Kuaishou's support team and sought their permission to teach on Kuaishou Classroom.

Kuaishou Classroom: From Traditional Lessons to a New Kind of Classroom

Since I began offering a course on Kuaishou, I have earned nearly 800,000 yuan.

My course is called "Excel Crash Course" and is priced at 89 yuan for a total of 10 lessons in the form of video recordings. The videos can be watched immediately after purchase and can be rewatched an unlimited number of times.

It took me a few days to sort out the syllabus. As I was formerly a lecturer, I already had a ready-made syllabus and courseware, but I wanted to tweak them to better suit students who were absolute beginners at using Excel. At the same time, I also improved them by incorporating the strong points of other teachers' courses.

My paid course is very different from my other productions. It is systematically taught and goes through every Excel toolbar one by one, thereby providing students with a complete understanding of Excel. Instead, the tips and tricks taught in my other productions are fragmented and not systematic at all.

After completing my formal course, students might feel that they have learned everything there is to learn about Excel. However, if they then watch my short videos on Kuaishou, they will realize that their knowledge is still only superficial.

To my understanding, many of my students perform white-collar jobs such as in finance or clerical work. My course is suitable for absolute beginners and allows students to master common Excel skills such as basic operations, table formatting, and data analysis.

On average, my students on Kuaishou do not have the same foundation in Excel as my earlier students in the training agencies. Many of them are absolute beginners, which is something quite new for me.

Before I started my formal course, I gave several free open lessons on Kuaishou. After nearly a month of doing so, I realized that some of my students did not even know how to use a keyboard. I had never needed to talk about the keyboard in my earlier lessons, but this time, I added content that explained how to use the keyboard in my video lessons. In my paid course, I would also explain how to open, close, and create a new spreadsheet on Excel, which I never had to do in the past.

Although some of my students have no foundation in Excel, I can tell that they are very keen to learn and will definitely become good at Excel in time. Persistence is the key; at times, a student might not understand a certain point the first time around, but would then understand said point when I explained it for a second time the next day.

The Secret to Success Is to Provide Valuable Content and Work Hard

My students on Kuaishou come from all over China, while some are overseas Chinese.

I now teach full-time on Kuaishou from my home in the countryside. I have terminated my contracts with my earlier training agencies and no longer accept invitations to conduct offline training.

My husband is a truck driver and makes a lot less money than I do. He is very supportive of me even though he does not understand my online teaching at all.

All my videos on Kuaishou were recorded by me alone. After I started teaching on Kuaishou Classroom, I hired two assistants to answer student questions, and so I now have a small team of three. They are very good friends of mine and are also Excel trainers on Kuaishou. From around 8 a.m. to 11 p.m., they help to answer any questions that students have while taking the course.

I think my course has sold well for two reasons: value and diligence.

Firstly, you have to create value for people and allow them to gain something in order for them to be willing to purchase your courses.

My method of selling my course is to keep on telling my followers that learning will help them to improve themselves. Among my formal students, many have given feedback that my course has helped to improve their work efficiency, to raise their salary, and to enhance their quality of life, and they are thus happier for it. Thanks to their word-of-mouth publicity, more and more people are attracted to my course.

Secondly, you have to work hard in order to get something done. Every day, I would livestream for three to four hours and interact with my followers, who are only willing to purchase my course because the knowledge I teach is helpful to them.

When I am livestreaming, I do not encourage my followers to send me gifts, since all they would get in return is a word of thanks. Instead, I tell them to purchase my course if they feel that I teach well—this way, they can improve themselves and acquire knowledge in return for showing me support.

Furthermore, whenever I upload a new tip-and-trick video to Kuaishou, I write in the description that my course is for sale and can be purchased by anyone who desires a more systematic study. By doing so, many people who watch my videos become interested in purchasing my course.

In short, you will definitely be able to earn income on Kuaishou if your content is good.

The Kuaishou support team is very friendly to us and is able to solve any problems we encounter. For example, our video lessons could not be viewed in full screen at first. After I contacted the Kuaishou support team regarding this matter, it did not take long for them to make this feature available. Kuaishou has done a very good job at responding to users' needs—every time I report a small problem to them, they reply to me or fix the problem in a timely fashion.

I have already started recording videos for a new course on Kuaishou Classroom. It is also a systematic course on learning how to use Excel, albeit it is more detailed and complete than the earlier 10-lesson course which is priced at 89 yuan that was already purchased by more than 10,000 people. I will continue to offer more and better courses in the future.

ANBA THE VETERINARIAN: SPREADING KNOWLEDGE AND FINDING LOVE ON KUAISHOU

Anba is said to be the first veterinarian on Kuaishou. He started using Kuaishou in 2014, offering short videos of pets. Five years later, Anba has around 100,000 followers. Although this is not as high a number as that of other pet anchors who may have up to 20 times more followers, Anba is able to make a profit of more than 1 million yuan—a sum that is greater than that of many small and medium-sized enterprises—from these 100,000 followers.

How is it possible to make so much money from so few followers?

The answer is precision.

From the very beginning, Anba focused on the medical treatment of pets and the popularization of veterinary science. His followers are all pet owners and lovers, and so they are all precise, potential customers. High-quality followers like them may not be large in numbers but have very strong purchasing power. Anba's story serves as a positive inspiration for people who hope to find business opportunities on Kuaishou.

PROFILE

Kuaishou name: 私人宠物医生 安爸 (Private Veterinarian Anba)

Kuaishou ID: Anbayisheng

Hometown: Yanji City, Jilin Province

Age: 28

Education: undergraduate

Topic: veterinary medicine

Production style: veterinary cases and treatment

Message to his loyal fans: You just have to be yourself. On Kuaishou, you can gain like-minded followers without having to follow trends or imitate others.

Business model: sell pet supplies through Kuaishou Store

Narrator: Anba

I Became a Veterinarian Because of a Childhood Regret

I am an ordinary veterinarian. Before I downloaded Kuaishou, my days were more or less spent treating cats and dogs and handling their bodily waste. My income was limited and my profession was not afforded much respect.

After I started using Kuaishou, the thing I enjoyed doing most was to upload short videos on pet-keeping knowledge. My viewers showed their appreciation for these videos by giving me "little hearts." The trust that my loyal fans have in me has given me an unprecedented sense of identity with my profession. I had never thought that, one day, I would be able to find career success and love by spreading knowledge.

When I was a child, I always wanted to be a soldier who fights in real battles to defend the motherland. However, something happened later on that completely changed the trajectory of my life.

I was still in school back then. Using the "lucky money" I received from my family during the Spring Festival, I bought two puppies. Snowball was a snow-white Samoyed, while Invincible was a handsome black Alaskan Malamute—both of them were highly obedient. Because they had never been bathed, they both had an odor on their bodies. I thus decided to give them a bath one day. The next day, however, Snowball stopped eating and had diarrhea while Invincible was also in low spirits, and so my elder brother and I brought them to a pet clinic. The veterinarian told us that both puppies had contracted canine distemper and canine parvovirus, which were very serious viral diseases with high mortality rates. In order for them to stand a chance of survival, they required five injections a day for five straight days. The treatment cost 400 yuan a day per puppy, meaning we would have to spend 800 yuan each time we brought the puppies for treatment.

I could not believe it at all. How could they be dying from just a little ailment? And why was the treatment cost so expensive? Skeptical of the veterinarian's advice, we brought the puppies home. However, that night, Snowball began to have bloody stools, and so we quickly brought the puppies back to the pet clinic that same night and had to knock for a long while before someone opened the door. We managed to persuade the doctor to give the puppies the necessary injections even though we had only brought 600 yuan with us, and promised to pay the remaining amount the next day.

Subsequently, we borrowed money from our classmates and friends and were finally able to raise enough money for the full treatment. Despite this, Snowball and Invincible left us anyway. What made me feel the most terrible was seeing Snowball effortfully wagging its tail at me just before she departed this world. At that time, I felt so angry at myself for not taking good care of them and for being unable to do anything to save them.

From then on, the world lost a potential military officer and gained an aspiring veterinarian with a deep sense of mission. Perhaps due to my childhood regret, I have all along been performing my job out of my love for pets and not out of a desire for monetary gain like some other practitioners in the pet industry. This is also the reason why I am able to gain loyal fans on Kuaishou.

I Chose to Be a True Disseminator of Knowledge on Kuaishou

Strictly speaking, I was the first veterinarian on Kuaishou. I first started using Kuaishou in 2014, when it was not as popular as it is today. Back then, it was just an emerging app for short videos, and there was not a single person who uploaded pet videos. Thus, when I casually uploaded a video of my puppy being bathed, the video swiftly made it onto the Trending page and garnered more than 200,000 views. I was greatly shocked when I checked my phone after work and saw the endless stream of comments and likes pouring in, and I even thought it must have been a system error.

After that encouraging first experience, I began to share more videos of my dog's daily activities in my spare time. My videos often made it on to the Trending page and I quickly accumulated more than 30,000 followers. That number might not seem like much nowadays, but back then it made me the most followed pet vlogger on Kuaishou. Later on, I started to wonder if I could popularize pet-keeping knowledge through my Kuaishou videos so as to prevent the tragedy of Snowball and Invincible from happening again. I thus tried making a video for popularizing veterinary science, but because Kuaishou did not support long-form videos at that time, I came up with a method of using "images + sound recording" to popularize pet-keeping knowledge. To date, this method is still being used by veterinarians on Kuaishou.

After uploading the video, I anticipated with great excitement that it would be very well-received. On the contrary, however, the video received next to no comments and likes and only a pitiable number of views—reality mercilessly extinguished the idealistic spark that had just been kindled in me.

I was very confused. Whenever I uploaded videos of cute pets, they would immediately make it on to the Trending page and bring me lots of new followers. Yet whenever I uploaded a science popularization video, it would receive little attention. After trying many more times, I finally understood that there was a mismatch. The reason for the popularity of my pet videos was that everyone enjoyed watching them. They did not have any hard-and-fast conditions or requirements, and as long as the pets were cute and interesting, everyone would be amused enough to tap on the Follow button.

However, veterinary science popularization videos were different. The people who would watch these videos are, in all probability, pet owners. Moreover, they have to be interested in the particular topic on show. For example, if my video is about cat health, then most dog owners would not be interested in it.

In between satisfying my vanity and upholding my ideal, I once considered giving up. However, I eventually chose to persist with my ideal and keep to the promise I had made to myself, which was to be a good veterinarian so as to take care of pets just like Snowball and Invincible.

As time flew by, the pet vloggers on Kuaishou increased in number and became very sought after. Some vloggers who previously did not have as many followers as I did now had more than 10 times as many followers. At times, people would advise me to post more funny pet videos to provide a quick boost to my number of followers. However, I remain adamant not to do things for the sake of increasing my follower count and receiving more gifts, but rather only for the sake of my ideal.

At some point in time, a few pet owners added me on WeChat and asked me to help treat their sick pets. They told me that my videos on Kuaishou gave them the impression that I am very professional and reliable. Strangely enough, I was indeed able to help cure many pet diseases that the local pet hospitals of these owners were unable to. I am not sure if this is really because of my veterinary knowledge and skills or because other veterinarians are not responsible enough.

Hence, I gradually made a little name for myself in the pet-keeping circle on Kuaishou. Many people began to "@" me in their comments, hoping to receive prompt veterinary guidance from me. As time went on, more and more people sought my advice on all kinds of pet-keeping problems, and so I started livestreaming on Kuaishou at 9 p.m. every day to answer such questions for free.

Later on, the internet became rife with news about fake pet food. As more people became worried about buying such bogus products and causing the deaths of their own pets, I began to receive enquiries about whether I sold pet supplies. This was because people trusted that I would not harm pets for the sake of profit. Bombarded by such requests, I decided to set up an online store.

In truth, the pet-keeping problems that most people encounter are more or less the same, such as how to treat a dog with a cold or a cat with herpes, or whether a woman should be taking care of her pets on her own when she is pregnant. Faced with too many similar questions, I could not continue to provide answers one-on-one, and so I tried providing courses in a WeChat group. What I did was compile the most frequently asked questions so as to craft a relevant syllabus, and then post a few previews on WeChat Moments after the courseware had been finalized. Those who were interested in these courses could buy them for 50 yuan each, with each lesson limited to 100 people. I boldly stated that anyone who takes my courses will master the knowledge being taught.

At present, Kuaishou has also launched Kuaishou Classroom, and I am in the midst of trying it out. It would certainly be more convenient to provide lessons and transmit my knowledge and experience directly over Kuaishou.

Kuaishou Is Less About Watching Videos on Hot Topics and More About Truly Entering a Person's Life

In four years, I have transformed from a little-known veterinarian with an annual income of 18,000 yuan into a we-media veterinary celebrity with an annual income of approximately 1 million yuan. My online store has also become highly rated and sells at least 3,000 kilograms of dog food every month.

Moreover, my courses are also immensely popular among ordinary pet owners. I have sold more than 4,000 lessons at 50 yuan each, which is way more than I ever expected.

My business team now consists of seven employees. They are responsible for providing customer service for the online store, managing inventory, retaining customers, and marketing to new followers.

It is all thanks to Kuaishou that I have become a respected vet. Over the past four years, I have not only achieved career success but also found love. I got to know my wife through the Same City feature on Kuaishou. She likes dogs very much, but because her mother did not allow her to keep one, she became highly envious of pet owners. By chance, she found my videos of my own pets on Kuaishou's Same City page and followed me. Because we lived close to each other, she would come over to walk my dogs when I was too busy with work. After a period of frequent contact, we decided to get married.

I specially livestreamed our wedding on Kuaishou so as to share our happiness with my greatest fans. After all, I would not have met my wife if it was not for Kuaishou.

Perhaps influenced by me, many veterinarians today have also downloaded the Kuaishou app and begun sharing their daily work. As a result, people now realize that vets consist of not just balding middle-aged men, but also handsome or pretty young people.

I am grateful to Kuaishou for empowering ordinary me and my ordinary job. On other popular short video platforms, an ordinary person like myself might never make it on to the Trending page without following the trend of popular topics or producing something funny. However, I feel that there is little meaning in attracting a large number of followers in this manner—such followers are just drifters who cannot possibly be monetized. They are not attracted by the creator's life but rather by a certain hot topic, and thus they leave as soon as said topic is no longer hot. This kind of relationship does not involve any trust and naturally does not lead to interaction. Instead, Kuaishou is more like a group of people entering a person's life, and then getting to know one another and becoming friends.

Kuaishou has all along been a byword for the grassroots because of how down-to-earth it is as an app. On Kuaishou, ordinary people just have to be themselves; they are able to gain like-minded followers without having to follow trends or imitate others.

I'm just a vet with no skill in analyzing big data. Nevertheless, it is evident to me that most of my more than 100,000 followers—which is not considered a large number today—are high-precision followers who have the same interests. Whenever I upload a veterinary science popularization video, they actively interact with me, and whenever I recommend a certain pet care product, there are buyers almost immediately. This feeling of being trusted unconditionally is something I have never felt on other platforms.

QIAO SAN: I TEACH VIDEO PRODUCTION ON KUAISHOU AND MAKE MONEY IN DOING SO

Qiao San is a person who has been interested—and quite talented—in art since childhood. After graduation, he opened a restaurant in order to make a living. However, he later decided to become a Kuaishou video maker after he was impressed by an outstandingly produced music video. Since then, he has gained more than 1.48 million followers on Kuaishou by teaching mobile photography and mobile video editing techniques through his videos, and now earns a monthly income of around 50,000 yuan.

Under his influence, a few of his students have gained hundreds of thousands—if not millions—of followers on Kuaishou. Having gone from a catering entrepreneur to a video creator on Kuaishou to a teacher on

Kuaishou Classroom, Qiao San no longer has to make a choice between pursuing his artistic aspirations and making a living—his life has truly been changed for the better.

PROFILE

Kuaishou name: 乔三（手机摄影）(Qiao San [mobile photography])

Kuaishou ID: XBQQQQQQ

Hometown: Kangle County, Ningxia Hui Autonomous Region

Age: 28

Education: undergraduate

Topics: mobile photography, video production

Production style: transmitting knowledge on mobile photography and mobile video editing by means of video lessons and demonstrations

Message to his loyal fans: the secret to success on Kuaishou is to create good videos through application and more so action

Business model: as a teacher on Kuaishou Classroom, sell courses related to mobile photography and video production, conduct livestreams, provide guidance on how to film short videos, establish cooperations related to post-production, and so on

Narrator: Qiao San

A Music Video Bonded Me to Kuaishou

I graduated from the art department of Huangshan University. I came up with the idea of starting my own business as I preferred a career where I was not so controlled by others. And besides, many of my relatives were business owners as well. However, my first business venture was unrelated to my background in art. Instead, I opened a restaurant together with two of my friends back in my hometown in Gansu Province.

That took place in 2017, when the people of Northwest China were still only beginning to use new platforms on the internet. It was also around this time when I first found out about Kuaishou. Initially, I uploaded a few videos containing scenes of my work in the restaurant and also my daily life—this went on for approximately two months.

Unfortunately, I did not gain many followers and my videos never made it on to the Trending page during that period of time, and so I took a break from uploading videos to do some reflection. I spent the next year or so looking for a new entry point. This finally came in early 2018 when I watched a phone-recorded music video on Kuaishou that still impresses me to this day. It was highly outstanding in terms of production and editing for its time. It gave me the inspiration and confidence to make videos that were just as good.

Having been fond of photography since my college years, I had learned some related knowledge from my roommates who were also passionate about photography. This was why mobile photography officially became my theme on Kuaishou. The music video that I watched can indeed be said to be what truly bonded me to Kuaishou and made me decide to take video-making seriously.

I Discovered a Demand for Video Production Tutorials During My Own Process of Exploration

At the start of 2018, there were still not many people teaching mobile photography on Kuaishou. Among them, some purely taught without providing examples, whereas others provided examples without offering any analysis or explanation. What I chose to do instead was to share my own photos and at the same time explain how I took them.

My most important principle is to apply myself fully when making videos. However, application alone is not enough; it has to be backed up by practical action. At first, I followed a lot of streamers and studied their photography techniques. I also downloaded various photography-related apps to learn the professional knowledge required when taking photos. In my opinion, it is very difficult to take good photos without a basis of professional knowledge, and this requires time to slowly cultivate and learn.

In February 2018, I began to take photos of flowers, plants, and people every day. I took photos of everything I saw and everything I felt would serve to improve my technique. Subsequently, I compiled my photos into videos. However, it was then when I realized that other people's videos were better than mine in terms of color and dubbing, and thus I figured that I also had to learn the technique of video production.

I downloaded more than 30 software applications of varying sizes. Whenever I found out about a certain software on the internet or was recommended a software by others, I would immediately download it and study it myself.

The first visible video on my Kuaishou homepage is dated April 12, 2018, and was filmed in Xining City, Qinghai Province. I did not publish my earliest videos—which were only meant for practice—and I have also hidden some videos. Thus, the videos I have shared are those that I am relatively satisfied with. I remember that on the way home one night, it was drizzling and so I took a few photos in the fine rain using a new photography skill I had learned that same day. When I got home, I immediately edited the photos and compiled them into a clip, which I then uploaded to Kuaishou when it was close to midnight. Unexpectedly, it made it onto the Trending page the very next day and brought me more than 7,000 new followers. This made me very happy at that time and motivated me to work even harder at improving my ability by learning new skills and knowledge.

Therefore, I firmly believe that on Kuaishou any piece of work that you fully apply yourself in producing will definitely be seen by others.

Kuaishou Classroom Has Transformed Me into a Teacher Who Is Paid for His Knowledge

Ever since I was a child, I have always been fond of the internet and enjoyed studying new products. In 2017, I began wondering whether I could increase my income by livestreaming on Kuaishou, just like other people I had seen. However, I was never able to find a good point of entry. This only changed after I decided to focus on mobile photography as my theme. After I uploaded a few of my works on Kuaishou, I was offered some gig work on video post-production projects and earned a considerable amount of commission from them. However, my first official "pot of gold" came from Kuaishou Classroom.

In June 2018, I received a private message from the official Kuaishou team. It said that they had just launched Kuaishou Classroom and thus required a few teachers to do beta testing. Believing that this was an opportunity for myself, I filled in my personal information after further consideration and added the official support team to my contact list. With the team's guidance, I set up my first class. It was a lesson on producing videos using a mobile phone and was priced at 99 yuan. Back then, 19 people signed up for the class, thus netting me 1,881 yuan.

However, I only had 11,000 followers at that time, and so I figured that I had to attract more followers in order to expand my audience. From my experience, it would be impossible to attract new followers quickly if I were to produce new content from behind closed doors, completely oblivious to the perspective and taste of each potential follower. Hence, I observed other high-quality productions on Kuaishou in order to find out what people were looking for.

My summary was: First, the thumbnail must be attractive enough to arouse user curiosity. Second, the cover title must be consistent with the video content. It must also be concise in length and should be phrased as a question if possible. And third, the background music matters a lot, too.

A further tip is to make use of Kuaishou's built-in camera feature—this would make it relatively easier for a video to get on the Trending page.

The effects of following these tips are highly evident. In June 2018, the first video that I produced while applying these principles received nearly 80,000 views and made it onto the Trending page. Prior to this video, the highest number of views I received for a video was approximately 40,000. Today, I earn an average monthly income of around 50,000 yuan through my livestreams, coaching, and video courses on Kuaishou.

Thinking back, Kuaishou has witnessed the changes in my life since 2017, when I first conceived a plan and then further resolved my direction the next year.

Kuaishou Has Bridged the Gap between Ideal and Reality

I have been interested in painting since I was a child and was always ranked first in painting classes. However, there was not much of an artistic atmosphere in the village I lived in, and coupled with a few family reasons, I thus faced several obstacles in my path to learning how to be an artist. The pursuit of art requires substantial financial support, which I certainly lacked while struggling even to make a living. Later on, when I opened a restaurant as my first business venture, my knowledge and interest in art were also given no room to shine.

However, by producing Kuaishou videos on mobile photography, I became engaged in art once again and turned it into my career. Now that it generates a regular stream of income, it can perhaps be considered my second business venture. Thanks to Kuaishou, I no longer have to choose between art and life.

My mother and my restaurant's co-founders were all very supportive of me. When I first started on Kuaishou Classroom, I was a little worried that I would not be successful. However, my friends showed confidence in me and encouraged me to go for it, thereby giving me the resolve to succeed. Their encouragement and support have accompanied me throughout every important milestone in my growth on Kuaishou. I hope to pass on the same encouragement and support to more people in the future.

Today, among those students of mine who became content producers after learning from me through my livestreams, my courses, and my productions, more than 10 have become popular on Kuaishou. The "worst" among them have around 10,000 to 40,000 followers, while the fast-risers among them have 200,000 to 400,000 followers.

More and more people are choosing Kuaishou over other platforms, and this is possibly because the positive energy it radiates is infecting more and more people.

MAMA YAN: A CATERING TUTOR WHO SELF-DEVISED 84 KOREAN DISHES

After leaving Fushun Petrochemical Company in 1999, Yan Jun successively opened several retail businesses in clothing, fast food, and specialty snacks. Eventually, she settled on running her own Korean restaurant. By offering snack-making tutorials on Kuaishou, she has gained 46,000 followers who affectionately call her Mama Yan.

Today, she earns almost as much from Kuaishou as she does from her restaurant. The four courses she offers on Kuaishou Classroom have netted her close to 200,000 yuan in income.

On the platform, she patiently provides guidance to people who want to start a business but do not know how to begin. Kuaishou has enabled her to realize her value in life and receive warmth from the world.

PROFILE

Kuaishou name: 闫妈妈街边小吃 (Mama Yan's Street Snacks)

Kuaishou ID: Yanmama6969

Hometown: Fushun City, Liaoning Province

Age: 49

Education: senior high school

Topic: street snacks

Production style: providing tutorials on making snacks that people are fond of

Message to her loyal fans: utmost sincerity is my secret to getting the most out of Kuaishou

Business model: open a Korean restaurant and provide tutorials on Kuaishou Classroom

Narrator: Yan Jun

The Enthusiasm of Kuaishou Followers Made Me Join the Platform

I am the owner of a Korean restaurant in Fushun City, Liaoning Province. I am also known as Mama Yan on Kuaishou. "Keep forging ahead, never give up, and keep going" has been my motto throughout my journey of entrepreneurship. After quitting my job at Fushun Petrochemical Company in 1999, I started my own businesses: a clothing store, a fast-food restaurant, and a highly popular store selling Fushun Mala Ban (a kind of hot-spiced stew). I have been the proprietor of a Korean restaurant for the past four years. At the same time, I also serve as an entrepreneurship tutor on Kuaishou. This has unexpectedly given me a great sense of achievement and a lot of fun.

My initial decision to try out Kuaishou was inspired by the enthusiasm of my daughter's followers. My daughter runs a social eating stream on Kuaishou—all of her videos are about our homemade cuisines such as rice balls, pork belly rice, fried chicken, and mixed noodles. Over time, she has accumulated more than 60,000 followers.

Thanks to the influence of her videos, many of her followers have visited our restaurant from as far away as Jinzhou, which is 180 miles away in road distance. When they arrived, they would display a lot of warmth and might even give my daughter a cordial hug. I was particularly infected by their warmth and was highly impressed that people who had only ever met on Kuaishou could be so nice to each other when they met in real life for the first time.

This was why I told my daughter that I wanted to join Kuaishou as well. She was very supportive of my idea and helped me out a lot in areas such as recording, operating, and livestreaming on the platform. At that time, I joined the platform because of the enthusiasm of its followers. Today, everyone affectionately calls me Mama Yan—I never imagined that I would be so welcome.

Utmost Sincerity Brings People Closer

In May 2018, I published my first video on Kuaishou—it was about our homemade spicy chicken feet. If memory serves me right, I only had 30-odd followers back then, yet the video was viewed in excess of 40,000 times. I was so encouraged by this that I immediately got started on my second video, which was about mala ban (a kind of hot-spiced stew). Because I would stutter when I was nervous, I had to re-take the opening line of "Hello Everyone" seven or eight times before I got it right, and so the recording took me more than an hour. Although producing this video was not easy, it eventually brought me more than 10,000 new followers—and this was only the beginning.

Later on, something happened that was particularly moving to me. Because the livestreaming tripod that I used was quite a shoddy one, my livestreams would sometimes be interrupted. In the summer of 2018, a young couple from Tonghua City visited our restaurant. The wife, who was around 27 or 28 years old, had brought a few fruits and gifts. She greeted me with utmost sincerity, saying, "Mama Yan, I have come to see you."

I was surprised and moved by this, as I had never expected that my followers would come to visit me.

I learned later in the conversation that the couple had driven eight hours just to see me, and they also gave me a new livestreaming tripod. I could feel the sincerity and warmth in their hearts. In the end, they stayed only half an hour and drove home without eating anything.

Kuaishou is a place with a really great atmosphere. It has brought together a lot of talented ordinary people who sincerely share their skills and experience with everyone else, while the followers are also very sincere and enthusiastic. There is no doubt that Kuaishou has shortened the distance between people, allowing us to influence each other and improve together.

This is why I have always applied and will always apply my utmost sincerity when making Kuaishou videos.

Achieving Greater Value on Kuaishou

When I first entered the catering industry, the internet was still not yet developed and thus there were no online tutorials on running a restaurant or designing a menu. Back then, I had to figure everything out on my own. Today, the 84 dishes offered in my Korean restaurant are all devised by me. Most of my friends in the catering industry have commented that other people run a restaurant to make money, whereas my purpose is to "do something."

This is why I began to wonder if I could increase my own value on Kuaishou by providing guidance to people who want to start a business but do not know how to begin. They are just like me back then—full of aspiration and energy but lacking a goal and unsure of where to start. Therefore, my mission today is to conduct livestreams that provide guidance on how to start a business and how to establish clear goals.

During my livestream sessions, I teach basic kitchen knowledge for free. I also share a few snack recipes, such as for wonton, mala tang, chili oil, and seasoning oil. This requires me to walk back and forth in the kitchen and so I have never been seated during a livestream before. When I get tired after a hard day of work, I kneel on a stool to relieve the swelling in my legs. A particularly concerned follower sent me a chair on which I could sit or lie, as well as a silk banner to hang on the wall. I later found out that he was one of my students. He had learned from me how to make the seasoning for mala ban, and this has greatly improved the offerings on his online store.

Kuaishou Has Given Me Another Kind of Life

In my Kuaishou education course, I not only teach how to prepare cuisines but also pass on my relevant business know-how to my students, such as how to choose a store location, how to run the business, how to make early preparations, how to decorate the store, and what types of utensils to buy. These things are of crucial importance to the operation of a restaurant. The points I make are always highly detailed and thus require a longer time to explain. A course could last for 10 days with each lesson being 45 minutes long. At times, however, I would start lecturing at 8 p.m. and only end around midnight.

I have also assigned my students into different groups. During a livestream, my daughter would write down all of my students' questions, and I would then answer these questions in the pertinent group after my livestream has ended. In addition, beside my pillow are a notebook and a pen for writing down any sudden inspirations that I get during the night.

Because my work has taken a significant toll on my body, my family has always been quite worried about me. However, they have also been moved by the enthusiasm and trust shown by my students. In our daily conversations, we mention my students so frequently that they almost seem to be part of our family as well. We care for them just like they care for us—this is the force that keeps me going on Kuaishou. To this day, we have received more silk banners from my students than we could possibly fit into our house.

As good as our Korean restaurant is doing, the income I get from Kuaishou is nearly equivalent to the income from the restaurant already. To date, I have given four courses on Kuaishou Classroom, earning close to 200,000 yuan from them. This has brought great changes to my life and my family. Most importantly, however, I have gained far more enthusiasm and trust from my followers than I had ever received in the past. Such warmth and positive energy have pervaded all of my work on Kuaishou, and I hope to pass them on to more people in the future.

CHAPTER FOUR

KUAISHOU MUSICIANS: MUSIC–MAKING IS NO LONGER THE PRIVILEGE OF A FEW

CHAPTER OVERVIEW

Hu Zige might still be an unknown street singer and a disheartened middle-aged man were it not for Kuaishou. After he transferred his stage from the streets to a livestream channel, however, he gained the chance not only to tell his own story but also to interact with his fans. On top of that, he is now able to make enough income to solve his livelihood issues—all while doing something he likes.

In another example, two music enthusiasts "Dabing" and "Xiaorong" fell in love with each other after becoming acquainted through Kuaishou. They then got married and had a child. They livestream their singing—staged at the Canton Tower in Guangzhou City—on Kuaishou every day.

Uncle Benliang is not handsome but has a good set of vocals. Though he loves to sing, he cannot read a music score and always goes out of tune. He describes himself as "having no professional knowledge and just showing off my hobby online." Nevertheless, many people enjoy his performances, which is why he now has more than 10 million followers.

Kuaishou has helped these people to find success and obtain economic support while pursuing their hobbies. Although there are countless ordinary people like them, they have derived the possibility and value of being seen from Kuaishou. Singing and livestreaming have not only become a part of their lives but have also provided them with support and assurance—this is the best illustration of Kuaishou's concept of inclusivity.

SUCCESS STORIES·

Hu Zige: An Itinerant Singer Who Became Popular Overnight

Qu Xiaobing: A New Musician in the Internet Age Who Can Simply Be Herself

Liu Pengyuan: Kuaishou Can Give Scope to the Musical Aspirations of Many People

KUAISHOU MUSICIANS: MUSIC-MAKING IS NO LONGER THE PRIVILEGE OF A FEW

Yuan Shuai, manager of Kuaishou Music

Hu Zige might still be an unknown street singer and a disheartened middle-aged man were it not for Kuaishou. With the first guitar he ever had—bought more than a decade ago—on his back, he would wander the underpasses and food centers of the city all day long, paying no attention to drunken passersby and their song requests.

This continued until 2015 when a patron uploaded a video of him singing to Kuaishou, forever changing his life. Ever since he became a celebrity on Kuaishou Music, he has no longer had to be constantly on the move and exposed to the elements. Instead, simply by setting up his phone and turning on his livestream, he has countless followers—both online and offline—awaiting his singing performance in anticipation.

On Kuaishou, there are millions of people who love music and display their talents on camera just like Hu Zige does, and they even change their lives in doing so. Among them are musicians and songwriters who have made music their lifelong careers, as well as internet celebrities who enjoy singing in public. However, the majority is made up of ordinary users who simply enjoy singing, listening, and vibing to music.

Music-Making Is No Longer the Privilege of a Few

For many people, the word *musician* brings to mind a person who has made songwriting and performing their life, who has received professional training, and who is skilled at singing and songwriting. However, according to the official statistics, only 1.7 percent of the users who publish their musical works on Kuaishou every day are actually like that. The vast majority are instead ordinary people who regard music as a hobby and who appreciate, cover, and dance to the songs they love.

Don't underestimate the power of everyday music lovers; they and their followers make up tens of millions of the daily active users. One of them is Uncle Benliang of Guangrao County, Shandong Province. He may not be handsome but he has a good set of pipes. And though he loves to sing, he cannot read a music score and always goes out of tune. He describes himself on his Kuaishou account as "having no professional knowledge and just showing off my hobby online." Nevertheless, many people enjoy his performances, which is why he now has more than 10 million followers. As someone with great musical attributes, he certainly deserves to be classified as a musician.

In the past, publishing a musical work required going through a cumbersome process of songwriting, recording, contract-signing, and distribution. In the WeMedia era, however, everything from songwriting to distribution has become much easier, giving musicians greater freedom than before. Even so, disseminating music still requires elaborate packaging and strategic promotion.

Today, the emergence of Kuaishou has eliminated the middlemen for song distribution and packaging, instead providing a channel and platform that are relatively low in cost. Users can produce their own unique musical works simply by using a mobile phone to film and upload a video. At the same time, Kuaishou's positive community atmosphere, comprehensive feeds, and zero-distance interaction with followers provide users with the best feedback and encouragement possible.

In this way, Kuaishou has greatly enriched the subjective meaning of being a musician. From professional singers and artists to street singers such as Hu Zige and further on to ordinary music lovers such as Uncle Benliang, we have discovered to our surprise that every one of them has a unique talent that deserves to be unearthed and exhibited. Be it a lovely voice, a unique instrumental talent, amusing acting skills, or just a personal life story, they each have a special something that makes them an outstanding musician on Kuaishou.

Kuaishou Has Two Magical Weapons for Improving the Lives of Ordinary Musicians

There are certainly many professional singers on Kuaishou—in just the past two months, about 70 stars of considerable influence have registered an account on Kuaishou. To this group of users, however, Kuaishou is more of an ordinary platform for publicizing their songs, and thus they only make use of a small portion of Kuaishou's services. In comparison, it is the ordinary musicians who get more value out of Kuaishou.

First of all, Kuaishou upholds a content distribution logic that is based on equality, affording every high-quality video the opportunity to get on to the Trending page and be seen by many people. Secondly, Kuaishou is different from other short video platforms where the musicians primarily monetize their content through advertising. While advertising is the most efficient means of monetization for the top musicians, this is rarely the case for those further down. Having tens of thousands of followers might not seem like much on Kuaishou nowadays, but musicians can still net a monthly income of close to 10,000 yuan by livestreaming to a follower base of this size.

By shifting his stage from the streets to a livestream channel, Hu Zige has gained the chance not only to tell his own story and interact with his fans but also to earn an income and solve his livelihood issues. He is now able to "make money just by doing something he likes."

In another example, two music enthusiasts Dabing and Xiaorong fell in love with each other after becoming acquainted through Kuaishou. They then got married and had a child. They livestream their singing—staged at the Canton Tower in Guangzhou City—on Kuaishou every day.

Kuaishou has helped these people to find success and obtain economic support while pursuing their hobbies. Although there are countless ordinary people like them, they have derived the possibility and value of being seen from Kuaishou. Singing and livestreaming have not only become a part of their lives but have also provided them with support and assurance—this is the best illustration of Kuaishou's concept of inclusivity.

Two Major Responsibilities of the Kuaishou Music Department

In 2018, we established the Kuaishou Music department so as to better protect the rights of our music-making users and provide direct, policy-based support to our up-and-coming musicians.

The two major responsibilities of Kuaishou Music are to enforce commercial copyrights and to publicize and distribute musical works.

Firstly, most of the works published on Kuaishou are accompanied by background music, but due to copyright restrictions, the platform basically does not allow the independent use of background music. Kuaishou Music is thus responsible for managing copyright risks and providing legal means for using music sources.

Secondly, Kuaishou has a unique advantage in publicizing and distributing music. The platform has already become a new battleground for the releasing of songs. By making use of its existing capabilities in publicity and distribution, Kuaishou can obtain more resources to support its users. In this way, users can earn income simply by livestreaming on Kuaishou and singing their favorite songs.

Of course, copyright support is not enough on its own. Unlike video companies such as Netflix that have a procurement department,

Kuaishou thrives on content contributed by ordinary users. Therefore, Kuaishou attaches greater importance to the value created by its music-making users.

Kuaishou is committed to supporting original musicians around the world in their aspirations. In 2018, it launched the Musician Program, which is said to be its "accelerator for original music." Users who are certified as musicians can get their works accurately recommended and earn a royalty income on their original works. In addition, Kuaishou has many external partners with capabilities in the production, release, and copyright management of songs. Budding musicians can thus be swiftly put in touch with these partners to receive training and support in the packaging and release of their songs.

In 2018 alone, Kuaishou selected 20,000 of its top music producers for the Musician Program. In 2019, this was expanded to nearly one million producers, including many music enthusiasts who regularly publish music-related short videos on Kuaishou.

Thanks to the traffic resources and exposure that Kuaishou is able to provide, every musician now has the opportunity to showcase themselves and their works to the world.

Kuaishou Music's Continually Evolving Community

Because of the large number of music-making users and their followers on Kuaishou, any song that becomes popular on the platform is able to reach hundreds of millions of people. With such an enormous user base, Kuaishou has taken the music market by storm and will inevitably become a force to be reckoned with. It will have a direct influence on the ecosystem of music production, publicity, and distribution, and provide music-makers with more choices.

In the past, new songs in China were basically promoted on traditional music-playing platforms such as QQ Music and NetEase Cloud Music. Nowadays, however, such promotion is often carried out through the background music in short videos that are viewed by countless users every day. As people gradually understand the huge potential that lies in this, short video platforms are becoming the main battleground for music promotion.

In accordance with this demand, Kuaishou has established collaborations with many external companies, while at the same time more and more music-makers are paying greater attention to their activity on Kuaishou.

More importantly, with the help of the internet revolution, Kuaishou Music has provided cultural products that everyone can enjoy, ensuring that equal information is available to users who live in urban and rural areas alike. This indirectly bridges the gap between urban and rural dwellers and satisfies the diverse demands in the music ecosystem.

In the future, Kuaishou Music will establish more partnerships with most companies in China that deal with music copyright, production, publicity, and distribution, as well as various music-playing platforms. Furthermore, in order to make up for the lack of industry connections in the past, Kuaishou will offer its powerful capabilities in music publicity and distribution in exchange for industry resources, thereby providing better services to its music-making users.

Kuaishou will also place its focus on online work such as song recording, copyright sharing (between the platform and music-makers), linking talented musicians up with companies, and providing performance opportunities. After we have established the entire resource chain, music-makers will be able to gain even more income by taking part in offline activities.

Kuaishou is also in the midst of upgrading its technological reserves. It plans to combine AI technology and music so as to realize features such as real-time musical rearrangement and automatic insertion of background music into videos, providing users with a better musical experience. This has also been a focal point within the industry in recent years.

Guided by the principle of inclusivity, Kuaishou Music will brighten the future of every musician.

HU ZIGE: AN ITINERANT SINGER WHO BECAME POPULAR OVERNIGHT

As an itinerant singer, Hu Zige was once caught up in the dilemma between his aspirations and the realities of making a living. He made the decision to persist with his dream, which also meant choosing a life of abject poverty.

Fortunately for him, he still had a guitar as a companion.

The year 2015 proved to be a turning point in his life. One fine day, he accepted a request to sing for a table of patrons at a food center. While he was singing, someone took a video of him and uploaded it to Kuaishou. And just like that, he became popular in a way he had never expected.

Once a singer whom nobody was interested in, he now has a large number of fans because of Kuaishou. In fact, it is common for hundreds of people to crowd around when he sings in public nowadays.

Perhaps, what touches the audience is not just his songs but also the hardships and adversities he has faced in his life, as betrayed by his singing voice. Such vestiges of a person's life story have become an aspect of Kuaishou's community ecosystem.

PROFILE

Kuaishou name: Hu Zige's "From Acquainted to Separated"

Kuaishou ID: xiaohuzi99

Hometown: Fengyang County, Anhui Province

Age: 37

Education: primary school

Topic: outdoor guitar playing

Production style: one person, one guitar, one song

Message to his loyal fans: there are touching stories everywhere on Kuaishou

Narrator: Hu Zige

When I was young, I often felt a sense of malaise because I wanted to go out and see the world so as to find my own direction in life. Although my initial profession was unrelated to singing, I gradually found a direction that I liked and accepted.

I was born in 1982 in Fengyang County of Anhui Province—it's a place famous for the "Fengyang Flower Drum" song (a famous traditional Chinese folk song and dance from the late Ming dynasty) and also for being the hometown of Zhu Yuanzhang (the emperor of the Ming dynasty from 1368 to 1398). Back when I was young, primary school education was only for five years. Although I did well enough to get into junior high, I dropped out of school—just like many of my schoolmates—due to poor family conditions.

Subsequently, I had to bear part of my family's financial burden. Before leaving my hometown, I helped my parents to sell green chilies, tomatoes, eggplants, potatoes, and also some fruits. However, because there were many other people selling fruits and vegetables as well, business eventually became poor and unprofitable, and so my family contemplated leaving the village in search of a better life.

I persuaded my parents to venture out of our hometown to see the outside world and perhaps find better prospects. We thus went to Xi'an together—this was the first time in my life that I had traveled far away from my hometown.

After leaving my hometown, I decided to become a musician as an itinerant singer. This decision stemmed from my childhood interest. My parents, uncles, and aunts all enjoyed singing and dancing, while some of them could even play a few instruments. Influenced by them, I was fond of music from a young age. I have heard the saying that musical genes are hereditary—while I do not know how true it is, I certainly do come from a musical family.

I have never received specialized training in music or any guidance by a famous teacher; none of my uncles and aunts are professionals either. I simply enjoyed listening to my parents singing when I was young, and then enjoyed singing myself when I grew up.

Becoming Famous Overnight Thanks to Kuaishou

In 1999, the villages and towns in my area were not very well-to-do and thus many people ventured out to make a living by using their own capabilities. After moving to Xi'an, I was deeply fascinated by the sight of itinerant singers busking on the streets with a guitar in hand.

I did not know how to play any musical instrument back then, but nevertheless I realized that guitar-playing was a pleasant accompaniment to singing and thus thought it would be great if I could learn to play the guitar. As the days passed, I would watch other people playing the guitar every day and would often ask them questions on how to play the guitar while singing. Some of them would ignore me as they felt that it was unnecessary to talk to someone whom they did not know—but that did not put me off from asking questions the next time. And indeed, a few of the more enthusiastic ones would give me advice on how to play the guitar. As a result of this gradual process, my interest in playing the guitar increased over time.

I bought my first ever guitar after discussing the matter with my father. I still remember very clearly that I bought it for 168 yuan at Minsheng Building in Xi'an City. Thenceforth, my career as an itinerant singer began, accompanied by this guitar.

Instead of the big night markets that other singers prefer, I would go to the smaller ones and perform songs that were trending at that time. Although I was still a novice at the guitar, I practiced very hard to build up my playing-while-singing skills.

On my very first night of performance, I earned 16 yuan. This sum boosted my confidence and made me love music more.

Eventually I left Xi'an and returned to my hometown for a short while before going to many different cities across China such as Zhenjiang and Ji'nan. In 2000, I went to Nanjing and would spend nearly seven years there.

On April 16, 2007, I set off for Suzhou from Nanjing. I remember most clearly that I traveled by high-speed rail, which had only just begun operation at that time. The reason I decided to go to Suzhou was because a couple of friends had told me that making a living as an itinerant singer would be easier over there.

I ended up spending eight years in Suzhou, between 2007 and 2015. I sang on the streets, in food centers, and in hotels—wherever I could sing was my stage. However, I rarely sang in bars because the patrons there considered me to be a street singer or a food center singer who was not up to the mark.

An unexpected opportunity arose for me in 2015. One day, a food center patron who had listened to my singing the previous night called me on the phone and invited me to sing for him and his friends at their dinner gathering that night, to which I accepted. While I was singing, the patron filmed my performance using his phone and uploaded it to Kuaishou. In just one night, the video garnered several million hits.

As I did not know the slightest thing about the internet at that time, I was oblivious to what was going on. However, many of my relatives and friends who were already using Kuaishou messaged or phoned me to ask if I had uploaded my own video on Kuaishou, to which I replied that I had not. They explained to me that they had seen a video of me on Kuaishou and were very excited that I was able to be seen by more people over the internet.

The next day, many people gathered to watch my performance at the same food center, noting that I was the singer in the video that became popular the previous night. To be honest, my newfound attention was a little too much to take at that time. I had always led a free and easy life previously, and so I was quite stupefied.

From getting no attention to suddenly having a large number of fans, my life went through a great turning point. However, I still did not have my own Kuaishou account. This was until a few fans came up to me and asked me if I had uploaded the popular video myself, to which I answered in the negative and said that it must have been someone else, as I did not even know how to use Kuaishou at all. The fans then suggested that I download the app on my phone.

I thus applied for a Kuaishou account. As soon I announced my Kuaishou account ID, many people began to follow me. They live in various cities throughout China such as Zhangjiagang, Nantong, Shanghai, and Kunshan, while those who live nearby would often come down to watch my live performances. It was from that time on that I grew in popularity until the present day.

The Best Songs Are Those that Sing About Life

At the food centers where I perform, I have encountered many people who refused to pay up. They have even scolded or assaulted me after requesting and listening to my songs. They would hit me with beer bottles and insult me in various direct and indirect ways. Once, when I was performing with a friend in Ningbo City, we were suddenly assaulted by a man and woman. Later on, they simply said that they were drunk and did not remember the incident. I felt especially aggrieved at that time.

Although persisting with my dream was not easy at all, I continued to have faith.

Things are different these days. Nowadays, my fans often come from afar to listen to my singing and interact with me. I feel very happy and touched to receive such love and support.

I began using Kuaishou in July 2015. The period from 2015 to 2017 was when my follower count grew the most. Many people felt that my singing voice was pleasant to the ear—perhaps thanks in part to my unique throat-singing technique—and thus followed me on Kuaishou. Hence, the more songs I sang and uploaded, the greater my follower count became.

I did not pay much attention to my clothing and was not meticulous in maintaining my beard. When I first started singing, I was quite thin and thus gave off the impression that I was not mature and steady enough. Later on, I decided to grow a beard so as to look more mature and give off an artistic vibe. My wife is someone who likes cleanliness and keeps the house especially neat and tidy. Because she likes the purity and cleanliness of white, I also like to wear white pants.

Being an outdoor livestreamer, I have many opportunities to meet my fans in real life. A lot of people come from far and wide just to listen to my singing. I personally believe that the best form of communication with my fans is to interact with them face-to-face. At times, many of my fans sing along while I am performing. To get the crowd going, I sing, dance, talk, and laugh together with them. When my wife sees a lively crowd, she often records and uploads a video of the scene to Kuaishou so that more people can experience the vibrant atmosphere.

From 2016 to 2017, there were as many as 400 people at the venue of my livestreams. Often times, there would be people who could not get in because of how packed it was.

Music comes from our lives. I believe that a singer must have feelings and sentiments in their life for them to be able to sing well. The value of music lies in singing each song with application and sharing it with more people.

If I ever get the chance to go on televised competitions such as *Sing! China* or *Xingguang Dadao*, I would certainly take part positively. If not, I will stick to my original aspirations and continue livestreaming and singing as well as I can—these are my job duties and my interests after all.

Today, my living conditions are much better than before, while the life of my parents and children have also improved considerably. Although we are still living in a rented house, my wife and I are thinking about settling down in Suzhou City for the sake of our children. We have even considered changing our children's household registration to Suzhou so that they can attend school here.

I have composed a song called "Memories of the Past." Although it is probably not my best work, it encapsulates my deepest sentiments. To me, every real sentiment is rare and precious.

QU XIAOBING: A NEW MUSICIAN IN THE INTERNET AGE WHO CAN SIMPLY BE HERSELF

Once upon a time, musicians had limited ways of getting exposure and so most of them remained at the bottom of the industry, where making a living out of music was impossible.

On Kuaishou, however, a musician called Qu Xiaobing has amassed more than five million followers and earned several million yuan over 200 short videos and 50 musical pieces. She is a successful example of a musician who explored and found new channels of monetization.

With the new possibilities available to musicians, the view count and influence of short music videos have shown a significant increase. In fact, on some music platforms, it is a regular occurrence for the most played songs to be dominated by songs from short music videos.

Today, musicians no longer have to worry about monetizing their craft. In Kuaishou's Musician Program, there are many stories such as that of Qu Xiaobing. As long as a musician is talented, there will be fans on Kuaishou willing to pay for their works.

PROFILE

Kuaishou name: 曲肖冰（歌手）(Qu Xiaobing [singer])

Kuaishou ID: quxiaobing

Hometown: Changzhou City, Jiangsu Province

Topic(s): recording original music

Production style: I say what I want to say and am always myself

Message to her loyal fans: Kuaishou accepts people at all levels and that is why it can be successful in the long term

Business model: singing songs to accumulate fans, working as an internet-age musician, and planning to expand to multi-channel networks in the future

Narrator: Qu Xiaobing

In 2018, I joined the Kuaishou Musician Program. For just the song "Liking You Once Again," Kuaishou paid me a dividend of approximately 1.6 million yuan.

At that time, Kuaishou told me they were going to promote my song, but they did not promise that it would make it on to the Trending page. Kuaishou would never artificially place a song on the Trending page; the process of deciding which songs to recommend is completely fair because it is performed by algorithms rather than by human intervention. It is precisely because Kuaishou treats all users equally and would never make a deal with artistes that it can be successful in the long term.

My Connection to Kuaishou

A few years ago, I would record the songs I sang, turn them into videos, and upload them to Kuaishou. All of this was done from my very own recording studio, where the good acoustics meant that the quality of my productions was higher than average, and thus, I was able to amass followers very quickly. One video alone could bring me up to 100,000 new followers. At that time, I was the only user on Kuaishou who filmed videos in a recording studio.

Of course, it was not long before many people did the same. This led to the creation of many musical works with the same style. Seeing as it was no longer creative to film videos in a studio, I began trying to film videos for traditional-style music. In time, Kuaishou became filled with videos of traditional-style music. I then began to experiment with an orchestra, which requires a great deal of expertise and thus cannot be easily imitated. For a period of time, I was also fond of aerial videography. It is only by doing different things from others that one can get ahead of the competition.

I amassed a lot of followers on Kuaishou by singing. Although I have never received formal training in music, singing has been my career for eight years and counting.

When I created my first single, all I wanted was to release an original song that I could call my own. I got one of my friends who was experienced in producing background music to compose the melody while I wrote the lyrics myself. I worked on only one song and it was just to amuse myself. Aside from Kuaishou, I also released the single on QQ Music, where I had published a few of my earlier musical pieces already.

A few copyright companies also gave me permission to perform the female cover of several trending songs, including "Silently," "Sorrow of Separation," "Aries," and "Saying Goodbye Before Dawn."

I Became a Boss Instead an Artist

When I was a child, I dreamed about becoming a celebrity who held concerts for a living. Later on, however, I felt that the life of a celebrity would be very tiring—having to be on the move and meet many different people every day was not something I could get used to. This is also why I rarely take part in concerts and variety shows, even when I am afforded the chance these days.

Recently, a few television shows and web shows invited me to sing their soundtrack songs, such as the song "Looking At Each Other" from the television series *Heavenly Sword and Dragon Slaying Sabre*.

I feel free and unrestrained nowadays—I do not have to put on a front and am able to make money through music. Most importantly, I am able to do what I like, and so I feel quite satisfied with life.

Because I am often busy, I seldom livestream these days. But whenever I have the free time, I start a livestream to sing for and chat with my fans.

I am currently living my ideal life—just doing what I like and not necessarily having to perform on stage. I intend to keep on improving my musical attainments; when I become professional enough, it will certainly be visible to my audience.

In 2018, I founded my own copyright company. It has since established collaborations with more than 100 internet singers. Together with Kuaishou, it provides resources that can help these singers produce high-quality songs. I have also signed some artistes such as Ban Yang, whom I share a deep friendship with. We have been making small and gradual improvements together, from the earliest single "Destined to Be Lonely" to "Wandering", and later on from "Lovesick Song" to "With Mountains." He is a highly talented singer-songwriter; I hope that he can perform at a music festival in the future so that everyone can witness the case of an emcee's successful transformation.

We now have many professional production teams which are each in charge of different musical styles. At the same time, some of the artistes we have signed are suitable for commercial performances and online variety shows, while others are suitable to be independent musicians. I position them differently so that they can develop in the directions that suit them best.

Kuaishou is pretty awesome; it has helped me to record my life, to achieve success in my career, and also to gain followers who enjoy listening to my music.

I wish all of my loyal fans on Kuaishou a bright future and continuous progress through innovation.

LIU PENGYUAN: KUAISHOU CAN GIVE SCOPE TO THE MUSICAL ASPIRATIONS OF MANY PEOPLE

Independent musician Liu Pengyuan has persisted on the path of music-making for more than a decade. He was formerly a popular contestant on talent shows such as *The X Factor China* and *Duets China* and also fared well at various singing and playing competitions. After joining Kuaishou, he rediscovered the joy of making music together with everyone, as he had at the start of his career. This long-lost feeling not only moved him deeply but also brought him precious friendships and new creative inspirations.

He has continually built up and shared his music portfolio on Kuaishou so that more people can hear and enjoy his musical works. Nowadays, he also encourages other independent musicians to join Kuaishou, telling them that the platform will help to find their audience, share their works, and increase the value of their music.

PROFILE

Kuaishou name: 鹏远 LPY (Pengyuan LPY)

Kuaishou ID: Lpy19870626

Hometown: Beijing

Age: 32

Education: undergraduate

Representative works: "Paradise," "Singing for You," "A Sad Pig"

Production style: focusing on music, singing while playing various instruments such as the guitar and the Chinese hand drum, and spreading tutorial videos and musical works that are filled with positive energy

Message to his loyal fans: the most exciting time in life is not the moment when you realize your dream but rather the whole process of persisting with your dream

Business model: livestreaming, giving lessons, and using Kuaishou to expand his influence and get more commercial gigs and other opportunities for cooperation

Narrator: Liu Pengyuan

Kuaishou Has Given Me a Bunch of Warm-Hearted, Loyal Fans

My name is Liu Pengyuan. I am an independent musician, a singer-songwriter, and a drummer. I have played the guitar for 17 years and was once described by Lo Ta-yu (a Taiwanese singer-songwriter) as "a human guitar." My friends think of me as a fanatical instrumentalist who goes crazy as soon as I pick up a guitar.

I am well-known in China because I have taken part in several talent shows such as *The X-Factor China* in 2013 and *Duets China* in 2015. To me, however, my life remains the same and as tranquil as it has always been. Every day, I spend much of my awake time singing and playing an instrument—as soon as I get out of bed, before going to bed, during performances, and even when I am giving a lecture on a podium. Indeed, my love for music borders on fanaticism.

Before I started using Kuaishou, I had never thought I would ever have so many adorable fans.

"You Are Finally Here; We Have Been Looking for You All This Time"

In 2016, I uploaded a couple of my videos to Kuaishou on a friend's account but did not take note of them subsequently as I was rather busy back then. Two years later, when the same friend uploaded another one of my videos to his Kuaishou account, he received many comments from people who said that they recognized me and wanted to know if I had my own Kuaishou account. Thus, I created my own account and uploaded a video that I personally liked. I received many comments saying: "You are finally here; we have been looking for you all this time."

I was deeply touched by these comments. After all, everyone likes to be appreciated by others, and heartfelt words of praise are all the more precious. I got to see the sincerity of my loyal fans on Kuaishou—they would show me support not only by liking my videos but also by sharing my singing videos with their friends of their own accord. This was why I was able to amass more than 100,000 followers in a very short time.

Feeling very excited back then, I would read every single comment I received. One person said, "I have been watching you play the guitar for more than 10 years and you are finally here." Another said, "I have been following you ever since I watched *The X Factor China*. Who would have thought that you can also play the drums?" Someone also asked, "Do you have any teaching materials? I want to learn music from you."

I gradually realized that the influence of Kuaishou far exceeded my imagination. As a musician, I have to hold concerts in many different cities across China. Often, the audience would take videos of the concert and upload them to Kuaishou. Many guitar teachers would then search Kuaishou for videos of me playing the guitar and send these videos to their students to learn from.

Later on, I began to livestream on Kuaishou at the request of my loyal fans. I would show everyone my daily routine and talk to my fans while playing an instrument. The environment encouraged learning from each other and getting along just like friends, and thus my relationship with my fans did not have to be sustained with gifts. Over time, we built up close friendships: I would share with everyone where I went to perform for the day what interesting things I saw and would also answer the questions of music learners. This brought my life a great deal of happiness, and I felt just as though as I had earned the approval of real-life friends. When we were happy, we would often celebrate together, and when the chat was going most pleasantly, I would offer a few gifts to my fans. These gifts were usually simple guitar-related items such as guitar straps.

There are more and more people learning to play the guitar from me on Kuaishou. Although their skill levels vary, our goal is much the same, and that is to find happiness.

I Am Touched by What I Have Amassed on Kuaishou over Time

It was my father who first got me interested in music. When I was young, I learned a few tunes from him and then began to explore and practice music on my own. While growing up, I was also fortunate enough to have Chang Kuan as a teacher. Because I regard music as life itself, I fully understood the feeling of being devoted to a craft and the value of having an expert to guide me in my pursuit of my dreams.

Today, Kuaishou has made it easier to gain access to expert guidance. This is because you can easily see the works of people who are better than you and begin a conversation with these people. This has torn down regional barriers and greatly lowered the cost of communication.

The truth is that many people have a musical dream deep within their hearts.

Kuaishou is certainly able to give scope to such dreams.

One of my fans left a very deep impression on me. Once, he told me over a private message that he was ready to quit his job as a civil servant so as to learn how to play the guitar from me full-time. He said that he had always liked music a lot and enjoyed singing and playing the guitar, albeit he had little time to do so, but after watching my videos, he was so moved by them that he wanted to "live for himself" for a while.

I refused him.

There are many fans like him on Kuaishou—they send me videos of themselves singing and playing and ask me if they could make a living through music. My advice to them is not to be impulsive, and if they really wanted to take this path, they must first find their own unique style and carefully evaluate if they have what it takes.

Some of my loyal fans come all the way down to my instrument store to learn how to play the guitar from me. There was a fan who would take a four hour taxi from Chengde City to attend bimonthly lessons taught by me. Each lesson was only two hours long, whereas his traveling time was eight hours each way.

I also have a middle-aged student who found me through Kuaishou. He, too, had musical aspirations when he was younger, but was unable to stick to them when work became too busy. However, watching my videos restored his motivation.

All of these moving stories began with Kuaishou and ultimately had a significant influence on my life. Later on, these students of mine became my friends because they offer me a lot of positive energy.

There was an incident that took place in 2018 that I remember most clearly. In December of that year, I was scheduled to stage a performance in Shijiazhuang City, but I had a high fever two nights before the event and thus only set off for Shijiazhuang the day before the event. After arriving in Shijiazhuang, I uploaded a video on Kuaishou stating the time of my performance.

It was the one-year anniversary celebration of an instrument store, and they had invited me as an honored guest. Their event began at noon but I arrived close to four in the afternoon, as they had not told me what time I was due to perform. Many people sent me private messages telling me that they had been waiting for me since noon. As soon as I walked down the stairs, many people crowded around, causing me to feel deeply touched.

By talking to them, I found out that there was a young fan who had specially taken a day off school to come and see me. There were also parents who had brought their children along to the event. After my performance ended, I had to hurry to catch a train, but because the organizers were too busy, it was ultimately a fan who drove me to the train station.

Having been in the music industry for so many years, I have become known by many people. Nevertheless, I feel that my fans on Kuaishou stand out as a highly special bunch. They are very down-to-earth and genuine, such that there is no distance between them and me. When I took part in talent shows earlier on in my career, the audience would regard me as an idol; at that time, there was a certain distance between me and my fans and the feeling was very different.

The Fascinating Chemical Reactions Produced
by Kuaishou and Me

After I became "famous" on Kuaishou, my income also grew considerably. Recently, I accepted performance invitations for a dozen or so beer festivals that were organized by a popular streamer on Kuaishou. In 2018, the owner of a certain brand personally sent me a private message on Kuaishou asking if I was interested in becoming their spokesperson. A few instrument stores have also invited me to perform at their one-year anniversary event, while a few music competitions have appointed me as a judge.

However, what makes me the happiest is getting to know many interesting people. During this process, my ideas about music have continuously broadened. On Kuaishou, my loyal fans and I would often produce a few fascinating chemical reactions.

In 2018, I livestreamed from the Kuaishou Music Festival in Xi'an. Knowing that I would be present that day, many of my loyal fans showed up to watch my performance. Their enthusiasm exceeded my imagination—some had brought me bottles of water while others had brought specialty snacks from their hometowns, causing the table assigned to me to be filled with gifts from fans. It is precisely this kind of attention that has tightly connected me with my fans, and the chain between us is none other than Kuaishou.

There was another incident at the same festival that left me feeling very touched. When shifting some equipment from one city gate to another, it was inconvenient to do so by vehicle and thus, I shouted out loud to my fans asking if they could help to carry a few drum kits or whatnot.

Unexpectedly, more and more people pitched in to help, and they were all my loyal fans on Kuaishou. It was at that moment that I felt so, so fortunate.

I have gotten to know many interesting souls through Kuaishou. In 2018, several outstanding Kuaishou musicians held a performance in Beijing, and I joined in as well. I felt truly lucky to be around such like-minded people. Because we all love music, we were able to have interesting conversations and eventually became good friends.

There is another incident that I have never forgotten. One day, a young fan sent me a private message asking me to choose a guitar for him. By chance, I learned that he had a terminal illness, but loved music just as much as me and would never miss any of my livestreams. On top of that, he was highly talented as well. I sent him one of my best guitars without hesitation and promised to practice the guitar with him. As the saying goes, music is the most beautiful language in the world, and it does not require deliberate expression. Thanks to Kuaishou, it has become very easy for me to find happiness.

I Plan to Release More Works on Kuaishou in the Future

The official Kuaishou team often organizes offline events—I participate in them whenever I have the time. For example, the Kuaishou Music Festival Tour is staged on the streets. The stage may not be quite so magnificent, but I like to perform that way because I can meet and interact with fans face-to-face.

There is a saying that "there are masters among folk people." Kuaishou is such a community for folk masters; these people may not be professional musicians in the traditional sense, but they contribute a lot to music nevertheless. Each of them has their own merits and offers new possibilities for music.

I have always believed that the most exciting time in life is not the moment when you realize your dreams but rather the entire process of persisting in your dreams. This idea has accompanied me throughout my entire musical career.

While on the path of music, my mentality once underwent change. There was a period of time when I often took part in competitions and clinched various awards. In 2013, I participated in a program on Hunan Television. At that time, I thought that it would better for me to have a big platform to perform on, but it turned out that they required me to sign a contract. Due to my desire for freedom, I ultimately turned them down. In 2015, I participated in *Duets China* and was assigned to Sitar Tan's group. Thanks to that show, I received the recognition of many people in the music circle.

Nevertheless, I had learned by then not to pin my hopes on an individual or a company. Previously, I had the notion that I could become popular just by getting on a certain show or becoming acquainted with a certain celebrity. However, as I gained more experience, I discovered that these things were far from being the key. Instead, it was more important to build myself up and accumulate followers on my own.

Nowadays, I encourage talented musicians to join the Kuaishou Musician Program. In the past, some of them would only share their musical pieces on WeChat Moments and thus did not get much visibility. I have told them to register a Kuaishou musician account and to try uploading their works on there. All of them are excellent music producers and singers, and thus their value can be better reflected on Kuaishou.

As for myself, I plan to release more of my own original songs in due course. I will cover many different styles of music from ballads to rock music.

Although I have been engaged in music for more than a decade, I am still a newcomer on Kuaishou. In the future, I hope to accumulate even more music knowledge, to produce more and better works, and to continue working hard together with my loyal fans!

CHAPTER **FIVE**

HAVING A KUAISHOU ACCOUNT WILL BECOME STANDARD BUSINESS PRACTICE

CHAPTER OVERVIEW

I n the print era, companies would advertise their products in the yellow pages or newspapers, and after the arrival of the internet age, they began to build their own web pages. Then, with the advent of platforms such as Weibo, Taobao, and WeChat, they became able to present even more content and publish instant messages, while their interaction with consumers also became more convenient than before. However, messages that are based on pictures and text are still not intuitive enough. As we enter the short video era, enterprises will become much better at self-expression. For an enterprise, a Kuaishou account can be utilized as a business card, an e-commerce channel for finding customers, or a localized channel for attracting customers to its brick-and-mortar stores. Just like having a company web page, having a Kuaishou account will become standard business practice for every enterprise. At present, there are tens of millions of enterprises in China; the question is: will at least 10 million of them adopt Kuaishou within the next few years?

HAVING A KUAISHOU ACCOUNT WILL BECOME STANDARD BUSINESS PRACTICE

Yan Qiang, vice president of Kuaishou Commerce

In May 2019, Sany Heavy Industry (a Chinese heavy equipment manufacturing company based in Changsha, Hunan Province) staged a livestream event on Kuaishou. Although it only had 2,000-odd followers, it managed to sell 31 road rollers that cost several hundred thousand yuan each within one hour. Subsequently, Sany Heavy Industry increased its multi-account operations on Kuaishou and even set up a special department for that purpose.

Sany Heavy Industry is not an isolated case; many other enterprises have also benefited from using Kuaishou. Many subsidiary stores of Huawei and Xiaomi have sold large numbers of phones through their Kuaishou accounts. Amusement park operators such as Fantawild and Haichang Ocean Park Holdings Ltd. encourage their employees to create Kuaishou accounts in order to showcase the company's events and attract customers. At the same time, major Chinese mobile home brands now receive a significant portion of their orders through their Kuaishou accounts.

Just like having a company web page, having a Kuaishou account will become standard business practice for every enterprise. At present, there are tens of millions of enterprises in China; the question is: will at least 10 million of them adopt Kuaishou within the next few years?

How an Enterprise Is Seen: From the Print Era to the Short Video Era

An enterprise cannot succeed in its operations without its employees, partners, and customers. Therefore, it is necessary for an enterprise to build connections and trust with them.

In the print era, companies would advertise their products in the yellow pages or newspapers, and after the arrival of the internet age, they began to build their own web pages. Then, with the advent of platforms such as Weibo, Taobao, and WeChat, they became able to present even more content and publish instant messages, while their interaction with consumers also became more convenient than before.

However, messages that are based on pictures and text are still not intuitive enough. As we enter the short video era, enterprises will become much better at self-expression.

Firstly, by using the "short video + livestreaming" model, enterprises can showcase themselves in a vivid, intuitive, effective, and interesting manner. An interesting example is Foxconn—what its employees do is merely to film the daily scenes in the company's cafeteria, yet this provides very important information to potential employees when they are considering whether or not to work for Foxconn. And indeed, many of Foxconn's recently hired employees decided to join the company after seeing these videos.

Secondly, Kuaishou is a hypermarket, with more than 300 million daily active users. Thus, enterprises can reach a large number of target users rapidly. The reason that Sany Heavy Industry was able to sell 31 road rollers is that 70 to 80 percent of the clients in the construction machinery industry are using Kuaishou.

Thirdly, Kuaishou attaches great importance to private domain traffic, which allows enterprises to form stable connections with users. By watching an enterprise's videos and livestreams over a long period of time, users build strong, trusting relationships with that enterprise. This greatly reduces the costs of maintaining customer relations and brings a steady stream of returning customers for the enterprise.

In short, for an enterprise, a Kuaishou account can be utilized as a business card, an e-commerce channel for finding customers, or a localized channel for attracting customers to its brick-and-mortar stores. We have correspondingly divided enterprise accounts into three different types, namely "Brand Accounts," "E-commerce Accounts," and "Local Accounts."

A Continuously Optimized Kuaishou Enterprise Account

Kuaishou has launched the Enterprise Account feature to better serve our enterprise users.

The core idea behind a Kuaishou Enterprise Account is to help enterprises "have content, followers, and business" and eventually become a place where enterprise users can gain long-term benefits.

A Kuaishou Enterprise Account is a commercial "hundred-treasure box" that caters to users with commercial needs. In terms of its overall policy, Kuaishou will provide Enterprise Accounts with a certain amount of traffic preference or support, as well as budgetary inputs in the form of cash. To be more specific, Enterprise Accounts will offer services that correspond to different types of enterprise users.

For brand-oriented enterprises looking to expand their brand influence, an Enterprise Account can directly help with brand promotion, such as by organizing "challenges," providing customized emojis, and setting up hashtag pages. Furthermore, it can provide related products and services such as headlines (promotion of creative works) and in-feed advertising services to increase the agility and maximize the value of the enterprise's ad delivery.

For e-commerce enterprises, an Enterprise Account can serve to increase the efficiency of their connection with customers and showcase all of their products in a comprehensive and intuitive way. It offers features such as Kuaishou Store, Video Promotion, and Livestream Sales; exhibits products neatly on the enterprise user's homepage; and provides access to the relevant purchase page. This makes it convenient not only for customers to understand and purchase products through videos and livestreams, but also for enterprises to interact with their followers at any time.

For localized enterprises, an Enterprise Account can reduce the costs of communicating with customers and make it easier for customers to find their stores. The homepage of an Enterprise Account comes with a phone inquiry feature and an accurate geolocation feature that helps customers navigate to the enterprise's brick-and-mortar stores, thereby satisfying the operational needs of localized enterprises.

Kuaishou will gradually seek to get the top enterprises from key industries, such as TAL Education Group, New Oriental, KFC, Haidilao, and DJI, on board its Enterprise Account Partnership Plan. In doing so, it hopes that these enterprises will serve as model examples.

Two of Kuaishou's Core Values

In less than half a year, the Kuaishou Enterprise Account has rapidly evolved, giving rise to the beginnings of a prosperous commercial ecosystem.

As a cornerstone product of Kuaishou's commercial ecosystem, the Kuaishou Enterprise Account will be continuously optimized and upgraded. New features such as "Discount Vouchers," "Buyer Groups," "@ Content Aggregation," and "POI Claiming" will be added in due course in order to keep attracting new and accurate follower groups, increase user loyalty, promote business transformation, and ultimately offer its users long-term value in two notable forms.

The first form is the value of a commercial ecosystem. The most common marketing technique used by enterprises on the platform is ad delivery, but this technique is fairly traditional and is often affected in volume and limited by factors such as changes to the economic environment or an enterprise's stage of development. More than just earning ad revenue itself, what Kuaishou cares about is how to build a long-term marketing mechanism and help enterprises earn even more revenue on its platform. For many self-serve advertisers of small- and medium-sized enterprises, a Kuaishou Enterprise Account is actually an ecosystem-based product for performing future commercialization, raising their ceiling, and expanding in breadth and depth. In this way, sustainable development of the commercial ecosystem can also be realized, allowing all stakeholders to benefit.

The second form is the value of a community ecosystem. More than just selling products and doing business on the platform, enterprises also have to offer high-quality video content that users enjoy watching. This makes users willing to follow them and builds long-lasting social connections with them.

This is precisely the development model of Instagram. In the later stages of its development, its users not only browse the content published by other ordinary users, but they also spend money on the content published by commercial users and build deep social connections with them. What we have learned from Instagram is that the establishment of Enterprise Accounts and the entry of enterprises onto the platform not only would not destroy the authentic, interesting, and diverse community ecosystem that Kuaishou has always had, but would even enrich the entire community.

ENTERPRISE ACCOUNTS: LIVESTREAMING HAS BECOME NEW TERRAIN FOR ENTERPRISES TO FIND CUSTOMERS

The short video era offers traditional companies new opportunities in sales and recruitment.

For example, through its livestreams on Kuaishou, Sany Heavy Industry has established face-to-face sales channels with users; their use of video has made it easier to build trust. Also, a growing number of used car sales managers regard Kuaishou as new terrain for finding customers. Meanwhile, Foxconn's employees serve concurrently as recruiters for the company by uploading various kinds of short videos on Kuaishou, thereby providing the company with a steady stream of manpower resources in an era of labor shortage.

Nevertheless, the reformation and disruption of traditional sales are only just beginning. At a time when short videos and livestreams have become all the rage, we can see the new markets opened up by enterprises. By tapping into short video communities such as the one represented by Kuaishou, a new kind of company-user relation has been born.

Sany Heavy Industry: Selling 31 Road Rollers in a One-Hour Livestream

In Spring of 2019, using a Kuaishou official account that they had only just created, Sany Heavy Industry sold 31 road rollers in one hour of livestreaming, with each road roller priced at 350,000 to 450,000 yuan. Given that they only had a few thousand followers at the time, this was certainly an astonishing feat.

It was the video of a young girl operating an excavator that had caught the attention of an intern sales manager at Sany Heavy Industry. The sales manager noted that the video got many likes, comments, and inquiries on the price of the excavator. Subsequently, during an internal sales meeting, she suggested to the company that they try finding their target customers on Kuaishou.

After doing some assessments, the company started on its "Kuaishou short video plan." Their first livestream turned out to be a blockbuster— after their engineers personally explained the functions of their road roller and the ongoing promotional event, the hour-long livestream received 31 road roller orders, all of which were successfully completed. This set a new record among construction machinery for the number of sales achieved via a livestream.

Having gained a taste of livestream sales, Sany Heavy Industry decided to go one step further and make practical training the focus of its short videos. Its center for interactive marketing created a Kuaishou account (Kuaishou ID: XC523188) that focused on technical training for its line of excavators, thereby solving practical work problems faced by seasoned and novice drivers alike. This further earned them the trust of their followers—many followers began inquiring about their products and prices through their Kuaishou account and eventually placed orders; one 57-second video alone sold five excavators.

On one hand, Sany managed this feat because 70 to 80 percent of the clients in the construction machinery industry are also using

Kuaishou. As of now, there are more than 450,000 Kuaishou users who have published content related to construction machinery, such as excavators and road rollers. On the other hand, they accomplished this because the ways of presenting short video content have become more diverse and thus the transmission of information has become more straightforward. Furthermore, Kuaishou's principle of inclusivity has enabled many ordinary truck drivers, excavator operators, and repairmen to become minor celebrities who set the pace for vertical users to interact and share all kinds of technical knowledge and information on the platform.

Sany's short video strategy on Kuaishou is an epitome of its allround push toward digital transformation. In the past, they had been among the earliest adopters of e-commerce within the construction machinery industry. Today, they hope to lead the way in digital transmission and marketing once again by using richer and more agile means to interact directly with clients and win the favor of more young clients.

The Most Essential Sales Secret: Selling Vehicles by Livestreaming on Kuaishou

Yang Jingrui is a used vehicle dealer in Huaxiang, Shijiazhuang. He started using Kuaishou two years before Sany Heavy Industry did. Nowadays, he can sell up to 40 mobile homes for several hundred yuan each on Kuaishou every year. His account, called "Brother Yang Talks About Mobile Homes," has nearly 600,000 fans, which thus ensures the sustainability of his mobile home business.

His customers come from all over China, including as far as Xinjiang and Tibet. His one-man business has earned tens of millions of yuan in revenue so far.

He became a mobile home celebrity on Kuaishou partially because of a recommendation from a friend who had started using Kuaishou even earlier on. This is also an important reason why Kuaishou's users keep on increasing in numbers—word-of-mouth communication produces a never-ending absorption effect.

Brother Yang Talks About Mobile Homes has itself become an example of successfully using Kuaishou to generate sales. Earlier on, at an end-of-month meeting with dealers, the general manager of the Huaxiang Used Car Market demanded that every dealer must download Kuaishou. At present, more than 10 dealers in the market conduct livestreams every day, and their sales performance has indeed been good.

Selling vehicles via livestreams is no longer a secret in the vehicle dealership circle; stories like Mr. Yang's are taking place throughout China as we speak. Livestreaming and short video e-commerce are changing the vehicle market by expanding the customer base of a vehicle dealership from its locality to all of China. And during this process, the channel layouts and marketing methods of vehicle brand manufacturers are also changing.

Shengye Mobile Home Company of Linyi City, Shandong Province, had also gained half of its clients through Kuaishou. One of their sales managers, Chen Jin, regards Kuaishou's livestream mechanism as his most essential sales secret. He requires each of the 20-odd salespersons under his charge to have a Kuaishou account and to upload at least three videos per day. Together with all franchisees, these salespersons have to undergo training on operating a Kuaishou account.

Chen Jin and his colleagues have seen their number of followers on Kuaishou increase from a few thousand to a few million. Each Kuaishou account is a company asset; when a salesperson resigns, they must return the account they were operating back to the company.

Shengye's sales revenue has skyrocketed thanks to Kuaishou. The vehicle output of their factories often ranks first in China, while the number of sales they make is more than 10 times that of a 4S store (in China, this is a dealership designation that refers to "Sales, Spare parts, Service, and Survey"). Their sales revenue in 2017 was a tenfold increase over that in 2016, which then doubled in 2018 to reach 240 million yuan.

When asked why Kuaishou is so effective at helping them increase sales, they said that when compared to online forums, graphics, and posters, short videos can increase a client's sense of experience and trust vis-à-vis the company to such high levels that hundreds of thousands of mobile homes and road rollers can be sold wholesale.

Foxconn: Recruiting New Employees by Livestreaming on Kuaishou

In 2009, Cheng Bin became an assembly-line worker at Foxconn. As the financial crisis had only just subsided back then, finding a job was not so easy and he even had to pay a factory entry fee.

Ten years later, the situation has reversed. Even a highly coveted place to work such as Foxconn is now facing a labor shortage. In response, the company has implemented an incentive policy that pays 1,000 to 3,000 yuan to any employee who is able to bring in a new employee. Cheng Bin immediately seized this opportunity. He created a Kuaishou account called "Foxconn HQ @Interviewer" to conduct recruitment, thereby opening up a considerable source of income for himself.

At Foxconn, there are many Kuaishou pros just like Cheng Bin. One of them has an account called "Foxconn Electronics Factory @Sprint 300,000," which successfully brought in 1,200 regular employees, earning more than 1 million yuan in incentives in just one year. For Foxconn, Kuaishou has become a more effective recruitment platform than any employment agency out there.

As new types of communication carriers, livestreams and short videos offer greater possibilities than anyone can imagine and do not merely provide entertainment content.

They possess unique advantages in showcasing an enterprise's culture and environment and are more visual and genuine than the content on traditional recruitment websites. Young people aged 25 and under who have begun to enter society and have together become a major force of consumption are internet natives who grew up with the internet and thus are more inclined to use the internet to make purchases and look for jobs. At the same time, they find it easier to accept livestreams and short videos as the modes of showcasing content.

New Terrain for Enterprises to Find Customers

In 2019, Kuaishou's innovative platform ecosystem for connecting enterprises and clients became a commercial sensation on the internet.

Enterprises and their agents are given an infinite number of contact points on the platform, enabling them to accurately reach their target users. The platform not only makes the world flat but also allows everyone to coexist in a "society of acquaintances"—within the boundaries of their mobile phone screens—where they can trust and carry out zero-distance transactions with one another.

To all enterprises, it therefore represents new terrain that awaits further development. At the same time, Kuaishou is providing ever-greater possibilities. Livestreams and short videos are just like wings that can help an enterprise fly higher and steadier than ever before.

EMPLOYEE ACCOUNTS: KUAISHOU'S "INTERNET CELEBRITIES" HAVE RECONFIGURED EMPLOYEE-ENTERPRISE RELATIONS

On August 1, 2019, Zhou Yantong uploaded a video on Kuaishou. In the video, a handsome animal trainer is trying to kiss a white dolphin, but the dolphin does not cooperate. The trainer thus had no choice but to feed a small fish to the dolphin, causing it to swiftly lean forward and plant a kiss on his lips. Within a day, this lovey-dovey video was viewed more than 190,000 times.

Zhou Yantong is a trainer at the Tianjin Haichang Polar Ocean Park (Haichang Ocean Park for short), and he operates a Kuaishou account called "Big White and Teacher Zhou." He himself is Teacher Zhou, while Big White is the name of an adorable white dolphin. The interactions between Big White and Teacher Zhou are filled with so much warmth that watching their videos never fails to melt the hearts of many of their followers on Kuaishou.

Big White and Teacher Zhou (Kuaishou ID: JoyZhou1) currently has 415,000 followers. Yet, there are other celebrity trainers from the same park whose Kuaishou accounts have even more followers than that. Since 2017, most of the 52 animal trainers at the park have created their own short video accounts. Five of them have more than 50,000 followers, among which an account called "Big Chun, Trainer of Dolphins and

Whales" (Kuaishou ID: cc13821182009), owned by a trainer called Zhao Yingchun, has more than 900,000 fans.

The Ocean Park has supported the growth of these online "celebrity trainers" in order to increase its own popularity and reputation through short video platforms such as Kuaishou. In May 2019, without the park doing much publicity, its first artificially reared dolphin caught the attention of tens of thousands of people. Videos of it being born underwater, learning to swim, and feeding on its mother's milk attracted a large number of likes and comments on the short video accounts of the park's celebrity trainers.

Compared to the meticulously managed "official accounts" of enterprise teams, the Ocean Park's use of the accounts of its online celebrity employees to perform communication appears very simple and effective.

On the same day that "Big White and Teacher Zhou" published their lovey-dovey video online, several thousand Direct Supply Accounts for Xiaomi electronic products carrying the words "Directly Supplied by Xiaomi" also published short videos on Kuaishou. By integrating offline and online resources, Xiaomi was able to embrace Kuaishou users.

Because many Xiaomi fans are loyal fans of Kuaishou, and also because of the strong interaction and stickiness of short video content, Xiaomi was able to find value on Kuaishou. The company successfully combined new retail concepts by distributing in bulk through offline channels and synchronizing the distribution with new marketing online, thereby increasing the sales of their electronic products ceaselessly—with Kuaishou serving as an important platform.

"Chat with Xiaomi" Showcases an Internet Marketing Spectacle

"Xiao'ai, I want to listen to 'Fly Far and High,'" said Xiaoxue in front of a Xiaomi speaker.

Xiaoxue is the manager of a Xiaomi Direct Supply store in Linyi City, Shandong Province. September 4, 2017, was a memorable day for him. That day, he focused his camera on a white Xiaomi AI speaker that was placed on a display counter and filmed an 11-second video, which he then uploaded to Kuaishou.

This was his first time uploading a short video to Kuaishou, and so he was certainly not experienced at all. Oddly enough, there was a housefly resting on the AI speaker, but as soon as Xiaoxue said the words "Fly Far and High," the housefly indeed buzzed off and "flew far and high."

The housefly unexpectedly became the biggest talking point of this video. One comment read, "Chase away that housefly, ha-ha." Another said, "Bro, was that housefly part of the script? It really cooperated with you and flew far and high." One of the unique features of a Kuaishou personal account is that perfection is not sought after; personalized expressions and some unexpected accidents can become tools of communication that are favorable for sales, provided that they do not harm the brand.

The newly registered account called "Xiaoxue the Technologist" (Kuaishou ID: mi93666666) only had a handful of followers when this video garnered more than 2,000 views. Encouraged by this, Xiaoxue went on to publish more than 200 videos over the next two years, with one video in particular garnering more than 3,000,000 views and 30,000 interactions. For a Xiaomi Direct Supply store that markets phones through direct appeal, this was certainly an amazing feat.

Empowered by Kuaishou, many managers of Xiaomi stores became local key opinion leaders (KOLs). To date, Xiaomi has more than 10 celebrity store managers who drive up the activity levels of the loyal fans and Xiaomi fans in their localities to great effect, thereby increasing their own stickiness and directly stimulating transactions.

Every year in April, Xiaomi holds its traditional Xiaomi Fan Festival, albeit 2019 was slightly different—the Xiaomi Fan Festival became more than just an offline carnival, as Xiaomi launched an event called "Let's Chat with Xiaomi Together" on Kuaishou. Hence, by integrating the offline festival with the online event, a unique spectacle of internet short video marketing was presented.

On the day that the event went live, it rapidly attracted the attention of more than 800,000 Xiaomi fans. Over the next 10 days, Xiaomi published more than 2,000 videos, which garnered more than 10 million views in total and gained more than 100,000 new fans. Meanwhile, the offline festival was held in 50 universities for more than 30,000,000 fans. In the final analysis, Xiaomi succeeded in integrating the offline carnival with the online event to create a festival for everyone.

Being on Point and Having Feelings

Unlike the Xiaomi model of using many direct suppliers to conduct sales in each and every region of China, the Tianjin Haichang Polar Ocean Park instead achieved success with a small number of employees. It strives to fully unearth the value of its celebrity animals and trainers and turn them into top internet celebrities in vertical domains.

Haichang Ocean Park operates six ocean theme parks and two all-in-one entertainment theme parks in cities such as Shanghai, Dalian, Qingdao, and Tianjin. In total, it keeps more than 66,000 large-sized marine animals such as belugas and polar bears—the most out of any theme park chain in China—and has drawn more than 110 million visits. In 2018, its theme park in Tianjin brought in the highest operating revenue among its theme parks in different cities; an important factor for this was the traffic it got on short video platforms.

According to Liu Qingqing, marketing director of the Tianjin Haichang Polar Ocean Park, most of the park's 52 trainers have created their own short video accounts since 2017, with five of them having more than 50,000 followers each. Encouraging its employees to film short videos and establishing internet celebrity employees has turned out to be a masterstroke in the park's marketing strategy.

Although many enterprises have tried to operate short video accounts, a large portion of them were unable to find suitable methods and tricks for doing so. When a beluga-themed short video by the Tianjin Haichang Polar Ocean Park "broke" the internet in 2018, many marketers of other ocean-themed amusement parks began to study why Employee Accounts were making a bigger splash than Enterprise Accounts.

"Fans like short videos taken by the employees themselves. Instead, many videos that were taken by enterprises failed to catch on in spite of the creative efforts made and publicity they were given."

Liu believes that the short video accounts of internet celebrity trainers have amassed large numbers of followers mainly because they are "on point" and "have feelings."

One example is trainer Zhao Yingchun. He is one of the earliest users of Kuaishou from Haichang Polar Ocean Park, having begun to operate a Kuaishou account since 2017. His videos are all about his life with three belugas, which he calls his "Eldest Son," "Second Son," and "Third Son." The daily routines of brushing the belugas' teeth and playing and performing with them have attracted the attention of millions of followers. In particular, one video of him affectionately splashing water at a beluga garnered more than 7.4 million views.

The most touching aspects of Zhao's videos are those that showcase the mutual interaction and feelings between him and the belugas. He says that every beluga has its own moods and personality: Third Son is an honest and frank boy who would never disobey a trainer's commands and is always on the go, whereas Second Son is more playful, clownish, and quick-witted, and would often tease rookie trainers by pulling them underwater or nibbling on their socks.

The story of the internet celebrity belugas and internet celebrity trainers has struck a strong emotional chord with fans. Zhao Yingchun said that

> "Many Internet users have gotten to know about belugas through my videos. Belugas are not as smart as other animals such as cats and dogs and do not understand spoken human language. However, they know how to communicate by acting pettishly and can discern a human's emotional state through their body language.

Many internet users have left comments telling the trainers to "take good care of the belugas" or have traveled thousands of miles to visit the trainers whom they have followed for a long time. A user from Mudanjiang City who calls herself "Chuxue" left a comment saying that she had been following "Big Chun" for more than a year, and in May 2019, she made a trip to the Tianjin Haichang Polar Ocean Park—and even bought VIP seats—to get a closer view of the belugas' performance.

There are many others who are just like Chuxue, and this thus prompted Haichang Polar Ocean Park to begin paying attention to Kuaishou's power of communication. They realized that their followers' love for the internet celebrity trainers was far greater than their receptivity toward brand advertisements, while at the same time, personal accounts operated by employees could garner a lot of traffic and exposure without much investment. With the increasing popularity of short videos, the brand awareness of the Tianjin Haichang Polar Ocean Park extended out of the Beijing-Tianjin-Hebei region. More and more tourists from all over China came to visit the park after watching the videos, thereby providing it with greater income and popularity.

At present, Haichang Ocean Parks in other cities are also actively training their own internet celebrity trainers. For example, a celebrity trainer called "Polar God" (Kuaishou ID: D-Beluga) at the Dalian Haichang Polar Ocean Park has amassed more than 960,000 followers on Kuaishou. These internet celebrity employees have become stars in the eyes of many animal trainers across China.

The Success of Every "Employee Account" Contributes to the Success of the Enterprise Brand

Because there are differences between an Employee Account and an Enterprise Account after all, the Tianjin Haichang Polar Ocean Park is still in the midst of figuring out through trial and error how to incentivize employees to keep on promoting their enterprise brand and how to manage the relations between the enterprise and the employees' self-operated media.

Liu Qingqing explains that what the park has done is bring out their employees' initiative in filming videos by having the marketing department provide support to the employees in content planning and creativity.

For example, the marketing department once guided the trainers on video recording by helping the trainers find the interesting points of interaction between them and the belugas, and also by discussing how to film an exquisite video. The success of every Employee Account contributes to the success of the enterprise's brand; employee endorsement helps to max-imize the influence of publicizing an enterprise's brand.

To encourage more employees to endorse the enterprise on short video platforms, the Tianjin Haichang Polar Ocean Park introduced bonus payments for trainers who amass more than 10,000 followers by filming short videos and livestreaming.

Once the matrix of employee-operated short video media is formed, the company will be able to plan and integrate content. In 2019, the Tianjin Haichang Polar Ocean Park began to further integrate its ex-isting employee-operated media resources by encouraging employees to base their videos on the company's marine animal resources and to spread more popular scientific knowledge to make the videos more pro-fessional and watchable. Previously, an Employee Account's livestream of the "water-entering ceremony" of an Adélie penguin named Jiubao, as well as a video of the birth of a dolphin, received widespread transmis-sion and attention. These are all part of the company's overall promotion and brand communication on new media.

Haichang Ocean Park's marketing department also plans to host stable follower groups for marine animal lovers on their employees' short video accounts. This plan includes organizing various types of competitive events based on short videos and personal stories of training animals, arranging fan meetings for their internet celebrity employees, and increasing the participation and interaction of groups of marine animal lovers using various methods such as giving away free tickets and gifts.

At the same time, the company will perform standardized manage-ment of employees' short video accounts in such ways as prohibiting commercial advertising and stipulating that an employee cannot con-tinue to use their account if they leave the company but remain in the industry. Although these regulations would inevitably affect the income and enthusiasm of employees in operating their accounts, Liu Qingqing found from the trainers themselves that the sense of honor and achieve-ment granted to them by becoming internet celebrity employees and re-ceiving company incentives was far more important to them than any material reward.

Therefore, an enterprise's use of Employee Accounts to conduct marketing, to incentivize employees to film videos, and to solicit the attention of followers is only the first step. Instead, long-term content management and follower conversion are the true objectives. At the same time, the issue of how to effectively balance the relationship between employee-operated new media and enterprise marketing cannot be neglected.

Xiaomi maintains relatively loose relations with the Kuaishou accounts of Direct Supply store employees in various regions. To date, Xiaomi Home and Xiaomi Direct Supply already consist of tens of thousands of stores, while new stores are being opened at ever faster rates in order to capture the market. A significant portion of the employees in these stores have created Kuaishou accounts; this is highly beneficial not only to the sales of Direct Supply stores but also to Xiaomi's brand image and the recognition of their products.

Every Direct Supply store employee's Kuaishou account serves to promote Xiaomi's products and brand, which is certainly something that the company is happy to see.

While Haichang Ocean Park needs to straighten out the relationship between the company and the employees vis-à-vis their Kuaishou accounts, this issue is much simpler for Xiaomi as their Direct Supply store employees are motivated to set up Kuaishou accounts due to the natural win-win relationship they have with Xiaomi.

The Kuaishou platform has empowered Xiaomi to successfully combine the new retail concepts by distributing in bulk through offline channels and synchronizing the distribution with new marketing online, thereby ceaselessly increasing the sales of their electronic products.

In recent years, with the saturation of the electronics market in first- and second-tier cities in China, Xiaomi has shifted its target customers to people in third- and fourth-tier cities in order to acquire new target markets. Xiaomi's brick-and-mortar stores, which consist of Home stores and Direct Supply stores, can be found almost everywhere today. At the same time, thousands of Xiaomi Direct Supply accounts are quietly popping up on Kuaishou. Compared with the rising costs of traffic acquisition on other platforms, the low-cost conversion provided by Kuaishou is highly attractive to Xiaomi's resellers. With its new retail strategy, Xiaomi is able to penetrate prefecture-level cities and small counties alike.

The marketing of an enterprise needs to be conducted where its customers are. Xiaomi and Haichang Ocean Park are not the only businesses to have realized this point, which is the golden rule of enterprise development in a market economy. Kuaishou's user base of several hundred million people has warmly embraced short videos and livestreams, bringing benefits to countless enterprises as a result.

Every enterprise has its own way of positioning its Kuaishou accounts, and new methods and strategies are continually emerging. Aside from Haichang and Xiaomi, more and more enterprises have begun to reconfigure their relations with their employees in order to make the operation of Kuaishou accounts a potent skill they can wield.

CHAPTER SIX

KUAISHOU'S POVERTY ALLEVIATION: SEEING EVERY VILLAGE

CHAPTER OVERVIEW

The internet has built an information highway for everyone. Kuaishou's form of "short videos + livestreams" has lowered the barriers to entry for sharing and recording online. Nowadays, as long as they have a smartphone and know how to use Kuaishou, people in poorer regions are able to see the vast world as presented on the internet, thereby broadening their minds and horizons. At the same time, they are able to record and share the lifestyles, foods, and scenery found in rural areas. Once a village is seen, it will be able to create connections. And once it can create connections, infinite possibilities will be born. Using Kuaishou, the poorer regions of China can be connected to the outside world, inadvertently bringing about miraculous growth for individuals and villages. To give a few examples, Yuan Guihua became an entrepreneur and is now building orchards and guest houses to help her fellow villagers attain wealth; Jiang Jinchun mobilized her fellow villagers to gather tea leaves and sell tea, kudzu root powder, and dried bamboo shoots; while Wu Yusheng found "the Seven Fairies of Dong Families" and helped their entire village rise out of poverty by promoting Dong culture and facilitating sales of their local fabrics and embroidery.

Interestingly, each of these villages rose out of poverty in its own unique way that was not designed by any poverty alleviation agency. Rather, it was a "best practice" that naturally came about through the numerous interactions between rural users and their followers. Such a practice is more accurate and vigorous than any other.

SUCCESS STORIES

Xueli the Smile-a-Lot: A Left-Behind Youth Who Promotes the Idyllic Beauty of the Countryside

The Seven Fairies of Dong Families: Connecting the Ancient Dong Villages to Modern Civilization by Using Short Videos

A Taste of the Mountain Villages: Kuaishou's "Lu Zhishen" Is the King of Poverty Alleviation in the Mountains

China's First Yoga Village: Kuaishou Made the Legend of Yugouliang Village Visible to the World

KUAISHOU'S POVERTY ALLEVIATION: SEEING EVERY VILLAGE

Song Tingting, vice president of Kuaishou Technology and director of the Kuaishou Poverty Alleviation Office

Yuan Guihua was 18 years old when she returned to the depths of her mountain home in Guizhou Province to work on the family farm after failing the college entrance examination. While herding cattle one day, she casually filmed a video and uploaded it to Kuaishou. Unexpectedly, the video attracted the attention of the outside world and has brought her several million followers to date. Her life thus made a turn for the better.

Calling herself "Xueli" on Kuaishou, she enables her followers nationwide to see the beautiful countryside and its high-quality specialty products through short videos and livestreams. She has helped her fellow villagers sell more than 2 million yuan worth of specialty products. Nowadays, she is building orchards and guest houses to help her fellow villagers escape poverty and attain wealth.

There are many people like Xueli on Kuaishou. For generations, their families have lived in remote and impoverished mountain villages. Kuaishou has enabled them to showcase the beautiful scenery, delicious cuisine, and folk customs of the countryside online. As a result, they have discovered that their lives are worth sharing and that many people are interested in the rural world. By entering the eyes of people online, the villages they live in have changed their destiny.

We can see, to our surprise, that Kuaishou has gradually assimilated into the daily working lives of people in poorer areas, becoming a new "farming tool" that they need in order to achieve a better life.

A New "Farming Tool" for People in Poorer Areas

The most significant characteristic of the contemporary age is the rapid development of the internet, which has brought fundamental changes to how we live and work. People in first- and second-tier cities were first to learn how to use it for e-commerce, food delivery, ride-hailing services, and many other innovative purposes. As for the people who live in remote and poorer regions of China, the limitations of their objective conditions have meant that they are one step behind.

Many people think that the poverty of certain regions is caused by their inaccessibility and lack of resources. In actual fact, technological improvement has made physical distance a nonfactor. With the continuous investments of the state in the poorer regions, the people there have become equipped with the infrastructure they need. These regions are a gold mine of cultural tourism, specialty products, and even intangible cultural heritage, but because of the psychological distance of the people there, these things have been unable to be showcased to the rest of China.

As observed by President Xi, the top priority in poverty alleviation is not something regarding material wealth but rather it's about changing mindsets and ideas. We believe that poverty alleviation should be about allowing poorer regions to enjoy the benefits of social development just like in other regions. The people at the "nerve endings" of China's territory should be enabled to see different lifestyles, to aspire for a better life, and to master and apply new technologies in order to improve their lives.

This is the vision that Kuaishou started out with. The internet has built an information highway for everyone. Kuaishou's form of "short videos + livestreams" has lowered the barriers to entry for sharing and recording online. Nowadays, as long as they have a smartphone and know how to use Kuaishou, people in poorer regions are able to see the vast world as presented on the internet, thereby broadening their minds and horizons. At the same time, they are able to record and share the lifestyles, foods, and scenery found in rural areas.

According to our statistics, by the end of 2018, one in five people from 832 poverty-stricken counties were active users on Kuaishou. More than 1.1 billion videos were posted from poverty-stricken regions, with total views amounting to more than 600 billion and the number of likes amounting to more than 24.7 billion.

At Kuaishou, we do not regard poverty alleviation as something extra we need to do, but rather as something that is closely related to our business development. In 2018, 16 million people earned an income on the Kuaishou platform, of which 3.4 million came from poverty-stricken regions. It was the ecosystem on the platform that drove us to work on poverty alleviation. As a result, Kuaishou has been hailed as the platform that "has an intrinsic motivation for poverty alleviation work" and has become a new farming tool that helps poverty-stricken communities earn higher incomes and improve their lives.

Kuaishou's poverty alleviation work is all about making this new farming tool better to use. Aided by the state's sustained efforts in building internet infrastructure, this is the mission that Kuaishou has always been devoted to, as it embodies our adherence to the principle of inclusivity. Kuaishou hopes to use warm-hearted technology to improve every person's unique sense of happiness. Driven by this mission, we have used "algorithms for good" to ensure that rural users from poverty-stricken regions—who often have few followers—can be seen by many people, as long as their content is good enough.

Once a village is seen, it will be able to create connections. And once it can create connections, infinite possibilities will be born.

Traffic Supports a Positive Ecosystem of Poverty Alleviation

The use of Kuaishou to connect poverty-stricken regions with the outside world has inadvertently brought about miraculous growth for individuals and villages alike. To give a few examples, Yuan Guihua became an entrepreneur and is now building orchards and guest houses to help her fellow villagers attain wealth; Jiang Jinchun mobilized her fellow villagers to gather tea leaves and sell tea, kudzu root powder, and dried bamboo shoots; while Wu Yusheng found the Seven Fairies of Dong Families and helped their entire village rise out of poverty by promoting Dong culture and facilitating sales of their local fabrics and embroideries.

Interestingly, each of these villages rose out of poverty in its own unique way that was not designed by any poverty alleviation agency. Rather, it was a "best practice" that naturally came about through the numerous interactions between rural users and their followers. Such a practice is more accurate and vigorous than any other.

To maintain its advantages and better fulfill the social responsibility of an internet enterprise, Kuaishou has set up a specialized Poverty Alleviation Office. And in 2018, Kuaishou announced the "500 Million Traffic Plan," pouring in 500 million yuan worth of traffic resources to give poverty-stricken counties a certain amount of traffic preference and boost the promotion and sale of local specialty products.

Thanks to the traffic support, the "mountain products" of many poverty-stricken regions achieved astonishing sales volumes. For example, the Aiyuan oranges of Sichuan Province became famous for their soft pulp and juiciness. Many farmers who grew Aiyuan oranges published videos of squeezing orange juice by hand on Kuaishou, attracting a great deal of attention and receiving many comments asking to purchase these oranges. In 2018 alone, 20 million kilograms worth of Aiyuan oranges were sold on Kuaishou, bringing in a revenue of 157 million yuan and thereby helping countless families improve their lives.

But that is not all. Kuaishou's unique model of "poverty alleviation through traffic" takes "poverty alleviation through education" as its core, "poverty alleviation through e-commerce" as an important means, and "the creation of poverty-stricken regional brands" as a supplementary approach. It is an accuracy-based model that seeks to mobilize a wide range of social forces.

Poverty alleviation must start with education. The Kuaishou platform itself contains many videos on agricultural technologies and services that are suitable for rural users to learn from. Kuaishou has also partnered with poverty-striven counties to launch Kuaishou University, which trains the local people to use the internet, master short video tools, and access various information channels. So far, Kuaishou University has provided training sessions in provinces and autonomous regions such as Guangdong, Inner Mongolia, and Shanxi, and has trained more than 2,000 short video producers from rural villages. In doing so, it has given impetus to the development of social e-commerce in poverty-stricken regions.

In 2018, Kuaishou launched the "Happy Countryside Strategy." One of its core modules is the "Happy Village Leader Program," which seeks to support 100 rural Kuaishou users to start businesses locally. To date, this program has reached 21 counties and municipalities in 10 provinces across China, nurtured 25 township enterprises and professional farmer cooperatives, trained 43 rural entrepreneurs, provided more than 120 local jobs, and increased the income of more than 1,000 poor households.

Thanks to the loyal fan economy in Kuaishou's communities, rural users who sell agricultural products are no longer just salespersons but have instead become savvy and honest marketing experts. In launching the "Seeds Plan," Kuaishou has mobilized all of its e-commerce experts, MCN agencies, service providers, and other experienced and willing users to help users from poverty-stricken regions promote and sell their products. To date, this plan has helped nearly 80 poverty-stricken regions in China sell their mountain products, directly improving the incomes of nearly 180,000 registered poor people.

Aside from providing point-to-point assistance to every poverty-stricken village, Kuaishou also pays attention to the overall regional cooperation. By working with the local governments of poverty-stricken counties and providing traffic support, Kuaishou has started on a project called "Log on to Kuaishou to Discover a Beautiful China," which seeks to empower individuals and regions using internet technologies and rectify the imbalance in development between cities and villages and between different regions. So far, Kuaishou has established regional poverty alleviation partnerships with places such as the Xilingol League of Inner Mongolia, Yongsheng County in Yunnan Province, and Zhangjiajie City in Hunan Province.

A Wider Range of Forces That Influence and Mobilize Society

Drawing on its technical expertise and principle of inclusivity, Kuaishou is developing a new approach to poverty alleviation. These systematically-developed poverty alleviation programs emphasize teaching people to fish, rather than giving them fish—using short videos and livestreams as tools of information inclusivization in the work of rural poverty alleviation, empowering rural farmers, giving impetus to social e-commerce and information sharing, and systematically stimulating intrinsic motivation for alleviating poverty in poverty-stricken regions, thereby realizing "hematopoietic" poverty alleviation and enabling every village to be seen.

In this pan-society war on poverty, countless beautiful stories, ingenious methods, and poster children have emerged. Short videos are one of the best ways to convey and publicize these experiences and methods. For example, Zhang Fei, the poverty alleviation secretary for poverty-stricken villages in Aba Prefecture, Sichuan Province, has brought dining tables deep into the clouds, more than 3,200 meters above sea level. The picturesque clouds in his videos have gained him over 10 million views, while his home has been dubbed a "restaurant in the clouds." Zhang Fei also showcases the scenery of the countryside through Kuaishou, attracting many tourists to visit and boosting sales of local agricultural products—ultimately increasing the incomes of the villagers.

In the future, Kuaishou will continue to partner with various sectors of society and launch more promotional campaigns for poverty alleviation. With its built-in social attributes and novel short video format, it will influence and mobilize more forces in society to join the fight against poverty.

XUELI THE SMILE-A-LOT: A LEFT-BEHIND YOUTH WHO PROMOTES THE IDYLLIC BEAUTY OF THE COUNTRYSIDE

Yuan Guihua is a bright-smiling woman in the mountainous area of Guizhou Province who calls herself Xueli—after the heroine of an adventure novel—on Kuaishou. A few years ago, she began to share her everyday life in a mountain village on Kuaishou. Through her videos, people can see the daily life of this tough woman: carrying bamboo on her shoulders while making bamboo wine, digging for loaches in paddy fields, herding cattle, and climbing trees. At the same time, her videos also exhibit the temptingly beautiful scenery, delicious foods, and idyllic lifestyle deep in the mountains.

Today, more and more people have found out through Xueli's Kuaishou account that there is actually such a beautiful and primitive paradise in the Qiandongnan Miao and Dong Autonomous Prefecture of Guizhou Province. Xueli has also marketed the specialty products of her hometown on the platform, and she plans to lead her fellow villagers to start a big venture next.

PROFILE

Kuaishou name: 爱笑的雪莉吖 (Xueli the Smile-a-Lot)

Kuaishou ID: yuanguihua

Hometown: Qiandongnan Miao and Dong Autonomous Prefecture, Guizhou Province

Age: 20

Education: senior high school

Topic: lifestyle, food, and specialty products of a mountain village

Production style: showcasing the real work and life scenes in a mountain village and conducting livestreams to interact with followers

Message to her loyal fans: After the rain comes the sun. Always believe in rainbows

Business model: help fellow villagers sell hometown specialty products, publicize our hometown, and attract tourists through livestreams

Narrator: Yuan Guihua

My Unique Life at 18

My name is Yuan Guihua, and I was born in 1998 in a wooden house in Tianzhu County, Qiandongnan Miao and Dong Autonomous Prefecture, Guizhou Province. Tianzhu is a poverty-stricken county. To reach my village, you have to get off at the nearest high-speed rail station, take a two-hour-odd long minibus ride to the county seat, and then drive another half hour or so into the mountains.

We used to only have mud roads. It took more than an hour to get to school from my home. We had to walk everywhere because there was no other form of transportation. But now, I have bought myself a small electric motorbike, so it usually only takes around 10 minutes to get home.

My nickname on Kuaishou is "Xueli the Smile-a-Lot." Xueli is the heroine in my favorite adventure novel, and I think she is exceptionally brave. I often introduce myself to people as a tough girl from the depths of the mountains. You can see on Kuaishou many scenes of my daily work, such as cattle herding, woodworking, bamboo weaving, tilling the land,

and carrying heavy loads. Many people are surprised that I am so strong despite looking so small and thin.

I spent my childhood in my grandparents' home. As a little girl, my grandfather taught me how to make baskets, chopsticks, and brooms with bamboo. As for my grandmother, she would often take me with her to harvest *Litsea pungens* (a Chinese herb) and sell it in the local farmer's market. Occasionally, I would find a job there to sort chili peppers for 10 cents per kilogram, meaning I could make 30 yuan in half a day. Working with adults enabled me to learn many skills at a young age.

My life at 18 was different from many others'. That year, I scored 427 points on the national college entrance examination. Dissatisfied with my score, I did not apply to a single university. My parents wanted me to repeat a year and take the exam again, but I refused because my family could hardly afford it.

I have an elder brother who was in poor health and an elder sister who had polio, so raising the three of us was not easy for my parents. In our village, if we did not attend university, there was only one path, which was to do odd jobs. But that was not what I wanted. I learned about Kuaishou in 2015 and created an account the next year. It was then that I wondered whether I could do something with Kuaishou.

I felt rather inferior at first. As a girl from the mountains, I had few talents, whereas other creators on Kuaishou had a talent for singing, dancing, or acting. However, after thinking it over, I realized that I also had some things to share with everyone—the joys of life in the mountains.

I remember that it was Father's Day when I uploaded my first video. Back then, we only had mud roads (since replaced by concrete roads). My father and I were driving cattle on the roads when I casually filmed a video. Unexpectedly, I found out just before going to bed that night that the video had garnered more than 500,000 views. Feeling most excited, I could not stop showing it to my family for some time. This also gave me great encouragement; I realized that my life was also worth sharing and that many people were highly interested in life in the mountains.

Subsequently, I shared a lot of my daily life in successive videos. For example, when helping my father with some labor work, I could carry a log as heavy as a hundred kilograms. After sharing such videos, my followers slowly increased. Someone left a comment saying that my videos made them miss their own childhood, while another comment said that the simple life in the mountains was what they yearned for. And someone else exclaimed that they never knew there was such paradise-like scenery in the mountains of Guizhou.

At first it was all just for fun and I did not think about how to make money using Kuaishou.

However, people began to ask me if they could buy the delicious mountain cuisine and specialties that constantly appeared in my videos. At first, I replied that I could send them some for free. But when thousands of people made requests, I could no longer afford to do so. I thought that since so many people liked the specialty products of my hometown, it would be a good idea to try to sell them; that way, I could help increase my family's income as well.

My follower count gradually grew from several hundred thousand to two million and then to three million, and more and more people wanted to buy our specialty products. When we became unable to keep up with the demand, we sought the help of our elderly neighbors. The young people of our village were all either doing odd jobs elsewhere or working in the county seat, whereas the elderly people had a lot of free time and knew how to make our specialty products at home. Of course, I had to check the quality of the products before I could sell them to my followers. In this way, my relatives and friends could earn a little pocket money, while people from outside the mountains could also get to enjoy the cuisine of my hometown.

And so, just like that, the foods that my village had grown accustomed to, such as cured meat, moldy tofu, anchovies, dried bamboo shoots, bracken fern, and rice wine, became sold throughout China. I felt extremely happy because I started to earn my own income, as well as some gifts from my livestreams. Not only that, but my family's living conditions kept on improving, while my fellow villagers also increased their incomes. Being able to help the whole village earn money on the internet by using this tradition-breaking method made me feel both immensely happy and fortunate.

After My First Start-up "Failure," Kuaishou Offered Me Timely Assistance

At first, my parents disapproved of my livestreaming at home instead of going out to do odd jobs because they felt that it was not proper work. I slowly proved to them that this was not the case, and they eventually began to support me after I earned some money from selling specialty products and could afford to repair our pigsty and fishpond. My sister-in-law has also joined Kuaishou—she amassed 40,000 fans in just a month after joining and is able to sell 50,000 yuan worth of specialty products every month.

I livestream for an hour or so once or twice a day. This is sometimes done in the doorway of my home, sometimes in the mountains, and sometimes in the market while I am selling agricultural products. My livestreams showcase the local customs and conditions, and the processes of making our specialty products and cuisines—many people have bought our specialty products after watching them.

By selling specialty products on Kuaishou, our family's annual income has increased from nearly 30,000 yuan to more than 200,000 yuan. My income alone provides for the livelihood of 11 of us, only excluding my elder sister's family of three.

However, I will not rest on my laurels. Since Kuaishou has provided me with such a good opportunity, and I am fortunate enough to occupy a small space on it, I intend to lead my fellow villagers to start a big venture.

There is a type of fruit that grows in our mountains we call the "blood vine fruit"; its other names are "demon fruit" and "kadsura coccinea." Its name in Hmong means *the fruit of beauty and longevity*. It is not only edible but also has high nutritional and medicinal value. However, its production is scarce, and it can only be found in some of the highest mountains around us—it sometimes can't be found for several miles. My grandfather likes to go into the mountains to gather wild fruits, including the blood vine fruit, and bring them back to grow.

I believe that the market for this fruit should be extremely large. After all, it is highly peculiar and few people have eaten it before, yet so many people are interested in it. I thus intend to build an orchard for blood vine fruits and industrialize this fruit together with my fellow villagers, who trust me greatly due to my experience in selling goods, and the assistance I have rendered to them in selling many of their goods. Hence, 33 villagers have established a cooperative with me, and planted 10 acres of blood vine fruits.

My prediction is that the cooperative will earn approximately 450,000 yuan in revenue if the blood vine fruit business succeeds. That would allow the villagers to increase their incomes, escape poverty, and attain wealth together. Our village could even become the "village of blood vine fruits." Nevertheless, no matter how positive-minded we are, the process of starting a business always comes with unexpected difficulties.

We had never planted blood vine fruits in the past, so we now have to deal with issues such as pollination and pest removal on a step-by-step basis. Our output is not high in quantity but reliable in quality. In 2018, I began trying to sell these fruits and received 1,000 orders during a one-hour livestream. However, a problem occurred during the delivery and we bore the full costs.

Earlier on, I had discussed this problem with my brother-in-law. I had experimented with packing the fruits in express delivery boxes, and the result was that the fruits did not go bad for a week. When picking fruits, we also avoided picking those that were too ripe. Nevertheless, despite further wrapping the fruits in newspaper and foam when packing them for shipment, many of them were damaged in transit. I provided full refunds to buyers who received at least two damaged fruits out of three. This incident hit me very hard; I was self-reproachful and upset to have let down my fellow villagers by failing on my first venture.

However, in the midst of my frustration in September 2018, I received a special admission notice to attend training at Kuaishou's "Happy Village Entrepreneurship Academy." This would be my first time going to Beijing, and I would be going to learn together with many other young people. Before that, the furthest I had been away from my hometown was Kaili City, which is less than 200 kilometers away from our county seat.

In Beijing, I learned a lot about online sales and marketing, such as how to deal with customers, how to do market analysis, how to ship goods, and how to calculate my actual annual earnings. More importantly, many lecturers who were successful entrepreneurs themselves told us that they had faced plenty of setbacks and were even penniless at some point in time. It was then that I realized my losses were not that bad and there was no need for me to be so disheartened. Therefore, I returned home enlivened.

Creating a Paradise and Receiving Guests from Outside

I now have another idea. Because there are many high mountains and a lot of beautiful scenery around my hometown, many of my followers are interested in coming to visit, so they will certainly require accommodation.

In the summer of 2017, four young fans from Heilongjiang Province visited me by car. I took them on a mountain hike, but one of them got heat stroke halfway through, while the others also had to rest every couple of minutes. They do not exercise often back home—life in the mountains is perfect for them to build up their endurance a little.

Another young lady came to experience what life is like here together with her son. Her son was very spoiled and rebellious, which was why she wanted to show him life in a village. On the first day, I had them try planting vegetables and loosening the soil with a hoe. Halfway through, blisters formed on his hands. I then took him to pick wild vegetables and water celery. As soon as he stepped in the mud, he could not pull his feet out on his own. Later on, he fell into a furrow and I had to jump down to pull him out—there was a scratch on his leg that did look kind of painful. It was at that point that he said he never wanted to come back here again. However, a week later when he was about to leave, the cabbages and radishes he had planted on his own began to sprout. That made him very excited, and he even took photos as a memento.

An owner of a fashion store also came to visit. After enjoying the scenery along the way, she expressed her wish to build a house in the mountains and bring her family to live here.

These visitors and their reactions boosted my confidence. I hope that more people, especially those from the cities, will be able to come and experience life in my hometown. We have plenty of fruits, such as muskmelons and watermelons, to share with them, while they can also try our homegrown cabbages and wild berries.

So, I began to build a guest house with the help of my parents and fellow villagers. Having been familiar with carpentry since I was young,

I have always wanted to build a house and be involved in every aspect of its construction, including finding lumber and crafting the furniture myself—only then would I consider it fun. Many of my loyal fans on Kuaishou have found it very interesting to watch as the guest house is being built day after day. The guest house now has 12 completed rooms, but there are still no bathrooms or showers. It will only open for reception when the infrastructure is complete.

In the Future: Keep Pressing on with My Business

Although I never left the mountains to live and work elsewhere, I feel that my life has become richer and more colorful by getting to know—and be known by—many people through Kuaishou. At the same time, I can now try many things that I could not afford to in the past—I have begun to learn the guitar and I recently shared two songs I played on Kuaishou. I have also bought some cheap paint for creating artwork. More importantly, I want to keep pressing on with my business.

I have helped my family and fellow villagers sell more than 2 million yuan worth of our specialty products through Kuaishou. I'm now thinking about how to turn these specialty products into brands. Although our products are purely handmade and we pay great attention to hygiene during the production process, we still need to get certain certifications and qualifications for the sake of buyer confidence, no matter which platform we sell on. Therefore, I now need to solve some problems regarding production licenses and distribution licenses.

The blood vine fruit orchard is still going strong to date. However, the logistics issues we faced have not been adequately solved, so the fruits are not available online for now. Nevertheless, many people have come here in person to purchase them. More and more people have discovered the benefits of the blood vine fruit, which is high in added value and can be brought home to grow in a pot. Its pulp is good for replenishing blood, while its leaves are extremely pretty and can be used as facial masks—we did our own experiments and found that the leaves feel cool, smooth, and comfortable when applied to the face. I hope to solve the issues regarding the mass production and delivery of the blood vine fruit, standardize the management of its cultivation, and also create a series of videos on it.

After a midsummer rain one day, a rainbow appeared in the sky. Sitting on the bamboo steps beside a pond with a guitar in my arms, I felt that everything about that moment was so wonderful. Subsequently, I uploaded a Kuaishou video with the captions: "After the rain comes the sun. Always believe in rainbows. If you see a rainbow, good luck shall come upon you."

THE SEVEN FAIRIES OF DONG FAMILIES: CONNECTING THE ANCIENT DONG VILLAGES TO MODERN CIVILIZATION BY USING SHORT VIDEOS

The "Seven Romantic Fairies of Dong Families" come from a remote, inaccessible, and poor mountainous village in Guizhou Province called Gaibao Village.

Wu Yusheng, the first secretary of Poverty Alleviation, created the Kuaishou account called "Seven Romantic Fairies of Dong Families" in 2018. Through short videos and livestreams, he has introduced to the outside world the ancient and distinctive traditional culture of the Dong villages, attracting the attention of netizens and the media. The account now has 260,000 followers. By assisting villagers in selling their local specialty products and clothing via the internet, Wu Yusheng helped Gaibao Village escape poverty completely by the end of 2018.

Gaibao Village hopes to have cultural exchanges with other ethnic minorities in the future in order to jointly rejuvenate the rural areas.

PROFILE

Kuaishou name: 浪漫侗家七仙女 (Seven Romantic Fairies of Dong Families)

Kuaishou ID: langmannvshen

Hometown: Liping County, Guizhou Province

Age: 32

Education: undergraduate

Topic: traditional cultures of ethnic minorities

Production style: capturing the daily lives of girls from Dong families and the traditional customs of the Dong ethnic group and livestreaming

Message to loyal fans: as a fusion of tradition and modernity, traditional culture must be carried forward and innovated upon without losing its original cultural roots

Business model: publicize the unique scenery and customs of the Dong ethnic group by using the Seven Romantic Fairies of Dong Families as image ambassadors, use publicity to establish links between production and marketing, help local villagers sell specialty products such as embroideries via the internet, develop tourism resources, and spur economic development

Narrator: Wu Yusheng

My name is Wu Yusheng, the first secretary of Poverty Alleviation in Gaibao Village, Liping County, Guizhou Province. My other identity is as an atypical livestreamer on Kuaishou; I'm the person behind the Kuaishou account called Seven Romantic Fairies of Dong Families.

When I first started using Kuaishou, filming short videos was just a pastime of mine and I never expected that Kuaishou would one day become the focus of my work. Since 2018, Kuaishou has become the base camp for Gaibao Village in connecting with the outside world and achieving poverty alleviation and prosperity.

A Derelict Secretary for Poverty Alleviation

On February 14, 2018, which is the second-to-last day of the lunar year, I visited Gaibao Village for the first time. Back then, I had just received a transfer order to become the secretary of Poverty Alleviation here.

The journey from Liping County was 100-odd kilometers long and took four hours. My initial impression of Gaibao Village was its inconvenient transportation, serious shortage of living supplies, and poor economic development. However, because of its isolation from the outside world, it retained the very primitive and ancient local culture of the Dong ethnic group. Coupled with the beauty of its scenery, it seemed as though as I had entered a paradise.

From the perspective of a visitor, this is a very old and beautiful Dong village. However, when you actually step into their homes, you would see the hardship of their impoverished lives. A few years ago, some families were still using kerosene lamps instead of electricity, as they had barely a few yuan at home.

I was saddened to see that such a beautiful place was actually so poor.

After the Spring Festival, I officially took up my post in Gaibao Village. Almost every young person had gone elsewhere to do odd jobs, leaving only college students who were on winter vacation. I organized a survey team and spent a month visiting every household to conduct a detailed survey.

The results of the survey showed me that my work was going to be more difficult than I had imagined. It was virtually impossible to alleviate poverty and bring prosperity to these people simply by planting a few more trees and raising a few more pigs. Instead, the real treasures of the village were the rich ethnic culture of Dong families and the Grand Song of the Dong ethnic group (an international-level intangible cultural heritage), as well as the Pipa Song of the Dong ethnic group (a national-level intangible cultural heritage), the Dong Opera, the traditional handicrafts such as wax dyeing, and the paradise-like scenery.

As I had seen many Kuaishou videos regarding rural topics, I suddenly came up with the idea of using short videos to publicize the Dong culture and develop the tourism industry. Hence, I quickly proposed this idea to the village cadres and planned to raise funds for it.

However, everyone opposed my idea—after all, these people did not even use smartphones, let alone know about Kuaishou.

Nevertheless, I remained confident in my idea, because I could see that we had such a unique culture, and I was certain that outsiders would like it.

Since the fundraising had failed, I decided to go for a risk guarantee method—I promised that as long as the village was willing to start operating a Kuaishou account, any investment loss would be borne by me personally. In that way, I "borrowed" funds from the village to buy a tripod and a mobile phone suitable for filming videos. Subsequently, I began filming videos in many different parts of the village and posting them on Kuaishou.

After just over a month of doing so, our account gained a more than a thousand followers. Unimpressed, some villagers complained that as an official in the village, I was neglecting my duties by playing around on a mobile phone all day long. Not many supported me—my family members, my colleagues, and the cadres were all against what I was doing.

Although I was under a great deal of pressure at that time, I didn't bother to explain myself, because I thought explaining and arguing were futile. All I could do was keep going and stick to my guns.

The "Seven Fairies" Changed the Situation

One night, I heard someone playing the *pipa* (a four-stringed lute with 30 frets) outside and was fascinated by the song. The pipa songs of the Dong ethnic group are usually played and sung together by several people, but in the dead of night, what I heard was just one person playing and singing alone. The song was extremely beautiful to listen to and evoked a touch of sadness.

The next day, I asked the villagers about it. "The song I heard was quite impressive. Where did it come from?" However, nobody could give me a definite answer.

An old man told me a legend: A long time ago, people in the Dong villages did not know how to play the pipa. But one day, seven celestial fairies descended to the mortal world and bathed in the Gaibao River, leaving behind the echoes of a fairy song in the river water. After drinking the water, the young women of the Dong ethnic group became able to play and sing pipa songs, and they slowly spread pipa songs to all Dong villages.

For me, this story was simply too beautiful. At that time, I was constantly thinking about how to publicize the village, so this story combined with the song I had heard at night gave me an idea: I could create a narrative that the women in the Dong villages are all so pretty because they are descended from fairies. I immediately resolved to find seven fairies from among the Dong villages to serve as image ambassadors, who would introduce the Dong ethnic culture and the romantic life in the Dong villages.

I swiftly decided that the name of the new account would be "Seven Romantic Fairies of Dong Families" ("Seven Fairies" in short), which comes directly from the folklore of the Dong ethnic group.

Subsequently, I began to look for candidates, but it was much harder to do than I had expected. The eldest of the Seven Fairies, Yang Yanjiao, was someone I found among a pipa chorus while they were practicing. But after successfully inviting her, I failed to find a second fairy for more than a month.

The biggest problem was that the villagers, especially the elderly people, were very conservative and were thus opposed to my idea. They said that publicity could be done simply by taking a few photographs and it was unnecessary to find seven women. And of course, whenever the elderly people opposed an idea, the young people would shun it as well.

I found the fifth sister, Wu Mengxia, and the sixth sister, Wu Lanxin, on Kuaishou. They had been posting their own short videos on Kuaishou, so I contacted them and explained that they could publicize the culture of their hometown, drive the sales of agricultural products, and become more popular themselves by joining the Seven Fairies, which they could make a career out of. Back then, the family members of the fifth sister thought that I was a multi-level marketing scammer, and thus rejected me multiple times. As for the sixth sister, she quit her job as a troupe performer behind her parents' back in order to join the Seven Fairies. Their strong opposition to her decision after they found out meant that she had to spend time placating them every day.

After getting these women to join, videos of the Seven Fairies soon began to trend on Kuaishou. Once, a young man who was working outside the village phoned home and happily told his elderly parents that he had seen the village online thanks to the publicity videos of the Seven Fairies.

Although his parents did not know about Kuaishou, the news from the young man had a huge influence. It was then that the villagers recognized the Seven Fairies to be a good thing for the village. As everyone's attitude changed, the Seven Fairies soon completely fell into place.

A month or two later, the account amassed 30,000 followers and earned a stable income from its livestreams. Fans would ask if the pickled fish, meat, and ethnic clothing they saw in the videos were available for sale.

Soon, the media began to notice us. The fifth sister got on Hunan Satellite TV's *Happy Camp*, while all seven fairies were invited on a special Dragon Boat Festival program by CCTV in 2019. Various TV stations and media outlets competed to report on the Seven Fairies. The old folks in the village would often repost related news reports on their WeChat Moments and declare their pride in the Seven Fairies. After seeing their reactions, I felt heartened to have finally gained their approval.

Nowadays, my work every day consists mainly of visiting the villagers, handling village affairs, and conducting meetings. In the afternoons, we film videos of the Seven Fairies for two hours. The spiritual outlook of the village has changed; everyone is now thinking about how to develop the village's economy, and fewer people are spending their time on playing cards.

We have submitted an industry development plan to Kuaishou and received even more guidance and support on starting businesses. There are now many opportunities for external exchanges and learning, which are very important for a backward region to open up new horizons.

I have personally experienced a lot of growth during the process of creating the Seven Fairies. Previously, I had never filmed a video or conducted a livestream. My biggest gain is learning that one should never be afraid to try anything. Having accomplished my mission amid the pressure I was under, I will never shirk from any difficulties I face in the future.

Connecting the Ancient with the Modern and Linking the Present to the Future

Kuaishou has not only introduced the ancient Dong villages to the outside world but has also become a deep emotional link between a village and its villagers who are living elsewhere.

Most of the young people from Gaibao Village are doing odd jobs elsewhere, albeit they often return home to visit. Because the ethnic culture of Dong families is very deep-rooted, it is regarded as a must to return home whenever there is a festival. Many also return whenever a bullfighting competition is being held in the village. Each trip home sets them back 1 or 2 thousand yuan per person and causes them to skip work, and thus many of them actually do not have much money despite working elsewhere.

At first, I could not understand why these young people loved bullfighting so much. But after spending a year in the village, I have also grown fond of the bulls and become a bullfighting fan.

The Bullfighting Festival is a very large festival for the Dong ethnic group, with each village raising a mighty and majestic "Buffalo King" of its own. In 2018, the Seven Fairies livestreamed the festival on Kuaishou. At the start of the festival, the buffaloes were covered in red silk as they entered the bullring, with the villagers following behind. The people of each village then gathered among themselves inside the bullring. All in all, the large crowd and the deafening beating of gongs and drums made it an extremely lively occasion.

During that livestream, many followers commented that they could save on travel expenses, yet still be able to watch the spectacular Bullfighting Festival anyway. The young people from the village, too, did not have to return home to watch the bullfight—the livestream allowed them to keep up with what was going in the village while working elsewhere.

In July 2019, the director of CCTV's *Focus Report* came to film a program on Gaibao Village. We also conducted a livestream with many elderly villagers taking part. After watching the livestream, many young people living elsewhere commented that they badly missed home and were thankful to the Seven Fairies for allowing them to see their hometown. They also expressed how moved they were to see that their hometown was changing for the better.

Economic benefits are one of the changes brought about by Kuaishou. The incomes of the native families and poverty-stricken families increased thanks to Kuaishou. For example, during the autumn harvest of 2018, the publicity made by Seven Fairies caused the village-produced turmeric to be sold across China. In total, we sold more than 30,000 kilograms' worth of turmeric, earning more than 300,000 yuan.

Because the turmeric was sold through the professional farmer cooperative in the village, the 10 or so poverty-stricken households that were part of the cooperative immediately saw their incomes increase.

In addition, we also sold a few specialty products such as pickled fish, cured meat, and embroidered clothing, and earned a little income from tourism. By the end of 2018, the village escaped poverty completely.

For some of the poorest peasant households, they could finally afford to buy small appliances and fruits that they could not before.

Although the economic benefits gained in one year were fairly limited, the most important thing was that the villagers began thinking about how to develop the village on their own.

In July 2019, more than 1,000 villagers organized a large meeting on tourism development. At the meeting, everyone discussed how development could be done. We made plans to connect more than 20 scenic spots in the village together. The village has three large waterfalls and is naturally covered in fog, resembling the heavenly palaces found on television shows. Moreover, the view of the clouds and fog from the mountaintop is especially beautiful.

A few followers who had found out about Gaibao Village from the Seven Fairies account visited us in several successive batches, from as far away as Chongqing Municipality and Tianjin City. This allowed the villagers to personally feel Kuaishou's powerful capabilities of publicity—after all, in the past, very few people would have specially come from so far away to visit this village.

I can clearly feel that our ethnic confidence is increasing. In the past, it was rare to see people in the county seat or more distant places wearing the clothing of ethnic minorities, while the villagers would seldom introduce themselves as being from the Dong ethnic group, as they deemed themselves to be from a backward and remote place and did not want people to find out.

But things are different now. After the Seven Fairies gained fame, ethnic clothing became the trend. When walking on the streets nowadays, one is able to see many young people wearing ethnic clothing of their own accord and taking pride in doing so. This is a huge change from the past.

In 2018, we sold 40,000 yuan worth of Dong ethnic clothing—many people bought the clothing after seeing the Seven Fairies wearing it.

While publicizing the cultures of ethnic minorities, it is important to think about how to combine them with modernity. Traditional culture must not only be preserved but also imbued with the spirit of the times.

Today, my goal is to showcase the physical and human landscapes of the Dong people to the world. I also intend to develop a healthier mode of development. This consists of harmonizing publicity with production and marketing, scaling up and professionalizing production, and developing tourism.

We are currently working on processing a few agricultural products and expanding the scale of our crop planting. At the same time, we have chosen pickled fish, cured meat, and embroidery as the three products which production we will try to professionalize.

Enabling the Seven Fairies and Gaibao Village to Achieve Greater Success

As General Secretary Xi said, "Civilization is colorful because of exchanges, and rich because of mutual learning." These words inspired me a lot. We cannot simply focus on the Dong ethnic culture but must instead go out and have exchanges with others.

In December 2018, we visited Qiaoai Village, which is a time-honored Miao village in Rongjiang County. There, we found a few local women to interact and livestream together with the Seven Fairies. In 2019, we also invited women from the Yi ethnic group to conduct a livestream together. It was only by going out and seeing other ethnic cultures that we could gain a more comprehensive understanding of the unique aspects of the Dong ethnic group by means of comparison. For example, each village of the Dong ethnic group speaks a language that is slightly different from other villages. Furthermore, some villages are known for their Dong Songs while others are known for their Dong Opera.

With the development of the times, many minority cultures are at risk of losing their traditions due to their small populations and under-developed economies. China has 56 distinct ethnic groups, each with an extremely rich ethnic culture and many precious and beautiful traditions that are worth passing down and inheriting.

My term of office in Gaibao Village is three years, of which one and a half years have already passed. Therefore, talent training is one of my current priorities. However, there are not many qualified people in the village, and we also face challenges regarding how to train young people to be more far-sighted and better at management, how to use their qualities well, how to groom them for the top posts, and how to retain them in the village.

Our Youth Management Committee now consists of 15 or 16 members, seven of whom are college graduates, including a few from key universities. Some of them are returning villagers, while some are from Guiyang City. Their goal is to drive the sale of agricultural products through the publicity of the Seven Fairies.

I have built an internet celebrity academy in the village for every worker and young person to undergo two hours of training here every day. I also specially engaged teachers to provide training and exchanges in geography, history, ethnic culture, intangible cultural heritage, and various other subjects. People from nearby villages are also welcome to attend this academy if they are interested.

This academy is not for financial gain but rather for broadening the horizons of the villagers. It is geared toward the future—the development of Gaibao Village, as well as that of other poverty-stricken regions, will ultimately depend on the locals as its backbone.

Once, the Seven Fairies published a video of a pesticide-spraying drone. It was an advertisement that DJI contacted us to do for them. It had a very positive implied meaning: the Seven Fairies can introduce the ancient Dong villages on Kuaishou to gain the attention and recognition of the outside world, while modern technologies from the outside world can also serve to better the ancient Dong villages.

A TASTE OF THE MOUNTAIN VILLAGES: KUAISHOU'S "LU ZHISHEN" IS THE KING OF POVERTY ALLEVIATION IN THE MOUNTAINS

Deep in the mountains of Hengfeng County, Jiangxi Province, Jiang Jinchun livestreams the villagers' production of dried bamboo shoots and sweet tea on Kuaishou. In this way, he has helped more than 200 farmers from over 50 villages sell their mountain products throughout China.

Jiang, who only has junior secondary education, had previously gone to work in Yiwu City, Zhejiang Province. However, he decided to return to his hometown so that his child would not become left behind. He never expected that Kuaishou could not only help him achieve his entrepreneurial aspirations, but also help more people escape poverty and increase their incomes.

PROFILE

Kuaishou name: 山村里的味道 (A Taste of the Mountain Villages)

Kuaishou ID: scvd8888

Age: 41

Education: junior middle school

Hometown: Hengfeng County, Jiangxi Province

Topic: the scenery, cuisine, and simple farming lifestyles of his hometown

Production style: using the image of "Lu Zhishen" to showcase the production processes of village cuisines + livestreaming to interact with viewers

Message to his loyal fans: I hope to do my best in helping more poor farmers escape poverty and increase their incomes

Business model: sell mountain products and local specialties through livestreams

Narrator: Jiang Jinchun

To Prevent His Daughter from Becoming Left Behind, He Returned to His Hometown and Started a Business

My name is Jiang Jinchun. In 2010, I left Yiwu City, Zhejiang Province, where I had been working for years and returned to my hometown in Jiangxi Province to spend more time with my family, especially my little girl.

I previously ran a small business selling Latin dance dresses in Yiwu. After I returned to my hometown, it became really inconvenient to continue managing my business in Yiwu, as it was too far away. Instead, I discovered that my hometown had a considerable number of specialty products, and thus thought about selling some agricultural products on e-commerce platforms. This plan, however, did not bear fruit until I came to know about Kuaishou.

I started using Kuaishou in 2015. I suggested to my wife that we could try filming short Kuaishou videos for a while. At that point in time, I had not thought about helping others to sell specialty products, because we were facing our own livelihood issues.

Our videos did not get us anywhere for the first three months, so I was somewhat frustrated. The turnaround came in May 2016, when many fans messaged me saying that I resembled the character Lu Zhishen from the novel *Water Margin*. They further suggested that my viewers would quite enjoy seeing me act as Lu Zhishen.

I thus went online and bought a few clothes and some makeup for myself. Indeed, videos of me acting as Lu Zhishen made it on to the Trending page and garnered more than a million hits. I kept doing this for a month or two, and saw my follower count gradually increase to 60,000 or so.

Back then, the poverty alleviation program in our village had just started. One day, a poor villager dug up a pile of bamboo shoots and I offered to help him sell them through my livestream. Unexpectedly, we sold more than 50 kilograms of them in just one or two days—nothing had made him happier.

By selling the bamboo shoots at 90 yuan per kilogram, he made as much money as he had in the previous half a year. The incomes of farmers in the mountains are not high, reaching a maximum of 10,000 yuan per year.

As my followers kept increasing, I gave up on my business selling Latin dance dresses and focused on filming short videos. On Kuaishou, I shared the scenery, cuisine, and lifestyles of my hometown, and sold specialty products such as sweet tea, camellia oil, and kudzu roots.

Initially, I sourced my products from within my village only. However, there were only a dozen or so households here that could supply my products and they did not produce enough. I thus began to search for suppliers in nearby villages. Later on, some people from nearby villages even delivered their goods to me for a fixed price. I paid them in cash and resold the products with a little markup. Everyone benefited in this way.

Nowadays, farmers in my area have grown used to the routine of delivering their kudzu roots and sweet tea leaves to my home every year. In 2019, I gathered 1,150 kilograms of sweet tea leaves, nearly 2,000 kilograms of kudzu root powder, and more than 500 kilograms of camellia oil.

How much is 1,150 kilograms of sweet tea leaves worth, you ask? A family can earn more than 9,000 yuan in less than a month just by selling sweet tea leaves—now do the math.

The more products that the villagers supplied me with, the heavier the weight on my shoulders became. In 2017, I sold more than 500 kilograms of sweet tea leaves and more than 350 kilograms of dried bamboo shoots. The next year, I sold 750 kilograms of sweet tea leaves. By 2019, every farmer from the nearby villages knew that I was a buyer of these products, so they harvested large amounts of these products and sent them to me. I had a hard time rejecting their products and thus bought them all. To date, I still have more than 350 kilograms of unsold specialty products—marketing them is why I livestream every day.

Selling Specialty Products to Help Increase the Villagers' Earnings

Dried bamboo shoots, sweet tea leaves, and pickled mustard are very common in the mountains, but they sell like hot cakes among my followers.

In recent years, 230 farming households from nearly 50 villages have sold their agricultural products outside the mountains by going through me. Among them are a few dozen poverty-stricken families, some of whose incomes have risen by more than 20,000 yuan per year.

The topic of poverty alleviation means a lot to me, personally. Our region, which is deep in the mountains, used to be very poor. I was born in 1979, and at 18 years old, I left my hometown to do odd jobs after graduating from junior middle school. People in my village used to chop firewood for a living—it was only possible to chop two loads of firewood per day. Each load of firewood could be sold for two yuan, so they made four yuan a day, which works out to 120 yuan a month. The only other ways to make money were to herd cattle or steal a few logs to sell. Such a life was very tough.

This is why there are still six unmarried men among the 17 households in our village—no woman will marry into a family from such a poor mountain village.

Later on, things started to get better. Beginning in the 1990s, more and more people left the village to do odd jobs. By 2001, the only ones left in the village were elderly people and children—everyone else went to provinces such as Guangdong and Zhejiang to find work.

During my first stay in Yiwu City, I found a job as a deliveryman. My pay back then was 700 yuan a month, which made me extremely happy because I would have had to chop several hundred loads of firewood back home to earn that much.

Having tasted the benefits of doing odd jobs elsewhere, the working-age villagers hardly ever returned home. This led to the problem of having many left-behind children back in the village. It was while working in Yiwu that I met my wife, a graduate from Jingdezhen Ceramic Institute. Reluctant to live away from our child, we decided to return to my hometown and seek a living here.

The living conditions of my fellow villagers slowly improved, thanks to the money from doing odd jobs elsewhere. However, there were still a few poverty-stricken households. I could not bear to see them living in such a miserable state, so I helped them sell their mountain products.

There were limited sources of income in the village. We were situated in a forest region and thus could not grow rice. Foods such as sweet tea leaves, kudzu roots, and dried bamboo shoots were harvested or dug up for personal consumption but were not for sale. Some people also chopped wood to sell, but this was bad for the environment and became prohibited when the "Grain for Green" program was launched. It was therefore necessary to find new sources of income.

Having spent many years outside the village, I knew that our mountain products and agricultural products were very popular among city dwellers. The key was to find a channel to showcase and market these products. Traditional e-commerce is not intuitive enough and cannot truly generate trust and interest among potential buyers. Personally, I felt that Kuaishou was the kind of platform I was looking for.

After I became popular on Kuaishou, my elder brother and his son also returned home from doing odd jobs in Hangzhou City, Zhejiang Province. Seeing that my agricultural products were selling well, they began filming Kuaishou videos, too. Similarly, an herb dealer in a nearby city and a clothing seller in Yiwu returned home to film Kuaishou videos—and it was I who taught them how to do so. Although I was no professional, I could tell them based on my own experience how to hold a mobile phone so that it would not shake while filming a video.

Later on, the government took notice of me. In 2016, people from the county government brought a few journalists to interview me. They commended me for helping so many farmers sell their goods. In 2017, our county's party secretary awarded me the "Most Beautiful Entrepreneur" prize. He proclaimed that my work since returning home helped the locals increase their incomes.

My efforts were also recognized in the academic world. Some scholars deemed that my way of doing business has not only invigorated the rural economy and enriched myself, but most importantly, allowed city dwellers to purchase fresh and unique specialty products. Thus, it can be said that I killed multiple birds with one stone.

The e-commerce division of our county's Poverty Alleviation Office also invited me to give a lecture on my experience in poverty alleviation as a young entrepreneur. This made me feel very honored.

The Government Assisted in Branding My Business and Helped My Fellow Villagers Earn an Income All Year Round

When I first started selling agricultural products on Kuaishou, I paid no mind to the packaging of my goods and simply sold everything in bulk. But as my followers increased, the consumers became more demanding. Some buyers said that my products did not have any of the necessary labels and threatened to file a complaint against me.

The local government and food safety administration learned about the situation and tried to help. They explained things to the buyers on my behalf, saying that I was just helping poor mountain villagers sell their products and that these products were authentic. However, the buyers were not reassured and insisted on filing a complaint.

Later on, the county's party secretary also learned about the situation and specially visited my home on three occasions to think up a solution together. Since 2019, the kudzu root powder that I source from other farmers has been professionally packaged by an enterprise brought in by the government. After the packaging is completed, a record of traceability has to be properly done, including information such as the production site, the names of the farmers who dug up the kudzu roots, the time of packaging, and the production date. In this way, my loyal followers can feel more assured when buying this product.

I have encountered many difficulties over the years, but fortunately, the local government has helped me a great deal and given me the confidence to carry on. Otherwise, I would be running around like a headless chicken, unable to find a way out.

After solving the packaging problems, logistics issues still remained. Because our village is deep in the mountains, no courier company is willing to come here. Thus, I have to drive one and a half hours to get to the county seat to ship the goods every day. And when I get back home, I have to go collect the kudzu roots from the farmers. There is no way I can afford to hire a helper, so I have to do everything myself.

I pay great attention to quality control in order to not let my followers lose trust in me. Take the sweet tea leaves, for example. Every farmer is now required to dry the leaves in a specialized pan, whereas in the past, the leaves were simply placed on the ground, which was certainly an unhygienic practice. As a principle, I no longer accept leaves from any farmer who does not use the pan.

I am now very busy every day. My wife and I currently live in an apartment in the county seat so that my daughter can attend school here. We get up every morning at six to get breakfast ready and send our daughter to school. We then drive for one and a half hours to get back to the village. Subsequently, we conduct a morning livestream to show our followers how our specialty products are made. After livestreaming for an hour, we start to do packaging work. At noon, we conduct another livestream and then do some more packaging work. Around two in the afternoon, we begin making our way down the mountains to ship the goods. After that, we return to the county seat to pick up our child from school. This is what my day's work looks like. My wife is in charge of customer service, and thus for the rest of the day, she answers queries, such as regarding parcel status or the steps for preparing sweet tea.

Our mountain products are all very seasonal. In spring, we collect the sweet tea leaves before the Tomb-Sweeping Festival. A dozen or so days later, we begin to dig up bamboo shoots and dry them. During summer, we make dried pumpkins and dried pomelo peel. After the Mid-Autumn Festival, we pick wild kiwis and chestnuts in the woods. And then in the winter, we dig up arrowroots and process it into powder. There's plenty of work to keep us busy all year long, which also means that we can earn an income all year round.

The county party secretary awarded me the "Most Beautiful Entrepreneur" prize because long-term solutions, like planting fruit trees, are unable to generate income within one or two years and thus cannot solve the immediate income issues. Instead, my business pays the farmers in cash instantly, which is why so many of them are willing to be my suppliers.

My hometown is a part of Hengfeng County, which is nicknamed the "Kudzu Capital" because of its endless supply of kudzu roots. In the past, nobody went to dig these roots up because it was very tiring work—you had to go up the mountain, dig up the roots, carry them down, and then process them into powder. Young people simply could not handle such tough work. But now, because there is a market for kudzu root powder, people are willing to do the digging work.

Dried bamboo shoots are also an important source of income for us now. There is bamboo all over the nearby mountains, but no one wanted it. About two decades ago, bamboo was used to make clothes racks, but nobody does that these days. This is why we have an abundance of bamboos shoots here, and we now make them into dried bamboo shoots and sell them for money.

Many of my buyers from Northern China had never eaten dried bamboo shoots before, but they have now grown very fond of them. I sourced more than 500 kilograms of dried bamboo shoots this year and have sold every last one of them.

Support from Kuaishou Has Expanded the Influence of Poverty Alleviation

Aside from the local government, Kuaishou's official team has also given me a lot of assistance in running my business.

It was in 2018 when Kuaishou's official team took notice of me. This was because I often shared a lot of photos, such as a photo of the government awarding me a prize, and they were seen by Kuaishou. Kuaishou has a public welfare department called Kuaishou Action—they sent a team to inspect my operations in order to verify that I was truly helping the farmers. After the verification was complete, they put in even more efforts to help me with publicity.

Subsequently, more media outlets came to cover my story. A Beijing TV Station (BTV) reality show even sent some celebrities to my hometown and filmed an episode called "Looking for Lu Zhishen in the Mountain Villages" in order to publicize my hometown. It made our village more famous than ever before and attracted many tourists to visit out of their admiration for our village. With the assistance of the government, some farmers have built holiday homes and farm stays to provide accommodation and meals.

Shortly after that, CCTV-13, CCTV-2, Jiangxi TV, Youth.cn, and Xinhua News Agency all covered the story of me and my hometown. During the 2018 World Internet Conference held in Wuzhen, my story was included in a photo exhibition as an example of the internet changing the lives of Chinese farmers, causing it to be seen by more people, including a few internet moguls.

However, I would never use celebrities or famous people to pull publicity stunts in my Kuaishou videos, as I do not think it is right to do so. A farmer should behave as a farmer; after all, it is our simple and organic lifestyle that consumers are attracted to. If I wanted to pull publicity stunts, I should not be in the business of selling mountain products—and I would probably have it easier in other businesses.

CHINA'S FIRST YOGA VILLAGE: KUAISHOU MADE THE LEGEND OF YUGOULIANG VILLAGE VISIBLE TO THE WORLD

"Whenever you do something, there are two possible outcomes: you either become a joke or become a legend. If you give up halfway, others will only see you as a joke. But if you stick to your goal and put in unwavering efforts, you would quite likely become a legend admired by the world."

—From *The Legend of Yugouliang Village*, by Bai Wei

To many people, Lu Wenzhen used to be a joke. He was first brought into the spotlight by a news report two years ago titled "The Secretary of a Poor Village Teaching Senior People Yoga." Yugouliang Village is a national-level poverty-stricken village with fewer than 100 households. That the village secretary would lead a group of empty-nest seniors with an average age of 65 to practice yoga was simply inconceivable.

In order to persuade the elderly people to practice yoga, Lu Wenzhen not only wrote a song called "There's a Place Called Yugouliang" but also set up a WeChat official account for the village.

To everyone's surprise, the Social Sports Guidance Center of the General Administration of Sports of China (GASC) later gave Yugouliang the title of "China's First Yoga Village." Many journalists from media outlets such as Xinhua News Agency, *People's Daily Online*, and CCTV-2 were thus attracted to the village to conduct interviews. Zhao Zhannan, the vice chairperson of Zhangjiakou City Photographers' Association, took a series of photos over the course of more than two years. Her photographic work attracted the attention of *China Daily* and *South China Morning Post*, while international media outlets such as the *New York Times*, the *Globe and Mail*, the *Sunday Guardian*, and *Hindustan Times* also reported on it. Luo Zhaohui, China's vice minister of Foreign Affairs and former ambassador to India, also wrote an article that talked about the practice of yoga in Yugouliang.

The combination of keywords such as "farmers," "yoga," "seniors," and "poverty alleviation" made Yugouliang the talk of the town for a while. However, coverage on print media alone meant that dissemination was limited in volume and monetization was difficult, and thus the villagers could not derive much income from it. It was only in 2019, when the villagers set up two Kuaishou accounts, that the exposure of the village soared.

In less than half a year, the Kuaishou account called "Yoga Granny of Yugouliang" (Kuaishou ID: z15133389889) amassed 156,000 followers. It also launched a seven-episode video tutorial for yoga learners at the beginner to intermediate levels. The tutorial is priced at 19 yuan and has been bought by 638 people.

The director of Yugouliang's Women's Federation, Jin Xiuying, runs another account called "Yugouliang, China's First Yoga Village" (ID:1045021298). On August 2, 2019, she brought a group of elderly yoga practitioners to take part in the Third Zhangjiakou Tourism Industry Development Conference while her daughter livestreamed the event using a mobile phone. More than 5,000 people tuned in to watch the elderly people practicing yoga.

It can be said that Kuaishou is transforming the previously poverty-stricken lives of Yugouliang's villagers.

Village name: Yugouliang

Hometown: Zhangjiakou City, Hebei Province

Topic: elderly people practicing yoga

Production style: filming the yoga activities of elderly people

Message to their loyal fans: we will use Kuaishou to help Yugouliang escape poverty

Narrator: Lu Wenzhen

There are many accounts on Kuaishou that showcase the rural life, but the account that showcases the village of Yugouliang is very special. Before the village showed up on the platform, nobody would associate the words "farmers," "seniors," "yoga,", and "poverty alleviation." Without seeing it with your own eyes, it would be very hard for you to imagine an elderly woman in her 80s twisting her limbs with great flexibility. In the village, a group of elderly women who are all around 70 years old are able to do forearm stands and splits with no problem at all. They can also easily raise their legs to plant the soles of their feet on the back of their heads. Their flexibility makes you forget about their age and even makes you feel as though you are the one who is abnormal.

After videos of these elderly people were published, someone asked in the comments if they had some kind of secret to longevity. Another person believed that there must be a decades-old tradition of yoga practice in Yugouliang. And there was also someone who was concerned for the health of these elderly people's limbs.

What most viewers did not know was that these seniors had been doing yoga for only three years. It all began with the poverty-alleviation campaign that came to Yugouliang three years ago.

The Extent of Poverty in Yugouliang Was Beyond My Imagination

I visited Yugouliang Village for the first time in February 2016, three days after the Lantern Festival. When I entered the village, what I saw was deeply troubling. There were no cars in sight, and worse, no food kiosks or eateries. It was freezing cold that day. Only at noon could you see a handful of old people taking a slow walk in the sun.

The farmland was covered in snow; even if the snow melted, it would offer few prospects. The land was arid and lacked a source of irrigation. All they could rely on was natural rainfall, yet drought occurs 9 out of 10 years in these parts. Crop yield was low—an acre of land could produce only 300 kilograms of crops in a growing season—so it was a wonder how the people had survived. The young people had all left for the cities to make a living, leaving behind only a few seniors who were mostly 60 years old and above. These seniors could barely walk out of the village even if they wanted to. They grew their own food at home and had barely enough to eat for each meal. To them, simple and shoddy meals had become the norm.

Prior to visiting the village, I had not heard its name before, and only knew that it was a national-level poverty-stricken village that required targeted alleviation measures. Yet, the extent of poverty here far exceeded my imagination.

I was a teacher at the Shijiazhuang Posts and Telecommunications Technical College, so topics like farmers, agriculture, and poverty alleviation were practically foreign to me. After seeing the situation here, I had completely no idea how to begin changing things for the better.

Prohibited from Digging Wells, Scared of Being Scammed for Their Handiwork, and Unable to Find a Way to Alleviate Poverty

During my first week in the village, I went door-to-door visiting the residents to understand their circumstances, listen to their ideas and needs, and find out what they had and what they could do.

I learned from these visits that what they wanted most was to dig a well to irrigate their fields. They believed that their lands were actually very fertile, and that once these lands were irrigated, farming alone would be enough to lift them out of poverty.

Although this was what everyone wanted, digging a well was not in line with the state's policies. Groundwater in the village area had already declined to a critical extent, and thus digging new wells was prohibited. In fact, some of their existing wells had to be closed. Therefore, their wish could not be fulfilled.

If this wish could not be fulfilled, what other wishes did they have? Some women mentioned the idea of making handicrafts such as cross-stitches. So, we then contacted a wholesale market and prepared to find a distribution channel to sign an exclusive distribution agreement with them.

However, after we had made an agreement with the wholesaler, a problem arose. One of the women asked whether signing that agreement with the wholesaler would mean that their earnings would be deducted if they failed to complete the orders. She was afraid that her efforts would be in vain if the already meager compensation would have deductions taken out. Given that the villagers all had poor eyesight and various problems with their backs and legs, it might have been very difficult for them to fulfill the requirements in the agreement. Therefore, this wish could not be fulfilled either.

Achieving Good Health and Poverty Alleviation Through Innovative Yoga for Seniors

During the course of my visits and surveys, I began to take note of the health issues faced by the villagers. More than 60 percent of the poor people in the village had been dragged into poverty by illness and poor health.

I gradually discovered that the people here spent a third of their day on their *kangs* (a traditional long platform for living, working, entertaining, and sleeping that is commonly used in Northern China). They would eat their meals, watch television, and chat with other people while on their kangs. Because of sitting cross-legged for long periods of time, their legs had become abnormally flexible and were extremely flat when in the cross-legged position. This detail gave me a flash of inspiration, and somehow made me think about yoga movements.

I told the villagers about my idea, but they did not even know what yoga was. Thus, I used my mobile phone to search for yoga videos and photos, and then told everyone that this was a way to build up one's body.

The seniors were all in poor physical shape. Thus, in the name of building up their bodies, I arranged for all of them to practice yoga—this was my original idea.

Later on, I discovered that all of them seemingly had the genes for practicing yoga. Regardless of gender or age, all of them could perform the yoga movements to a very high standard after just a little training. A woman in her 70s was easily able to cross her legs, as could a 91-year-old woman with bound feet. (Feet binding is a Chinese custom of breaking and tightly binding the feet of young girls in order to change the shape and size of their feet.)

This was certainly a novelty. Anybody would be surprised that yoga, farmers, and poverty alleviation could be linked together. Moreover, yoga is very suitable for elderly people—if done properly, there would be practically no safety risks.

The Majestic Emergence of "China's First Yoga Village"

It was a very long and arduous process from making the decision to improve the villagers' health with yoga to eventually getting everyone enrolled and committed. In the middle of it all, I had to slowly teach them about yoga and its postures, as they had completely no idea about it at first. Many imaginable and unimaginable things happened along the way. Nevertheless, this process constantly touched and inspired me to keep going.

One day, there was an old empty-nest woman who had been sick at home for days before her neighbor realized it and sent her to the hospital. That incident hit me very hard. I thought to myself that no matter how many children an elderly woman has, or how rich, powerful, capable, and filial her children are, she cannot count on her children when she is in need if they are simply not around. This thought stirred me to write a village song I named "There's a Place Called Yugouliang." After getting it professionally recorded, I was surprised to find that it was very well-received among the seniors—and that was because the lyrics of the song were about matters that were highly relevant to them. The song thus increased their positivity toward practicing yoga, and from then on, we would play the song during their yoga practices every day. Even an 80-year-old senior was able to practice yoga while singing the song.

Because WeChat Moments only allows the of uploading nine photos per post and limits video to a dozen seconds or so, I felt that it would be quite a pity—and a potential cause of unhappiness—to leave out everyone except nine people. Thus, I set up an official WeChat account to post our song along with photos and videos of everyone practicing yoga. The development and efficiency of today's media truly exceeds my imagination—in less than a week after the account was set up, I got a call from the Social Sports Guidelines Office under the GASC, who said that they had taken note of what we posted. Coincidentally, the GASC was about to regulate the yoga industry in China at that time. They did not expect there to be yoga students in rural areas already, especially among the seniors. Even more so, they did not expect that yoga could be linked to the work of poverty alleviation. Therefore, they called to find out more about the situation.

The call was made from a landline telephone number that started with 010, so at first, I thought it was a scam or an ad. However, upon picking up, I heard the voice of a very polite lady, who introduced herself as being from the Social Sports Guidelines Office and asked for my name.

I did not believe her at all, because I did not know a single person from the GASC and certainly had no dealings with such a high-level agency.

I asked her to repeat herself and she obliged, only adding that her surname was Li. She introduced herself, explained why she had called, and talked about what the GASC was doing at the moment. After listening to her explanation, I believed her completely.

Before ending the call, she mentioned that if the GASC ever came to Zhangjiakou to inspect the fitness levels of the people here, or to prepare for the Winter Olympics, they would try to schedule a side trip to Yugouliang and meet our yoga seniors. Her words gave me tremendous confidence in what I was doing.

I wrote a report to the GASC to present the work we had done so far, including why we were using yoga to fight poverty and how we planned to improve people's health in order to prevent the phenomenon of falling into poverty due to illness.

As we entered 2017, various governmental institutions held events to celebrate the 19th CPC National Congress. For that occasion, the GASC organized the "Most Beautiful Sportsperson" award and called for all local authorities to submit nominees.

Ms. Li from the GASC called me again on February 13, 2017, to tell me about this award. She suggested that I write an article about our plan to fight poverty with yoga and attach 10 photos along with it. That way, the Social Sports Guidelines Office could recommend the story to GASC's Press and Publicity Department.

I was overwhelmed by that good news. It would be more than I could ever hope for if the GASC gave us such recognition and included Yugouliang in its promotional campaigns. I wrote the article at once, sent it out, and soon got a reply from them saying that they had polished the language and changed the title to "Yugouliang: The Most Beautiful Yoga Village." In the text, we were also referred to as "China's First Yoga Village," which sounds even more impactful. This represented a turning point for our village.

The article was published on February 15, 2017, on a WeChat official account run by the National Yoga Exercise Management Committee under the Social Sports Guidelines Office. Soon, the story was picked up by several Chinese news agencies such as Xinhua and Sohu. On February 19, HEBTV called to invite us to film a show. So, a week later, I brought 22 villagers over to Shijiazhuang. They were all very excited because it was their first ever trip to the city, and many had never even been on a train before.

When the program aired a week later, everyone from the village gathered together to watch the show. They had never dreamed of appearing on television and were curious about how they looked on air. They also rushed to call their relatives to share their excitement.

On March 19 of that year, reporters from CCTV-2 came to the village for a day and a half to make a documentary, and thus they stayed a night in the village. The villagers were even happier than when we celebrated festivals.

During the filming, a reporter mentioned that the Publicity Department of the Communist Party of China would be watching that documentary and that he believed our work was very meaningful. That report became a 15-minute feature that aired on CCTV-2 on April 29, 2017.

In September that year, CCTV aired a six-episode documentary called *Amazing China* to welcome the 19th CPC National Congress. The fifth episode, which focused on the sense of happiness and attainment of the masses, played a clip of our village that lasted 10 seconds or so. Today, as the influence of our village keeps increasing, more and more media outlets are coming to cover our story on their own initiative.

A Yoga Granny Unexpectedly Became a Kuaishou Celebrity When Her Grandson Casually Uploaded a Video

When a famous internet singer came to our village to do a livestream in the summer of 2018, I realized that short videos could reach an even larger audience. Earlier on, a county official had also suggested to me to conduct livestreams, but I felt that the village did not have the necessary conditions yet, as we had not created a fixed syllabus for teaching yoga. If we were to conduct livestreams, we would have to teach yoga in a standardized way and obtain the approval of yoga experts first. After all, it would not be right to mislead people by teaching them the wrong things.

A young man who had experience in conducting e-commerce marketing livestreams came back to the village during the Spring Festival period. His grandparents were both very good at yoga, so he took some short videos of them with his phone and posted these videos on Kuaishou. In particular, a video of his grandmother practicing yoga on a kang brought him many new followers.

Having gained some followers, he began posting videos every once in a while. Some villagers were impressed by his videos and began using Kuaishou as well. Some of the best yoga practitioners in the village also started filming Kuaishou videos, with their whole family taking part as well.

When I returned to the village after the Spring Festival, I also started paying attention to Kuaishou and would often take a look when I had nothing much to do. Later on, I also registered an account—and this was how a few yoga-related Kuaishou accounts were created.

We posted many videos of local farmers practicing yoga, which was quite a novelty. Their clothes were very countrified, but they could do difficult and eye-catching yoga poses with great flexibility. Since we often get very strong winds here, most villagers would usually wear a headscarf. Therefore, I made it the signature of the yoga seniors in Yugouliang— they would put on a headscarf whenever they were performing yoga for a video. Whenever Kuaishou viewers saw that headscarf, they would know that the performers were from Yugouliang.

In May 2019, we hosted a group of tourists from Taiwan—all of whom were yoga lovers. During their stay, I gave each of them a signature Yugouliang headscarf, much like Tibetan people presenting a khata (a type of long scarf made of silk) to their honored guests. These guests had all arrived in clean white yoga outfits while the villagers were wearing their very colorful rural clothes, so the pictures of them together turned out to be very pretty.

Embarking on Kuaishou E-Commerce to Further the Fight Against Poverty

In 2018, we raised some money through crowdfunding to grow quinoa. Later on, someone suggested to me that instead of seeking outside money, we could engage an internet celebrity during the autumn harvest to conduct a livestream in order to market our products.

This matter reminded me that we could indeed promote our goods through livestreams. Nowadays, two Kuaishou accounts set up by the villagers, namely "Yoga Granny in Yugouliang" and "Yugouliang: China's First

Yoga Village" are already generating income. And in less than a month, our yoga tutorials for beginners sold more than 1,000 copies and made more than 20,000 yuan. We are also striving very hard to market several types of agricultural products before the harvest season, including quinoa, potatoes, and oat flour.

We are now thinking about how we can sell our oat flour via livestreams. Oat flour is very healthy and is suitable for people with diabetes. People in Yugouliang hardly ever suffer from diabetes, which can be a key point in our marketing strategy. We also welcome potential partners to work with us on this project and help improve everyone's health.

Our village is still some ways off from achieving stable poverty alleviation. Nevertheless, Kuaishou has played a crucial role on this journey. We believe that yoga and poverty alleviation will, in time, become even more popular thanks to Kuaishou.

CHAPTER **SEVEN**

KUAISHOU'S INTANGIBLE CULTURAL HERITAGE: SEEING EVERY HERITAGE

CHAPTER OVERVIEW

For thousands of years, our ancestors amassed countless treasures of experience and wisdom on this land. Now, with the progress of the times, these treasures are becoming in danger of being lost due to their inability to adapt, which is a most distressing state of affairs. However, on Kuaishou, the inheritors of intangible cultural heritage are given a new platform where they can record and share intangible cultural heritage via short videos and allow unique cultural skills to be imparted. Kuaishou is currently keeping a faithful record of the unique skills of various folk craftsmen, such as the Shehuo Festival, which is in peril of being lost. Kuaishou makes it easier for craftsmen to find inheritors who like their unique skills, and also helps a wider audience better understand the charm of intangible cultural heritage. The value of traffic empowerment lies in nothing other than recording and sharing. From building up connections and establishing mutual support among individuals to engendering self-identity and the confidence and strength to create value in individuals, this chain of "energy transfer" continually affects every user of intangible cultural heritage on Kuaishou, arousing their intrinsic motivation to use the internet to explore new possibilities for disseminating intangible cultural heritage. By means of its inclusive distribution of traffic and authentic attributes of a sharing community, Kuaishou has become an important platform for every inheritor of intangible cultural heritage to express themselves and monetize their value. For those craftsmen who had simply kept their heads down and worked, they have finally found a gateway that leads to the market.

SUCCESS STORIES

Wei Zongfu: Kuaishou Has Breathed New Life into the Daoqing Shadow Play of the Wei Clan

Chen Libao the Suona Player: I Gained 500 Times More Students as Soon as I Got on Kuaishou

Ajie the Opera Singer: I Only Realized I Had a Prodigy at Home After Using Kuaishou

KUAISHOU'S INTANGIBLE CULTURAL HERITAGE: SEEING EVERY HERITAGE

Zhang Fan, head of Kuaishou Corporate Social Responsibility

There is a father-and-son duo on Kuaishou whose family has been singing Qu opera and leading a troupe to tour many different villages for generations. The father is in the prime of his life and is proficient at playing the *quhu* (a stringed instrument)—he is the backbone of the troupe. The son, Chaochao, is a handsome young man born in the 90s and is proficient at playing various instruments. Every time Chaochao goes to perform in a village or county, he films a few backstage videos and adds in captions to encourage himself, his father, and the troupe to keep going.

At times, offstage scenes appear in his videos. For example, the camera often pans to a square that is full of elderly men and women seated on their own small stools, fanning themselves with a cattail leaf fan as they take in the joys and sorrows of the opera. Chaochao's videos are very popular. Each video has garnered about 100,000 views on average and made many young people take notice of Qu opera, which is an intangible cultural heritage that is ancient and steeped in a unique regional flavor.

On Kuaishou, there are countless inheritors of intangible cultural heritage in various forms of folk art just like Chaochao. Kuaishou's inclusive algorithmic distribution mechanism has built an information highway that enables people with the same customs and cultures to break through spatial limitations in order to see authentic, shared scenes and produce emotional resonance. The platform also enables people with different customs and cultures to see, via authentic and first-hand sharing, different forms of expression of the same feelings, emotions, and experiences among different cultures, thereby deepening mutual familiarity and understanding.

Today, many different types of inheritors of intangible cultural heritage are exploring new opportunities on Kuaishou.

Kuaishou Gives Birth to a New Video on Intangible Cultural Heritage Every Three Seconds

I have been following the Kuaishou account of a Tibetan singer-instrumentalist who plays a six-stringed harp since I found it on the Same City page for the Ganzi Autonomous Prefecture. Xi Daojia, as he is called, livestreams every night from 7 or 8 p.m. until midnight. He plays and sings song after song while facing his mobile phone, and occasionally co-streams with other Tibetan singer-instrumentalists. I gradually started to follow a few dozen Tibetan folk singer-instrumentalists from places such as Ganzi, Aba, and Hainan Tibetan Autonomous Prefecture after getting to know them through Xi Daojia's channel. Like him, they gradually shifted their main stage from racetracks, wedding ceremonies, and festivals to Kuaishou's platform, and in doing so, they can now record moments and stories that are interesting and vivid at any time.

Aside from the inheritors of intangible cultural heritage themselves, ordinary viewers are also enthusiastic about seeing the records of intangible cultural heritage. In March 2019, a statistics report released by

Kuaishou showed that, on average, one video on intangible cultural heritage was "born" every three seconds, and over the past year, 11,640,000 videos on intangible cultural heritage appeared on the platform, garnering 25 billion views and 500 million likes in total. Moreover, these videos were rich and diverse in content—among the top 10 types of intangible cultural heritage in terms of number of videos, Qinqiang opera had 940,000 videos, Yangge folk dance had 790,000 videos, Chinese dough figurines had 520,000 videos, and Yu opera had 430,000 videos. In addition, there were also videos on the Yi Torch Festival, temple fairs, hobbyhorses, Chinese chess, Jin opera, jade sculptures, and so on. In a video that filmed a play staged in Longnan Village, Gansu Province, there were only two live spectators, yet this video garnered more than a million views on Kuaishou.

These precious folk records are just like a huge database that bears the collective memory of all Chinese people, and they are continually evolving with the changes of the times together with intangible cultural heritage.

Indeed, watching Kuaishou videos about various kinds of human life can be quite addicting.

Whenever I go on a business trip to different counties and cities, I swipe to the Same City page on Kuaishou. There, I find the daily lives, joys, anger, and sadness of people within several hundred miles. And the closer I am to the mountains, villages, grasslands, and seas, the richer, fresher, and more exuberant the folk vitality in the area.

For thousands of years, our ancestors amassed countless treasures of experience and wisdom on this land. On Kuaishou, the inheritors of intangible cultural heritage are given a new platform where they can record and share intangible cultural heritage via short videos and explore new directions for intangible culture in the new age via the internet.

Kuaishou Enables Intangible Cultural Heritage to Be Inherited and Monetized

After the Seven Romantic Fairies of Dong Families amassed a large number of followers, they were able to earn an income from tips. At the same time, ethnic clothing has become popular once again, after nearly disappearing even from its place of origin. Influenced by such changes, more and more locals are participating in the cause of ethnocultural development of their own accord. In less than a year, Gaibao Village—where the Seven Fairies originated—has completely escaped poverty.

An elderly man that makes dough figurines has also amassed a million followers on Kuaishou. Most of his sculptures are modeled after heroes from myths and legends; their vivid colors and majestic appearances have attracted many young people to come and serve as his apprentices. Hence, he took in more disciples via Kuaishou and started a training class, and he has also begun to accept commercial orders. His craft can now be imparted, while his life is improving by the day.

Chen Libao is the suona player in Su Yang's band, and also for the movie *Song of the Phoenix*. In order for more children to experience the charm of traditional suona folk music, he explains the technique of how to play the suona in detail in every video, and also provides systematic suona lessons via Kuaishou Classroom. In just a few months, he has had thousands of suona lessons booked on Kuaishou. He has not only benefited many suona enthusiasts, but also monetized the value of his skill.

The value of traffic empowerment is nothing other than the value of recording and sharing. From building up connections and establishing mutual support among individuals to engendering self-identity and the confidence and strength to create value in individuals, this chain of "energy transfer" continually affects every user of intangible cultural heritage on Kuaishou, arousing their intrinsic motivation to use the internet to explore new possibilities for disseminating intangible cultural heritage. By means of its inclusive distribution of traffic and authentic attributes of a sharing community, Kuaishou has become an important platform for every inheritor of intangible cultural heritage to express themselves and monetize their value. For those craftsmen who had simply kept their heads down and worked, they have finally found a gateway that leads to the market.

WEI ZONGFU: KUAISHOU HAS BREATHED NEW LIFE INTO THE DAOQING SHADOW PLAY OF THE WEI CLAN

Wei Zongfu is a typical farmer and a teacher in a shadow play class, but even more so, he is a Kuaishou talent. Born into a family of shadow play masters, he bears the historical mission of imparting and promoting the craft of shadow play. However, due to his low income, he struggled to make ends meet and could not find a successor. He used to lament that the craft of shadow play would die if its craftsmen were to die out. But all of this changed after he discovered Kuaishou.

In less than two years, he has published 889 short videos of shadow play on Kuaishou, amassing 44,000 followers and earning an income of 150,000 yuan. Nowadays, he shares the happenings of his daily routine and performances on the platform, which he also uses to spread this traditional skill to more young people.

Kuaishou is quietly protecting intangible cultural heritage in its own unique way. Inheritors of intangible cultural heritage like Wei Zongfu are fortunate that a new stage that belongs to them has already been set up and the audience is swiftly being seated. People can now feel the ancient art of light and shadow through their mobile phone screen.

PROFILE

Kuaishou name: 魏宗富，道情传承人 (Wei Zongfu, Inheritor of Daoqing)

Kuaishou ID: 835521006

Hometown: Huan County, Gansu Province

Age: 52

Education: primary school

Topic: Daoqing shadow play

Production style: professional performance of shadow play

Message to his loyal fans: I hope everyone will come to watch shadow play on Kuaishou

Narrator: Wei Zongfu

Business Model: Offline performances + Online Livestreams

I often feel old these days. Shadow play is on the verge of death, yet I am incapable of saving it. On days when I am not performing, I sing a Daoqing opera (an art of chanting folk tales to the accompaniment of simple percussion instruments) before going to do farming work. Later in the day, when I have some free time, I gently caress the envelopes that the shadow puppets are kept in. And then at night, I play the ukelele to entertain myself.

This was my life until December 2017. That month, my daughter started using Kuaishou after seeing others doing so. She later told me to try performing on Kuaishou, since I had such great talent.

My children kept on telling me about the merits of Kuaishou—they told me that one could showcase one's talents, chat, and make friends on Kuaishou, and, thus, I could use this platform to get more people to watch shadow plays.

I did not understand the internet, let alone know how to use it. Back then, I was only using an old-style mobile phone. Soon, however, I decided to get a smartphone in order to give Kuaishou a try.

Shadow Play Would Die if Its Craftsmen Were to Die Out

I have witnessed the glory days of shadow play and also experienced its decline. Before the emergence of Kuaishou, shadow play was rapidly heading toward extinction.

A few decades ago, when I was performing with my great-grandfather, we drew full crowds for every show. We would sing from the afternoon till past dawn the next morning, at which time we would put shades on the windows and continue singing. Even then, the theater would remain so packed that many people would lean in through the windows.

The 20th century was when shadow play was at its most glorious. Huan County had dozens of shadow play troupes that went around the mountain villages to give performances. We could earn one yuan for every day of performance, which was a considerable sum in those days, albeit it was very hard-earned. Little donkeys carried all of the troupe's possessions, which could weigh as much as 60 kilograms in total.

Back then, every village in Huan County had a temple that would organize temple fairs at which shadow play was an essential element, regardless of whether a village was rich or poor. A temple fair without shadow play would no longer be considered a temple fair, as it would not be accepted by the villagers.

I was born into a family of shadow play masters. My great-grandfather was one of the four disciples of Xie Changchun, the "Daoqing Shadow Play Master" of the late Qing dynasty. After he became a master himself, he formed his own troupe. Over the years, he trained 84 apprentices to be masters and was famous for a period of time. Within our family, shadow play has been imparted to a fourth generation, in me.

I learned the skills of shadow play through rigorous practice with my grandfather when I was a child and began learning from him how to give a performance at 14 years old. By 16 years old, I could independently lead a troupe to give a performance. Nowadays, I perform at more than 140 temple fairs every year.

To the local villages, it is only when a shadow play has been completed that the sowing season for the year is considered to have truly begun.

Living conditions in the villages have improved over the years. There are now vehicles and televisions, and thus few people still watch shadow plays. The turning point was in 1996, when the shadow play from Huan County began to decline. That was the year when even the remote mountain villages in these parts were provided with electricity. Television became available to every household, causing shadow play performances to decrease as time went on.

In 2006, many people from the villages migrated for work. With few people left in the villages, even fewer continued to watch shadow plays, so our incomes became even more meager than before. My troupe saw our annual performances decrease from 300 to 150. Some of my former colleagues began finding other jobs and made opera singing a sideline. My own children are also unwilling to pursue shadow play as a career. After all, as I have also been convinced myself, practical considerations must be made alongside passion when deciding one's job or career.

I have already accepted the fact that it is impossible to find an apprentice. If it were me, I would not allow my children to become apprentices in shadow play, either. Otherwise, they might not be able to make ends meet for themselves in the future. An occupation that does not allow one to put food on the table has no realistic significance to any ordinary person. And when the last shadow player leaves this world, the art of shadow play shall follow suit.

The River in Me

The best way to present shadow plays online is not through photos and text, but rather through videos—only videos can convey their light-and-shadow culture.

I experienced the power of video for the first time through a movie whose production Su Yang had much to do with.

Su Yang and I have known each other for a long time. I got to know him by chance in 2003—he had enjoyed my performance in the county seat, so he came to talk to me. I even sold him a few discs I had burned myself. Later on, I regularly contacted him by phone to see if he needed any materials related to shadow play.

In 2016, he called to tell me of his intention to film the movie *The River in Me*. I was extremely excited to hear this. Starting in September that year, the production team visited my home and often stayed for up to 15 days at a stretch. They would follow me and film me while I was doing my farm work, singing in my spare time at home, or giving a performance at a temple fair.

We live in the mountains where there is plenty of space, so we put the production team up in a vacant cave house. Because they followed me around all the time, it felt as though my family had gained a few more members.

Things started off fine, but after a period of time, I got a little impatient. After all, I did not know how a movie was filmed and did not understand why so much time was needed to film this movie. And so I asked them one day, "How much more time are you going to need?"

Instead of replying to me directly, the director showed me a documentary called *Village Diary* and told me that *The River in Me* would take approximately the same time—over the period of a year, they would film the way I live and the way I perform.

I understood the significance of this project from then on. Just like in *Village Diary*, changes in my life and the extinction of shadow play were inevitable, therefore the video clips filmed by the production team might soon be all that is left. Hence, after that, I became very cooperative, hoping to make a good film to serve as a memento for myself, and as video materials for future generations.

In late October 2016, I brought the Xingsheng Troupe to Beijing to take part in a performance organized by Su Yang's show, *The Yellow River Runs Forth*. The film director Yang Zhichun was in charge of receiving us.

On our first day in Beijing, I performed a shadow play at Tsinghua University Primary School. The children all showed great interest in it. I remarked to my troupe members that these children were very bright and would certainly become elites in the future.

We also visited the Summer Palace, where, with great excitement, I experienced my first boat ride. There is not such a large lake in my hometown, so I had never had the chance to ride a boat before. Some of us even sang on the boat, and we were all in very high spirits.

That night, we went to give another performance at the request of the production team. I extended the performance to 30 minutes from the originally rehearsed 20 minutes, because Su Yang had said during the rehearsal that the story must be told completely, even if it has to be extended.

After three years of filming, the movie was finally completed in 2019. On June 17th of that year, its main production team visited my home to hold a special screening ceremony. The white projection screen that was used for the screening was none other than the scrim used on the shadow play stage. On its two sides was a couplet that read, "Singing a thousand ancient stories in one breath, commanding a million soldiers with both hands." I invited my fellow villagers to come watch the movie and livestreamed the event on Kuaishou, as usual. That day, I was so happy that I specially wore a suit to mark the occasion.

The next day, *The River in Me* was released nationwide. I had never imagined that I would one day appear on movie screens all across China.

Gaining New Life on Kuaishou

At first, I was a little unwilling to film Kuaishou videos. But later on, when I saw that countless followers cheered for me when a video of my performance was uploaded to the platform, I suddenly realized the magic of Kuaishou and began using it on my own initiative.

One night when I started a livestream, a follower requested a female voice for a Dan role. I had no choice but to ask my wife to sing along. This yielded unexpectedly good results. My wife now knows how to play the woodblock, handles the high notes better than me, and has a more accurate grasp on emotions involved in female roles.

Since 2017, I have earned 150,000 yuan in income. This includes my remuneration from performances in places such as Shanghai, Sichuan, and Xinjiang. Once, when I brought my wife to Shanghai to give a performance, she remarked that we would never have had the chance to visit Shanghai if it were not for shadow play.

These days, I receive many performance opportunities via Kuaishou. A loyal fan left a comment saying, "Our own plays are not up to scratch. Please come and sing at our temple fair; I think you sing very well." At first, I was afraid that this was a scam, but I later discovered that it was a real invitation.

Previously, when I was not getting many performance invitations, I also tried burning discs and selling them. When the internet came about, someone uploaded photos of my performances online, but this did not result in much. After Kuaishou emerged, however, people would watch the videos of my performances, and as a result, I received more invitations, made new friends, and earned some money. Some local shadow players also began using Kuaishou after seeing me earn money on the platform.

More and more people found my performances via Kuaishou, and I even recruited several apprentices through the platform. However, I still do not have an inheritor; these followers are merely interested in the craft and do not intend to become professionals. Finding a true inheritor is not an easy task.

Thanks to Kuaishou, many local troupes have come to my home to learn from me. Longdong University's College of Music also found out about me through my short videos and made plans to develop shadow play music together with me.

On October 20, 2019, I gave a performance in Beijing. For this performance, I specially used aluminum alloy to make a new detachable frame that is convenient for transportation. I also purchased new shadow puppets, remodeled my stage, and bought a pickup truck as part of plans to open a "cultural yard" back home. I did these things so I can build better connections with those loyal fans whom I have never met, and thank them for their love of shadow play.

CHEN LIBAO THE SUONA PLAYER: I GAINED 500 TIMES MORE STUDENTS AS SOON AS I GOT ON KUAISHOU

Chen Libao, a suona performer born in the late 80s, was made famous by the movie *Song of the Phoenix*. As a young wind instrumentalist in the China National Traditional Orchestra, he enjoyed a certain reputation. He once collaborated with the singer Tan Jing on the stage of *Singer*, moving many hearts with his song "Jiuer." He has a secondary identity as a livestreamer who teaches the suona. Tens of thousands of his followers are learning to play the suona from him, which is something that would have been quite unimaginable in the past.

PROFILE

Kuaishou name: 陈力宝唢呐 (Chen Libao the Suona Player)

Kuaishou ID: KS428742641

Hometown: Tangshan City, Hebei Province

Age: 32

Education: postgraduate

Topic: suona performances and course

Representative works: *Song of the Phoenix, A Pot of Old Wine,* "Jiuer"

Production style: suona performances and course, detailed and practical style of teaching

Message to his loyal fans: may more people listen to and enjoy suona music

Business model: suona courses, suona sales

Narrator: Chen Libao

After Joining Kuaishou, My Students Increased From Twenty to Tens of Thousands

My name is Chen Libao, and I was born in a small mountain village in Tangshan City, Hebei Province. When I was young, the suona would be played in my village at weddings or funerals. Influenced by that environment, I also took a fancy to the suona. Later on, believing that I was talented, my father hired a teacher from the Tianjin Conservatory of Music to train me. After graduating from senior middle school, I entered the China Conservatory of Music before going to work in the China National Traditional Orchestra. In 2013, I went back to attend postgraduate study at the China Conservatory of Music.

My first contact with Kuaishou was quite accidental. Two years ago, a friend published a video of a folk performer named Zheng Qingyi playing the suona. He is a Kuaishou livestreamer who performs the suona at a very high level. The reason that the orchestra has to go down to the countryside every year is precisely to find excellent folk performers like him and learn from their traditional folk cultures and skills. Therefore, in order to listen to him play the suona, I downloaded the Kuaishou app.

Kuaishou's recommendations also helped me to discover folk suona performers from places such as Inner Mongolia, Henan Province, Gansu Province, and Shaanxi Province. Among them are several high-level performers such as Song Xiaohong from Inner Mongolia, Wen Laowu from Henan Province, Ma Zigang from Gansu Province, and Wei Mingyou from Shaanxi Province. Whenever local events such as weddings, funerals, or temple fairs are held, they would use their mobile phones to livestream their performances. It was by watching their livestreams that I learned a lot about the folk culture and characteristics of the suona.

Someone then suggested that I give Kuaishou a try. I was hesitant initially, because I worked in a state-level institution and there had never been a Kuaishou livestreamer who was a public servant. Later on, however, I came around to the idea, so on November 28, 2017, I uploaded two videos in which I promised to livestream once I had gained a certain number of followers. The following month when I was giving a performance in Jiangsu Province, I started a Kuaishou livestream for the first time, when I had nothing much to do at night. To my surprise, I found it quite interesting and, thus, I have been livestreaming regularly since then.

Why do I say that it is "interesting"? I grew up in the countryside but have since lived in Beijing for nearly 20 years. On Kuaishou, many people from my village would talk to me and ask me about my childhood experiences attending school and learning to play the suona. Someone also asked me if I had ever worked in a field or ridden a tricycle. Questions like these brought back many childhood memories.

Age-related questions are the most common questions I get—many people are worried that they are too old or too young to start learning to play the suona. In my view, the suona is not just an instrument; it carries different meanings in the eyes of different people. For example, even if a village-born child goes to the city and lives there for decades, his childhood experiences would bring about different feelings in him toward the suona. I often say that anyone can learn to play the suona as long as they like it—everyone is equal before the suona.

Impartment and inheritance are topics that we are perpetually concerned about. The movie *Song of the Phoenix* explores the issue of how to impart folk traditions and human beliefs. As a matter of fact, change is a necessary condition for impartment and inheritance. For example, I only have 20-odd students in real life, yet I have tens of thousands of them on Kuaishou. Nowadays, students from all over China can learn more professional and systematic knowledge on playing an instrument, just by opening the Kuaishou app. This was certainly not the case in the past, when people like me had to go to faraway places like Beijing and Tianjin to study in a music academy.

Many art school students would send me private messages asking me about my livestream schedule and if I could give them a few tips. I would record their questions on my mobile phone and then answer these questions when I am livestreaming. Most of the time, I am able to address the doubts that they have. This kind of interaction has a great significance; face-to-face teachings cannot possibly have such a broad range of influence.

Achieving the Ideal of "Everyone Is Equal Before the Suona" on Kuaishou

When Kuaishou Classroom was officially launched in June 2019, its management team contacted me to teach a course there. Prior to this, many livestreamers with hundreds of thousands of followers had provided courses at a price of 10 to 20 yuan each, but few people actually bought their courses. I was thus a little worried that I would end up like them. However, many of my loyal followers offered me encouragement on my livestream channel, saying that they were confident my course would be fully signed up for, and that if this were not the case, they would each buy three copies of my course. This gave me a great deal of confidence. To my surprise, the course was fully signed up for almost as soon as it was launched online.

My course is conducted using livestreams only, with each lecture being about 90 minutes long. I set a theme and write an outline in advance, such as *what are the common problems faced by learners?*, or *which skills are harder to learn?* I then group similar questions together and answer them. Over time, I have also developed a habit of briefly pondering over what to talk about in the next lecture before going to bed every night.

When I first started doing online courses, my fees were in the range of 50 to 100 yuan. Later on, however, I fixed the price of my courses at 9 yuan each. To me, a difference of a few thousand yuan in my income is not really significant, whereas the price difference of my courses might weigh heavily on a portion of suona enthusiasts. As an illustration, the living expenses of my parents in the countryside are only 100 to 200 yuan per month. More importantly, I hope that everyone has an equal opportunity to learn how to play the suona.

My course is a part of Kuaishou's intangible cultural heritage courses. By the end of August 2019, a total of 12,506 people had purchased my course, while 3,219 people had purchased the "Suona Crash Course." I am very happy that so many people can get to know me via Kuaishou and derive confidence from me. Learning to play the suona is not that difficult but not that simple either. Nevertheless, this is what I tell people: as long as you want to learn to play the suona and you know about Chen Libao, you have the chance to learn it well.

I require my students to play just one line on the suona every day. However, do not underestimate the importance of this one line per day. For many people in the past, the song "Song of the Phoenix" was very difficult and required more than 10 years of effort to learn—but that was because we did not have a comprehensive teaching system and plan at first.

Instead, many suona beginners who attend my course are able to play "Song of the Phoenix" in full already, and among them is a student in his 50s. Although their renditions do not carry as much feeling as those of professional players, anyone who listens to them would know immediately that the song is "Song of the Phoenix."

Among my students, the eldest is 73 years old, while the youngest is only seven. They are all very keen to learn and, in turn, I am very willing to guide them. Some students have left a deep impression on me, such as a man in his 50s we call Brother Long. His life used to consist mainly of fishing and playing cards, but nowadays, he spends every day playing the suona in his basement and even co-streaming with me. There are also some students who have a million fans and get 10,000 viewers whenever they livestream—these are numbers that I as their teacher cannot match.

I have also been impressed by a seven-year-old boy named Xiaochang. He is from the same hometown as me, Tangshan, and is a child celebrity on Kuaishou. He plays the suona very well, and he comes to Beijing to learn from me twice a month. So far, I have taken in 10 or so offline students via Kuaishou, and they are all very much like Xiaochang—highly talented and very fond of playing the suona. I believe that they will make contributions to the future development of the suona.

Kuaishou Enables Folk Treasure Craftsmen to Be Seen

Every region has its own distinguishing features when it comes to playing the suona. It is not necessarily the case that professional players from the China National Traditional Orchestra and the China Conservatory of Music play the suona at a higher level than folk players. Previously, when our orchestra went to the countryside to collect folk songs and learn, the Ministry of Culture would introduce a few inheritors of intangible cultural heritage to us. Although there are not many such inheritors for the suona, they are all very famous in China's suona circle already. However, there are also many people who are doing the same things as them. These people have not been classified as inheritors of intangible cultural heritage but are nevertheless making their voices heard.

I have found many such people on Kuaishou; they come from all over China and have become good friends with me via Kuaishou. Some time ago, they held a temple fair in a village in Dingxiang County, Shanxi Province. I was invited to perform at the temple fair, where I also learned from their playing styles. Were it not for Kuaishou, I would not have gotten to know these people.

There are also a few folk musicians on Kuaishou, such as a horn blower from Shanxi Province named Wei Mingyou. I was amazed when I heard his performance on Kuaishou for the first time—his playing skills are absolutely top-notch.

Suona itself originated from the folk world and is rooted in the folk world. I enjoy sharing and interacting with folk craftsmen and their followers on Kuaishou, as this gives me a new sense of identification with the suona. I highly admire these folk craftsmen; regardless of their age, they are very well-liked by Kuaishou followers and certainly have some artistic value. They make a living with their authentic skills and craft, rather than by playing to the gallery or trying to please people.

Nowadays, I also go to places such as the National Centre for the Performing Arts, the Great Hall of the People, and the United States' John F. Kennedy Center for the Performing Arts to film videos and share them with my loyal followers. Because many of my followers have never even seen some of the places I often go to, I make it a point to showcase what is inside the buildings. I also take the opportunity to play the suona inside these buildings to let my followers hear what it sounds like in professional theaters—this is something that they are all very interested in.

New Ways to Impart Traditional Culture

In the past, the suona was considered clichéd, outdated, and forgotten. But on Kuaishou, I have found many people who are passionate about the suona.

Changing stereotypes regarding the suona requires the continuous efforts of suona players. I have personally taken some detours in my music career as well. I previously worked in a professional orchestra, but it was not possible to fully express my ideas while performing in a concert hall. Later on, I spent a while playing pop music and rock music, and attended various music festivals. On Kuaishou, I would upload a few creative pieces that are relatively modern and trendy, including collaborative performances with piano, percussion, guitar, and other instruments. In the folk tradition, the suona is usually paired with the sheng. However, I wanted to show everyone that the suona can also be paired with the piano, which is regarded as classy and sophisticated. In fact, many of my performances in the National Centre for the Performing Arts—and many other theaters—were done together with the piano. I only have one purpose in doing all of these things, which is to let more people hear the authentic sounds of the suona so that they might grow fond of the suona and realize that the suona can also be modernized.

For a period of time, I was occupied with an instrumental music competition that was broadcast on television. I had to go to CCTV to record the show every day and thus had no time to conduct livestreams. Many people messaged me asking why I had not been livestreaming and telling me that they missed me. I felt quite touched because the people who said those things were fans who were relatively old in age, and thus, their words carried a deep feeling. Hence, I would livestream for half an hour in the middle of the night, and, to my surprise, there would often be more than 2,000 viewers.

When I traveled to different cities to give performances in the past, only students from professional schools would come to watch. Nowadays, however, when I give performances in provinces such as Shaanxi, Shanxi, and Henan, a large group of Kuaishou fans go backstage to find me, bringing with them hometown specialties for me. This gives me a very cordial feeling.

One of most memorable experiences was when we went to Nujiang Lisu Autonomous Prefecture, Yunnan Province, to give a performance. Nujiang is located on the border between China and Myanmar. I never thought that I would have Kuaishou fans, let alone loyal fans, in such a remote place, so I felt very excited. A fan told me that were it not for my livestreams, it would have been impossible for him to learn to play the suona.

Many people do not know how to choose a good suona when they first start learning to play. This was why I began to sell suonas in April 2018. I had misgivings about doing so previously, because I was afraid that tongues would wag—after all, I was a professional performer and everyone knew me. But later on, I felt that the enthusiasm of learners would suffer a great blow if they did not have a good instrument. All of the suonas that I sell nowadays have been personally tested by me at the factory. I tune each and every pitch and only sell suonas that have been perfectly tuned. Some people even have waited three or four months for me to tune their suona before they get their hands on it. I am thankful to everyone for the trust they have shown in me.

I cannot represent the entire suona industry, but personally speaking, Kuaishou has indeed had a great impact on me. First of all, my original intention for using Kuaishou was to learn; for a professional performer, Kuaishou is a very good learning platform.

Secondly, Kuaishou has provided a learning opportunity for all suona enthusiasts. Nowadays, many fellow suona professionals commend me for having tens of thousands of students when they see me. Learning to play an instrument might not yield much material rewards for a person, but it can satisfy their spiritual pursuits.

In addition, I have offered professional-grade instruments at dirt-cheap prices to many people on my livestream channel.

Previously, no one from the national-level troupes would use Kuaishou. However, thanks to my influence, my university mates and colleagues have gradually joined Kuaishou. Some of them work in the China National Opera & Dance Drama Theater, some work in the China National Symphony Orchestra, while some are university teachers. Their addition to Kuaishou makes it possible to raise the quality of the education offered on Kuaishou—and this makes me feel very happy.

AJIE THE OPERA SINGER: I ONLY REALIZED I HAD A PRODIGY AT HOME AFTER USING KUAISHOU

When he was only two and a half years old, Ajie could already sing opera. At the age of five, he gave his first performance on Kuaishou—in the video, he sang a Qu opera called *Xiaocangwa*. The video garnered more than a million views and brought him tens of thousands of followers. He regularly finds the videos of professional performers in order to learn from them. He also likes to record videos and is accepting of any filming style.

Dong Huagai, the challenger for the Star Gold Award in the televised opera *Liyuan Spring*, contacted Ajie via Kuaishou. He said that the child has potential and must be properly developed.

In the summer of 2019, Ajie went to Zhengzhou and enrolled in a one-month standard opera training course in a school run by an apprentice of Niu Decao, who is a clown master in Yu opera. During that time, he unwittingly became a disseminator of intangible cultural heritage.

After school started on September 1, 2019, Ajie went to a boarding school to attend third grade.

Ajie went to Zhengzhou during the four-day break that was given after 10 straight days of school. His mother said that she would send him to learn opera at any price.

PROFILE

Kuaishou name: Ajie the Opera Singer

Kuaishou ID: 303384145

Hometown: Xiao County, Suzhou City, Anhui Province

Age: 7

Education: primary school (attending)

Topics: Qu opera and Yu opera

Production style: singing into a microphone in an old house and in the fields, occasionally adorning opera props, and revealing vivid and authentic expressions

Message to his loyal fans: our whole family is very thankful to you for your support toward our child and also to Kuaishou for giving our child a stage to perform on

Business model: selling products and earning tips from livestreaming

Narrator: Ajie's mother

Reconciling Learning, Playing, and Filming Kuaishou Videos

Ajie was able to sing opera when he was two and a half years old. Ever since he was young, he has had a great sense of music, and he is very talented. Songs are very easy for him; he only has to listen to a song once to be able to sing it. In the past, however, we felt that singing was just fun and games and did not take it seriously. But after we joined Kuaishou, we realized that we nearly lost out on a talented singer.

My hometown is a village in Xiao County, Suzhou City, Anhui Province—opera is not regarded highly there. My home has a total of one mou of land. Aside from farming work, my husband and I play the suona in our spare time. The village has suona troupes that get invited to perform at weddings, birthdays, and funerals in the vicinity. A suona troupe consists of seven or eight people, with each person earning 200 yuan for the usual two-day engagement. Summer is our off season, when we would have at most one or two performances per month, as compared to about 10 performances per month during our peak season.

I can not only play the suona, but also sing opera, albeit at an amateur level only. I enjoy singing Qu opera and Yu opera as a personal hobby, but have never received formal training in them. Nobody around me sings opera except my son Ajie. Seeing as he is able to sing every opera that I have sung, it is possible that he was influenced by me. He likes to imitate all roles, be it that of a young man or an old woman. On top of that, he learns operas really fast, such that he is able to sing an opera after listening to it only a handful of times on a mobile phone. I do not teach him anything; he listens to and learns everything on his own.

We started using Kuaishou in 2017. Back then, my husband said that many people were showcasing their talents and earning money on the platform. I doubted the possibility of this and even thought that he was up to no good, so I deleted the app after he had downloaded it the first time. However, he downloaded it again and insisted that it was really useful.

Ajie was five years old when he first started using Kuaishou. He was a little curious and enjoyed watching videos of professional performers. Thereafter, he would often search for videos of those opera singers and would use voice-to-text for Chinese characters he did not know how to write. After finding a video he wanted, he would sing along while the video was being played. And whenever he found a segment that he thought was sung well, he would ask me to download it for him.

When he first started recording videos, he sang the Qu opera, *Xiaocangwa*. The first video garnered more than one million views and brought him tens of thousands of followers—mostly because the character was quite an attractive one.

A view count of 500,000 to 700,000 would usually yield an increase of 3,000 to 4,000 followers, while a view count of more than one million should yield an increase of 10,000 followers. Under normal circumstances, there should be an increase of 1,000 to 2,000 followers per day, while some heavily viewed videos can yield more than 10,000 followers per day. Videos have an easier time yielding followers than livestreams; although a livestream can yield 1,000 followers or so, it is much more tiring to conduct livestreams than to post videos.

We are not like those creators who upload several videos per day, and this is partially because we are worried that our followers will get annoyed. Thus, we upload only one video every one to two days. Filming videos also requires all kinds of preparation work. As we do not have professional equipment, we film all of our videos using a mobile phone.

We learned how to use Kuaishou on our own by observing and understanding. We wanted to conduct livestreams, but an account could only do so if its videos had previously made it onto the Trending page. We heard that using an old house as the background of a video would make it easier for said video to get on the Trending page, so we traveled dozens of miles to find an old house for filming. On a hot summer day, our child walked out from the old house with his body completely covered in mosquito bites, which must have been especially painful. He has sacrificed a lot in order to get on the Trending page.

Some people have questioned me as to whether I had physically beaten Ajie in order to film a segment. This was because he could cry and laugh on cue, and his facial expressions were always on point. I replied that I would never beat my child in order to get on the Trending page and that any conspiracy theorist could come and watch when I started a livestream. As soon as Ajie starts to sing opera, his facial expressions would start to fit the role he is playing very well.

He has never gotten sick of Kuaishou—as soon as you mention filming a segment, he is willing to do it regardless of the filming style, so we have never needed to force him. His acting skills are really good, and it takes him only a few seconds to get into character. We believe that he is indeed a true talent.

I have also bought him a few custom-made sets of clothing that are based on the operas he sings. He only sings Yu opera and Qu opera, which are what he is good at, whereas other styles of opera are harder for him to learn. Moreover, I do not want him to expose himself to too many complicated styles at such a young age.

Ajie is about to turn eight years old now. Normally speaking, I would not allow his schooling to be affected by filming videos. Thus, before he started attending school, I filmed and saved many segments, and then uploaded each segment at regular intervals, with each video being about 57 seconds long. Afraid that he might become exhausted, I do not film long videos. And when I run out of segments, sometimes I film myself instead.

He has asked me if he can go out to play with other children, to which I answer that he certainly can. He feels that always having to film segments and conduct livestreams means that he has no time left to play. I told him that he could go out and play at any time. After all, it would be unwise to prevent him from having a normal life simply because of filming videos and livestreaming. His results in school are also very good. At times, he would come and ask me to film a segment on his own initiative. As his mother, I will maintain a balance between his studies, playtime, and filming Kuaishou videos.

Everyone in the Village Calls Ajie the "Little Streamer"

We have become quite experienced after using Kuaishou for over a year. Nowadays, we know that to film a segment, we must find a place with good lighting, choose a good position and background, pick the appropriate clothing, and control the singing volume. All aspects of the filming must be well-coordinated. Moreover, the thumbnail of each segment is also very important for attracting views. The videos that fare the best are those that are performed with certain plot scenarios; a few segments of him crying while singing have garnered a relatively high number of views. Fans enjoy our videos a lot because they feel that Ajie acts well and is able to affect people with his emotions.

Ajie often watches segments of himself singing opera and reads the comments left by fans. He greatly treasures this Kuaishou account. At times, he tells me not to scold or argue with haters, as that might lead to the account being suspended. Even at his young age, he is wise to these things.

If he feels that he did not do well in a particular segment, he tells me not to upload it. And if he is dissatisfied with a segment after uploading it, he deletes it and films it again. For some of our videos, we shoot several takes and then choose the best one to upload.

Ajie has truly changed a lot. Were it not for Kuaishou, he could never have learned so many things and become good at so many operas. By showcasing his talents here, he has become very well-liked and has also earned some money.

We now earn many more times what we used to prior to joining Kuaishou. Furthermore, our lives have changed greatly and our social status has increased. Everyone who lives within 30 miles of us knows about Ajie. When we are playing the suona in public, people mention to their companions that "Little Streamer's parents are here." And even when I bring him into the city, many passersby would recognize him as the popular opera singer.

His classmates and teachers also know about his performances on Kuaishou, and they call him the "million-fan internet celebrity." However, they treat him just like any other child. His teachers teach him or punish him at the appropriate times. For his part, his mentality has not changed; he does not know that he is famous and simply thinks that it is all for fun, nor do his friends treat him any differently. On occasions such as Children's Day, he will sing an opera during class performances.

Some online fans have even come to find Ajie in real life. In 2017 and 2018, many fans came to visit Ajie and stayed in my home for 10 to 15 days. They hail from provinces such as Hainan, Jiangsu, Shandong, and Henan, or even further than that. Some of these people bring their children along, while some are unmarried couples. Honestly speaking, I have never grown tired of receiving them because they are all Ajie's fans. No matter how long they stay in my home, I treat them as well as I can.

Receiving Professional Training and Inheriting
Intangible Cultural Heritage

After Ajie became famous on Kuaishou, he received the recognition of professionals. This reminds us that, as parents, we must keep on creating better learning conditions for our children.

Dong Huagai, the challenger for the Star Gold Award on the televised opera show *Liyuan Spring*, contacted us via Kuaishou and told us that Ajie was a child with potential and must be properly developed. He also expressed his wish to impart his knowledge to Ajie, but unfortunately, he was too busy.

Prior to this, I had never tried to find an opera teacher for Ajie. Furthermore, Anhui Province did not have an opera school. I thus asked Dong Huagai to suggest a school that was suitable for Ajie. He gave me the phone number of an opera academy in Zhengzhou City and told me to contact them myself. In the summer of 2019, I specially brought Ajie to Zhengzhou and enrolled him in a one-month opera training course for him to learn a few basic techniques. After all, Qu opera and Yu opera are both native to Henan. This was also my first time visiting Zhengzhou.

The principal of this academy was an apprentice of Niu Decao, a clown master of Yu opera. During the course, Ajie had to get up at six in the morning every day to practice leg presses, kicks, and other basic training skills. He would then spend the rest of the morning on voice training, and in the afternoon, he would practice the same basic training skills again. After all, no matter how good one is at opera singing, one would not be able to perform if one's body cannot keep up. He would get out of school at six in the evening and then repeat the same routine the next day. Aside from lunchtime, his mornings and afternoons were all spent training hard in school.

His teachers also think highly of him. They feel that he has an innate talent for performing and wanted him to take part in an opera challenge show on Henan Television. However, we did not sign him up for it because we felt it might be too tough on him.

After he returned from the opera academy, his followers could see that he had indeed changed. They said that there was a greater charm and appeal in his singing, performing, and various other aspects.

After school resumed on September 1, 2019, Ajie went to a boarding school to attend third grade. During the four-day break that was given after 10 straight days of class, we brought him to Zhengzhou to learn opera. If, one day, an opera master discovers him and wishes to develop him, we would definitely provide our full support.

Both Ajie and I started singing opera as a hobby. Because of Kuaishou, however, we unwittingly became disseminators of intangible cultural heritage. We have only now realized that both Qu opera and Yu opera are intangible cultural heritage and quintessence to Chinese culture, and more people are needed to impart them to the next generation.

Were it not for Kuaishou, we could never have realized that Ajie has an innate talent for singing opera. Kuaishou has enabled Ajie to be seen by more people. The encouragement offered by everyone has made us realize that we can still do better. People have told me that Ajie's future provides hope for the impartment of intangible cultural heritage and traditional culture. We thank all of our followers for their support for—and expectations of—Ajie!

CHAPTER EIGHT

KUAISHOU VILLAGES: A SINGLE SPARK CAN START A PRAIRIE FIRE

CHAPTER OVERVIEW

A t the physical level, the formation of Kuaishou Villages is a kind of extension in space and expansion in scale. But in a profound sense, it is an upgrading of traditional industries or even a remaking of industry chains. The rapid rise of the Kuaishou Village model has not only altered the destinies of many individuals, but has also changed the ecosystems of regions, professions, and industries.

Kuaishou Villages share a common characteristic, which is that they are all situated in traditional "featured villages and towns," wholesale markets, or industrial zones, all of which are centers of goods distribution or production. They thus have a highly convenient supply of goods and can keep on providing relevant products or services to consumers. At the same time, they have a certain logistics base. Because merchants are especially sensitive to information, centers of goods distribution or production are also places where the transmission of information is especially fast. For example, when a person has a profitable business, their business model would soon be imitated.

Kuaishou Villages have another characteristic, which is a fast speed of formation. Traditional featured villages and towns, wholesale markets, and industrial zones usually require a long time to be built up; they gradually come into being. The rapid growth of Kuaishou Villages can be attributed to the low barriers to entry and zero-cost strategy of its "short videos + livestreams" e-commerce model. In this age, e-commerce is rapidly improving. Not long after traditional offline sales methods had been replaced by e-commerce, traditional e-commerce forms—as characterized by their dependence on text or image search—rapidly evolved into version 2.0 and entered the age of short video.

SUCCESS STORIES

"Sister Yue" of Liangshan Prefecture: We Are Both from the Grassroots—if He Can Make Money, Then So Can I

Li Wenlong: I Became Famous Overnight Thanks to an Inspiration from *Dangal*

Huazai: How I Sold Dishcloths Throughout China and Even Southeast Asia

Haitou Town: How to Achieve 300 Million Yuan in E-Commerce Transactions in One Year

KUAISHOU VILLAGE: A SINGLE SPARK CAN START A PRAIRIE FIRE

Li Zhao, senior researcher at The Kuaishou Research Institute

Among the night market vendors of Yiwu City, Zhejiang Province, Yan Bo was one of the first to livestream on Kuaishou. While running his stall, he talks and laughs into his mobile phone. At first, his peers thought he was just goofing off. In August 2017, however, he sold 350,000 woolen sweaters via his mobile phone. This story spread throughout the city overnight. Fast forward to May 2019, when we visited Beixiazhu Village in Yiwu City, we discovered that more than 5,000 people in the village were livestreaming on Kuaishou to sell their goods. The village had become a Kuaishou Village in the truest sense.

In Haitou Town, Lianyungang City, Jiangsu Province, a fisherman named Kuang Lixiang uploaded a video of himself boiling mantis shrimp. The video soon garnered almost two million hits. Over the next two years, he would amass nearly two million followers, becoming the local "Promotion King" and even establishing a company that sells seafood. His success has led his fellow villagers to imitate him—his hometown of Haiqi Village, which consists of just over 2,000 households, now has more than 200 livestreamers. You can find people livestreaming everywhere in the village—be it on a boat, on a dock, or on a beach.

Stories such as those of Yan Bo and Kuang Lixiang are playing out endlessly in China's diverse featured villages and towns, wholesale markets, and industrial zones. Countless ordinary people have inadvertently been caught up in the trend of an age.

The rapid rise of the Kuaishou Village model, as exemplified by Beixiazhu Village and Haitou Town, has not only altered the destinies of many individuals, but has also changed the ecosystems of regions, professions, and industries.

The Formation of Kuaishou Villages

Yiwu City and Haitou Town share a common characteristic: They are both situated in traditional featured villages and towns, wholesale markets, or industrial zones, all of which are centers of goods distribution or production. They thus have a supply of goods that is highly convenient, and they can keep on providing relevant products or services to consumers. At the same time, they have a certain logistics base.

Take Yiwu, for example. It is a longstanding distribution center for small goods—the world's "capital of small goods"—and one of the most logistically-developed places in China. In 2018, the business volume of Yiwu's postal and express delivery services exceeded 2.9 billion packages, while more than eight million packages were shipped from Yiwu to destinations around the world every day. Located on the coast of the Yellow Sea, Haitou Town of Lianyungang City has a coastline that is

11.6 kilometers long. It has an abundance of all kinds of seafood, especially yellow croaker, horse crab, Chinese white shrimp, and seaweed.
Richly endowed natural resources like these are an important condition
for the formation of a Kuaishou Seafood Village.

In the pre-internet era, selling goods required having a brick-and-
mortar shop. However, shops cannot be moved, so they have a highly
limited reach and supply distance. In the internet era, the emergence of
traditional e-commerce platforms, such as Taobao and JD, and convenient logistical systems has given more freedom to the selling of goods
by breaking through the previous limitations in space. Yet, promoting goods required paying costly platform fees and embellishing them
with exquisite pictures and text. Therefore, not only were such promotions not intuitive enough, but the barriers to entry were also too high
for ordinary sellers.

As we enter the age of short video, the "short videos + livestreams"
method has made the showcasing of goods more genuine, intuitive, and
detailed than ever before. It not only shows you both the outcome and the
process, but it also allows for timely interactions. Furthermore, the filming of short videos and the conducting of livestreams are very simple to
do, enabling illiterate people to engage in e-commerce as well.

In this way, a simple and direct link between goods, livestreams, and
end consumers came into being. This might very well become the main
form of commerce in the future.

Kuaishou Villages have another characteristic, which is a fast speed of
formation. Traditional featured villages and towns, wholesale markets, and
industrial zones usually require a long time to be built up; they gradually
come into being. Instead, Kuaishou has relatively low barriers to entry, and
thus whenever a Kuaishou Village is successful, its model can be quickly
copied by the people around, hence the fast speed of formation.

An Opportunity to Introduce New Industry Chains

At the physical level, the formation of Kuaishou Villages is a kind of extension in space and expansion in scale. But in a profound sense, it is an
upgrading of traditional industries or even a remaking of industry chains.

Two years ago, there were only a handful of deliverymen—all from SF Express—in Haitou Town. Thus, the fish that Kuang Lixiang and his fellow fishermen caught had to be transported by truck to be sold in various places across China. Nowadays, however, Haitou Town can ship several hundred thousand orders via express delivery every day, and so a steady flow of fresh seafood is delivered to consumers in a precise manner. A large majority of these orders come from Kuaishou. The combined number of views of Haitou Town's short videos on Kuaishou is as high as 16.5 billion per year. In 2018, Haitou Town earned more than 1 billion yuan from e-commerce transactions, becoming the top seafood village in China.

The emergence of new e-commerce models will force industry chains to upgrade. In Haitou Town, a 33-acre seafood e-commerce industrial park is under construction. Traditional workshop production of seafood paste, such as shrimp paste and crab paste, has already been replaced by mala methods of production, which can better ensure the freshness and taste of the food. These days, mala seafood manufacturers are springing up like mushrooms, and as a result, new food standards have taken shape as well. New local brands have also been developed, with their annual output value reaching more than 300 million yuan.

Haitou Town is just a microcosm of a regional industrial zone that has been changed by the advent of livestreaming. If we turn our attention away from the fishing villages of Lianyungang and instead toward bigger, sprawling cities, we will discover that the changes brought about by Kuaishou are just as astonishing as in those places.

In Yiwu City, Zhejiang Province, Kuaishou is currently sparking the third revolution of this "city of small-goods distribution." This revolution is about the marketing of goods through livestreaming, and it follows two other revolutions, namely the rise of brick-and-mortar wholesale stores in the early days and the subsequent prosperity of e-commerce.

In the early years, Yiwu relied on the "front shop, back factory" model to shorten the cycle from production to sales and improve the efficiency of goods distribution. But now, livestreaming e-commerce has further reduced the segment of intermediary distribution between producers and consumers. This essentially improves the efficiency of product circulation and represents a revolutionary innovation of the sales paradigm.

"The e-commerce model for merchants in Yiwu is changing. Kuaishou Villages are a new form of e-commerce, just like Taobao Villages were back in the day," says Professor Jia Shaohua, who is a former vice president of Yiwu Industrial & Commercial College and has personally witnessed and participated in Yiwu's e-commerce development. He believes that e-commerce in Yiwu has undergone three revolutions. At first, the internet was used to display goods, mainly in the form of text and images. Then came videos, which were better able to demonstrate the advantages of a certain product. And now, the rise of mobile livestreaming has become an important mode in Yiwu's e-commerce development. "In terms of attracting traffic, text is not good as images, images are not as good as videos, and videos are not as good as real-time, interactive livestreams."

Jia thinks that "traditional e-commerce has nearly reached its ceiling" and "everyone who is doing e-commerce in Yiwu now faces transformational problems." He gives an example: A clothing merchant in Yiwu Market only received three orders per day. Deciding to take action to improve sales, the merchant gave livestream marketing a try. Although he spoke poor Mandarin, he achieved a turnover of more than 80,000 yuan. At present, Yiwu Market is divided into five districts, of which District 2 and District 5 have livestreaming platforms. Jia says that "e-commerce was done on laptops in the past, but it is now done on smartphones—this is an e-commerce revolution."

Yiwu has now become akin to a "Kuaishou City." Nevertheless, it is still extremely crowded, still pulling in investments, still full of innovative spirit, and still embracing the opportunities of the times.

We can feel the advent of the new era from the stories of people such as Yan Bo, Hou Yue, and Kuang Lixiang. They used to be bottom-level businesspeople, who could not be any more ordinary, but their lives became vastly different after they jumped on the bandwagon of livestreaming e-commerce. In Beixiazhu Village, there are countless such legends among the unmistakable Kuaishou livestreamers. This is the era's gift to trailblazers.

With their mobile phones in hand, more and more loyal fans of Kuaishou are trying hard to capitalize on this wave of short video e-commerce. They are advancing in the direction of the tide—their choices are the market's choices, and they have thus become the chroniclers and pioneers of this new era.

"SISTER YUE" OF LIANGSHAN PREFECTURE: WE ARE BOTH FROM THE GRASSROOTS—IF HE CAN MAKE MONEY, THEN SO CAN I

Hou Yue is a woman from a village in Liangshan Yi Autonomous Prefecture, Sichuan Province who is affectionately known as "Sister Yue" by her fans on Kuaishou. During her entrepreneurial days in Yiwu City, she got to know a lot of grassroots entrepreneurs via Kuaishou. Because of their encouragement, she has enriched her own life one step at a time.

Through the Kuaishou platform, she has brought small goods to every part of China, and in the course of doing so, she has not only achieved financial freedom, but has also helped more people take part in e-commerce entrepreneurship and earn an income from it. From realizing her personal values, to helping others, and to increasing the overall value of society, she has gone through three transformations in life.

PROFILE

Kuaishou name: 创业之家～悦姐 (Home of Entrepreneurship - Sister Yue) Kuaishou ID: houyue99

Hometown: Liangshan Yi Autonomous Prefecture, Sichuan Province

Age: 36

Education: technical secondary school

Topic(s): life records, goods displaying, entrepreneurial experiences

Production style: unembellished, genuine records

Message to her loyal fans: doing e-commerce is simple, as long as you are sincere

Business model: market small goods via livestreams and establish a "Home of Entrepreneurship" to train entrepreneurs

Narrator: Hou Yue

Misfortune Never Comes Alone—Amid My Confusion, I Met Yan Bo

My name is Hou Yue, and everyone calls me Sister Yue. I come from a village in Liangshan Yi Autonomous Prefecture, Sichuan province. My father died when I was nine years old, while my mother suffered from esophageal cancer and left me when I was 18. As a result, my younger sister and I only had ourselves to rely on.

Misfortune never comes alone. After I got married, my baby was born prematurely and with cerebral palsy. To treat my child, I had to spend more than 20,000 yuan every month. After four straight years of seeking medical treatment for my baby all across China, I had basically drained my family's savings.

To survive, I set up a vendor stall to sell goods. In the process of purchasing goods, I learned that Yiwu City in Zhejiang Province was the source of all kinds of small goods, so I decided to go there to make a living. At first, I tried to operate on several traditional e-commerce platforms, such as Taobao and Pinduoduo. I also opened a wholesale store, but it did not fare well and I eventually had to shut it down due to rental pressure.

Amid my confusion over what I could do, I met Yan Bo. He was the first person within the wholesale circle to find a business opportunity on

Kuaishou. At first, I thought he was a little weird—he dressed very casually in shorts and slippers, drove a small truck, and used Kuaishou on his mobile phone every day. Yet, he was very happy. Are these not the joys of a wayward youth? However, my opinion of him changed when he sold 350,000 woolen sweaters in one month. I began to feel that he was quite a remarkable person and started to take an interest in Kuaishou.

Yan Bo is an ordinary entrepreneur from Shaanxi Province. After his business venture in his hometown failed, he came to Yiwu to do traditional e-commerce, but ultimately could not earn enough to make ends meet. So, in order to feed his family, he set up a stall at the Binwang Night Market in addition to his regular e-commerce business. In his spare time, he would watch Kuaishou videos to unwind. Being a guitar enthusiast, he tried uploading a video of himself playing the guitar one day, and as it turned out, many people liked the video and exchanged ideas with him about guitar playing. Subsequently, he began to record his entrepreneurial life on Kuaishou, such as the packing and shipping of goods and the places he drove. At the same time, many people were willing to share their own entrepreneurial experiences with him.

One day, he set up a stall selling spinning tops at the Binwang Night Market and livestreamed it on Kuaishou. His tops, which could glow while spinning, quickly attracted the attention of his loyal fans on Kuaishou and sold unexpectedly well. One loyal fan thought the toy tops were clever and asked Yan Bo if he could buy a bunch of them to resell in his hometown. Some other fans were more interested in his e-commerce business and asked if they could become business partners with him.

By livestreaming on Kuaishou, Yan Bo inadvertently realized that livestreams could not only record his life, but they could also be used to market small goods and share the ups and downs of his entrepreneurial experiences with others. Hence, a new stage in his life began.

I thought to myself that if an ordinary grassroots person like Yan Bo could make money on Kuaishou, then as someone who is better looking and more eloquent than him, I should not fare any worse than him in e-commerce. I thus created a Kuaishou account called Sister Yue to record my own life and share my own stories. In doing so, I struck a chord with my fans and received encouragement from them.

Accumulating More Than 300,000 Fans by Recording My True Life

On Kuaishou, I just have to be myself. This is quite unlike other short video platforms where one must elevate or beautify themselves in order to attract followers. By showing the unembellished truth of my life, I gradually accumulated over 300,000 followers.

It was on the basis of mutual trust that I tried selling some of Yiwu's more competitive products. In my videos, I revealed the true cost of my goods—for example, I said that I would sell a pair of shoes that had cost me seven or eight yuan and make a profit of only 50 fen. The city of Yiwu itself has an ample supply of goods and low logistical costs, and since I mostly sold leftover stock and overstocked products, they were extremely competitive in price. I also designed and produced a few fashion accessories, and eventually set up a factory to manufacture them. As time went on, more and more of my loyal fans bought goods from me and resold them by setting up stalls in their hometowns.

On Kuaishou, I revealed all of the difficulties and setbacks I faced, the solutions I came up with, and the lessons and experiences I learned during my entrepreneurship period in Yiwu. I did so to benefit more grassroots entrepreneurs with regard to their own ventures. Although livestreaming has a low barrier to entry, and can be done by anyone, it nevertheless requires skill and continuous learning. By watching my livestreams, my loyal fans can learn from the bumps that I've encountered along my journey in entrepreneurship.

As an ordinary woman from out of town, at first, I had trouble paying rent, settling my family's debts, and taking care of my child. But now, my conditions have greatly improved. Some people who initially had no intention to be in business have copied my model and embarked on their own path of entrepreneurship after watching my livestreams.

Setting up a Home of Entrepreneurship to Help Entrepreneurs Sell Goods on Kuaishou

Together with Yan Bo and a few other partners, I eventually set up a training institution called "Home of Entrepreneurship" to help entrepreneurs market their products on Kuaishou and other livestreaming platforms. After a year of development, we have guided more than 600 trainees. In order to improve our professionalism and success rate, we came up with a curriculum, connected supply sources and supply chains, decorated store shelves, set up training classrooms, and added livestreaming equipment and warehouses. With that, the trainees could use our facilities to learn and practice how to film videos and livestream in order to market their goods. We thus became Yiwu's first livestreaming e-commerce team on Kuaishou.

On traditional e-commerce platforms, all we could do was take orders and talk about business. But on Kuaishou livestream channels, we are all good friends and fellow entrepreneurs, such that I have never thought of our loyal fans as clients. Authentic life records, face-to-face communication, and whole-process exhibitions are more reliable than traditional e-commerce. When we are livestreaming, we sometimes go to our factory to show the production process of our products, or to our warehouse to show the change in our stock.

Kuaishou livestreaming has greatly lowered the barrier to entry for doing e-commerce. In traditional e-commerce, it is necessary to take exquisite photos of one's products and write detailed product descriptions, and thus it is fairly demanding on ordinary merchants. But on Kuaishou, even illiterate people can engage in e-commerce.

For example, Yan Bo has a fellow villager who is a farmer living on the border of Shaanxi and Gansu provinces. Though already in his 40s, he cannot read a single word. His wife often criticizes him by saying that, due to his illiteracy, he has no chance to start a business or do e-commerce. Instead, we encourage him by saying that many stall vendors are also illiterate, yet their businesses are doing very well.

In actual fact, setting up a street stall is also a kind of livestreaming, except the audience is made up of the people who come to the market and browse the items in stalls. This differs from video livestreaming, whereby the audience is made up of people who are busy watching videos on their mobile phones.

Kuaishou has hundreds of millions of viewers every day. This is equivalent to a large bazaar that consists of hundreds of millions of visitors. Therefore, being illiterate is no hindrance to doing e-commerce—all that Yan Bo's fellow villager has to do is to speak into his mobile phone. We taught him how to sell placer gold from his hometown and some other local handicrafts on Kuaishou. At first, he was unable to read the comments left by users, so his wife would read them to him, following which he would reply to any questions via a short video. These days, he is able to make more than 3,000 yuan a day, and on top of that, he also helps his fellow villagers sell their goods. He now says that engaging in e-commerce is easy as long as you are sincere.

Helping Others Is Also Helping Yourself

I have inadvertently gained a lot of followers on Kuaishou. It was also on the platform that I found many people with similar experiences to myself, except that they were elsewhere, doing what I did previously. They would leave comments on Kuaishou to ask me about my relevant entrepreneurial experiences, such as how to set up a stall, how to find a source of goods, and other questions related to my current work.

Sometime later, I tried to conduct livestreams on Kuaishou, because I felt that livestreams were akin to face-to-face interactions and allowed me to answer my followers' questions in a very genuine manner. As luck would have it, I was running a wholesale business in Yiwu and there was a demand for my products among my followers, so we dealt directly with each other.

Kuaishou is truly a magical place in my opinion. Here, my followers can watch me every day—they can find out what I am doing and get to know me better, as though they are my neighbors, which leads to them being able to trust me more. As I have always adhered to the principle of "small profits, large turnover" in doing business, they are able to purchase goods from me at a much cheaper price than from their own local suppliers. Consequently, I am gaining more and more followers on Kuaishou, and my business is getting better and better.

These days, my monthly income is 200,000 yuan or so, which is a figure I had never expected. It can be said that Kuaishou was what made me successful. In the past, my family ran up a lot of debt because of my child's medical bills, but in recent years, I have not only paid off all the debt, but I also bought a house and a car. On top of that, I no longer have to worry about being able to afford my child's medical bills.

Kuaishou can also help me grow further. I used to consider myself an ordinary person, and all I thought about was how to earn money to support my family. Nowadays, however, I am beginning to focus on my own growth and on improving my capabilities. Moreover, I can share my story with more people and help others on their journey in entrepreneurship via Kuaishou, thereby increasing the value of my life.

LI WENLONG: I BECAME FAMOUS OVERNIGHT THANKS TO AN INSPIRATION FROM *DANGAL*

Born in Shanxi Province in 1994, Li Wenlong dropped out of high school in his senior year to become a soldier. After retiring from the army, he started a software business twice, losing more than a million yuan in those failed ventures and ending up with a ton of debt. Yet, he managed to earn a million yuan in one year and pay off his debt by selling fashion accessories on Kuaishou.

Judging from his entrepreneurial thinking, it was certainly not an accident that he achieved success by choosing Kuaishou. Rather, it was the wisdom of riding the trend that played a key role in his success.

Today, Li Wenlong has registered a company called Xiashoukuai Accessories and established his own brand. He attaches great importance to product quality and after-sales services, and he has stated that he does not do one-off deals. It is precisely because of this that he swiftly earned his first "pot of gold" from his business. Looking back on his entrepreneurial journey, he recalls the many bumps along the way, until everything paid off in the end. He therefore hopes that his entrepreneurial experiences can offer greater inspiration to young entrepreneurs.

Kuaishou name: 浙江义乌下手快饰品团长 (Head of Xiashoukuai Accessories in Yiwu City, Zhejiang Province)

Kuaishou ID: 20353635

Hometown: Shanxi Province

Education: high school (incomplete)

Topic: marketing fashion accessories on Kuaishou

Production style: use product differentiation to attract viewers and give his Kuaishou videos more talking points

Message to his loyal fans: in such a well-developed information society as the internet, what is true can never be false, and what is false can never be true

Business model: sell goods via short videos

Narrator: Li Wenlong

Because of Two Movies, I Started on a Journey of Selling Goods on Kuaishou

In 2018, I watched two very popular Indian movies: *Dangal* and *Secret Superstar*. *Dangal* tells the story of two female wrestlers, while in *Secret Superstar*, the female protagonist gained fame online by uploading videos of herself singing. Inspired by these two movies, it occurred to me that I could sell female fashion accessories by making use of my "gender perspective" as a male.

I chose Kuaishou for marketing our products because it is a platform where the product shown in a video is consistent with the product that customers receive. Conversely, there are some e-commerce platforms where the consumers are shown carefully edited images that have definite differences from the actual product. As videos are more intuitive and genuine than images, our loyal fans have more trust in goods that are marketed via Kuaishou videos.

Furthermore, I have carefully studied the video content that tends to trend on Kuaishou and discerned a few patterns that I can use. For example, I can use product differentiation to attract viewers and give our videos more talking points, thereby helping our videos get on the Trending page and achieve the purpose of promoting our goods.

After registering an account on Kuaishou, I discovered that the platform's commission mechanism was a lot fairer than that of other video marketing platforms.

On Kuaishou, the commission mechanism for livestreaming is significantly better than on other platforms. Kuaishou pays its merchants a pre-tax share and then handles the taxable portion. Kuaishou's powers of monetization are really strong—once in 2018, we received 2,000 orders in 15 minutes via Kuaishou. There is also a livestreamer with 10 million followers who is able to earn tens of millions of yuan per month.

Good Prevails Over Evil: Believe in the Power of Brands

Although the Kuaishou platform can bring in referral traffic, the most critical thing for my company continues to be improving on our own strengths. Our products may be slightly higher in price, but we absolutely guarantee their quality and after-sales services. For example, if our products are damaged or lost during shipping, the customer may choose to get a full refund or a replacement. This was the reason that we lost some money initially. However, after we established our brand, our business picked up and we were able to ensure sustainable profits.

Thanks to the huge traffic from Kuaishou, my monthly turnover has reached more than 300,000 yuan. The popularity of Xiashoukuai has also attracted many imitators. Republished or pirated versions of Xiashoukuai's videos have been widely disseminated; from the perspective of communication effect, this is actually beneficial to us, as it is equivalent to providing us with free advertising and helps to grow our reputation.

Of course, pirated videos infringe on our copyright and are illegal. However, in such a highly-developed information society as the internet, what is true can never be false, and what is false can never be true—pirated videos cannot become authentic videos, and good always prevails over evil.

HUAZAI: HOW I SOLD DISHCLOTHS THROUGHOUT CHINA AND EVEN SOUTHEAST ASIA

"Chen Zhihua looks very simple and honest. I think highly of him," says Li Yong, deputy director of the Expert Committee of the China Association of International Trade and co-chairman of the China-Europe-America Economic Strategy Research Center of the China Association of International Trade.

In Yiwu Market, there are thousands of shops selling the same goods, thus there is severe homogeneity and fierce competition. Without innovation, these shops would be susceptible to being phased out.

Since the beginning, however, Chen Zhihua has consciously managed his brand and protected his intellectual property rights. This has certainly set a good example for the merchants of Yiwu in their own business development. Through his practices, Chen tells everyone that it is only by protecting one's patents and intellectual property rights that one's efforts will bear fruit in the end.

What Yiwu lacks at present is its own brands. With proper management, the future will be limitless for young people like Chen Zhihua, who can innovate and protect their creative ideas.

PROFILE

Kuaishou name: 椰壳抹布创始人：荣叶华仔 (Founder of "Yeke" dishcloths: Rongye Huazai)

Kuaishou ID: A18757803388

Hometown: Ningde City, Fujian Province

Age: 33

Education: high school

Topic: demonstrations of how to set up a vendor stall and how to sell goods

Production style: focus on live demonstrations and whole processes

Message to his loyal fans: keep innovating and finding ways to protect your creative ideas

Business model: sell dishcloths through livestreaming, register the trademark of Yeke dishcloths, and develop more products in the future

Narrator: Chen Zhihua

I am known as "Rongye Huazai" on Kuaishou and I am from Ningde City, Fujian Province. I have run a street stall and a wholesale business and have also acquired nearly 10 years of experience in e-commerce sales.

Once, when my friends and I were having supper after our basketball game, we saw someone watching short videos and found it very interesting. After asking, we were told that the platform was called Kuaishou. My friends and I soon downloaded the app and were astonished at how fun it was to use. We all knew that the platform would become a hit one day. Hence, I also wanted to take part in and be a witness to the development of the platform. Together with my friends, I began to explore various video styles. After amassing 50,000 followers, however, I ran into a bottleneck because I did not know how to monetize my videos.

One day, I saw someone on Kuaishou demonstrating how to set up a vendor stall and how to sell goods. This provided me with a sudden inspiration. I had previously engaged in traditional e-commerce, where I wrote textual descriptions and uploaded photos of my products, but none of them were as intuitive as short videos. Thus, I thought to myself that I must seize this opportunity.

Paying Attention to Trademark Protection and Preventing Counterfeits

After doing some research, I decided to sell dishcloths. My reasoning was this: Firstly, everyone has to clean their dishes, so the market is huge. Secondly, dishwashing is especially demonstrative; I can demonstrate not only how to use my dishcloths, but also how to set up a vendor stall for selling them. Thirdly, our dishcloths are especially effective; our tests have shown that they can clean the stains of more than 50 percent of the various types of oil on the market, and more than 90 percent of commonly used vegetable oils. And fourthly, after-sales communication is convenient; consumers can communicate directly with me via short videos, unlike in traditional e-commerce, where the seller cannot even be seen.

My line of Yeke dishcloths has become especially popular ever since I promoted it on Kuaishou. It is now selling well in supermarkets and street stalls across all provinces in China, and it is also sold in Malaysia and other Southeast Asian countries. At present, it has to be produced concurrently by three factories in order to meet the demand.

I began selling and promoting Yeke dishcloths in May 2018, but it was not until November of that year when one or two competitors emerged. There are two reasons for this: firstly, the excellent quality of Yeke dishcloths is hard to match, and secondly, my self-devised sales method is hard to replicate.

I have come to realize that if I intend to keep on innovating, then I have to find ways to protect my creative ideas. Whenever something became popular in the past, many people would copy it. Therefore, I applied for trademark protection for my Yeke dishcloths before I started on livestreaming e-commerce—otherwise, my hard-earned rewards would be quickly stolen by others.

In the future, I intend to develop more products and market them from unique perspectives. While adhering to my principle of producing high-quality products, I will create products that are an even better value for money and that possess unique characteristics. More importantly, I will provide my customers with greater assurance, so that they would help advertise our products on their own initiative. At the same time, I will invite more entrepreneurs to come and interact and learn from one another.

Kuaishou Has Shaped Millions of People from the Grassroots

By livestreaming from my dishcloth stall, I have enabled my customers to see not only the functions and effectiveness of my dishcloths, but also how I market my products. Even when it is raining and I cannot set up a stall outdoors, I film videos at home to demonstrate the functions of my dishcloths and how I market them. This provides my viewers with a complete set of methods on how to sell dishcloths and also allows them to communicate with me if they have any questions.

In just one year, I have amassed 200,000 Kuaishou followers, while more and more wholesalers have begun to operate their own Kuaishou accounts and engage in livestreaming e-commerce. By marketing my dishcloths via short videos, I have been able to make money not only for myself but also for a few of my loyal followers who learned from my demonstrations and obtained a supply of goods from me.

I have personally taught many people who get their supplies from me how to market the goods and how to attract traffic via Kuaishou. Furthermore, I help them solve any problems they have. Should they still be unable to sell the goods, I even provide after-sales services for them to return the goods to me.

As the saying goes, it is better to teach a man how to fish than to give him a fish. On Kuaishou, I also teach people how to start a business and how to make Kuaishou work for them. By marketing dishcloths, I have attracted more and more entrepreneurs to join Kuaishou and caused a tiny miracle in this profession. Therefore, Kuaishou has shaped not just me, but also many other grassroots entrepreneurs.

Doing e-commerce on Kuaishou is actually just like setting up a street stall. To achieve strong sales, there are a few things you must take note of. Firstly, your products must be low in price and high in value for the money. Secondly, your products must have their own unique selling points. And thirdly, the effects of your products must be genuine and reliable. Aside from dishcloths, I am also developing other products these days; I will certainly make sure that all of my future products fulfill the above requirements.

If you have done livestreaming e-commerce before, you know that user comments are visible to everyone and cannot be deleted. Thus, counterfeit or low-quality products are swiftly and easily called out. This is different from answering a reporter's questions on television, where you can control the scope of questions, or even prepare for the questions in advance—and even then, unexpected situations often crop up. If a large number of negative comments appear during a livestream, it would be practically impossible for the livestream to continue.

This is why I believe that a business can only be sustained by adhering to the principles of honesty and the idea that the customer is king.

HAITOU TOWN: HOW TO ACHIEVE 300 MILLION YUAN IN E-COMMERCE TRANSACTIONS IN ONE YEAR

The development of the Caiyun Seafood brand is not only a remarkable story of how a traditional fisherman turned his fortunes around by using Kuaishou, but also an excellent example of the ascent of a traditional Chinese fishing village amid the trend of fresh-food e-commerce. In 2018, Haitou Town ranked first among Chinese towns and villages for the number of short-video views garnered on Kuaishou. Caiyun Seafood is one of the top channels from Haitou Town—it has nearly two million followers and is known for its spirited style and excellent ability to promote goods. Every time it conducts a livestream, it receives more than 1,000 orders. On a good day, it can receive a total of more than 4,000 orders, with sales exceeding half a million yuan in value. Only three years ago, it was still just a business handed down from a father to a 90s-born fisherman who made his living on the waves.

While e-commerce giants such as Tmall and JD are still ramping up their fresh-food offerings, and emerging competitors are still struggling with scale and profitability, Caiyun Seafood and Haitou Town have already completed the transformation from offline wholesale supply of goods to direct e-commerce delivery by using the "livestreaming + e-commerce" model. In 2018, Haitou Town achieved more than 300 million yuan in e-commerce transactions.

PROFILE

Kuaishou name: 彩云海鲜 (Caiyun Seafood)

Kuaishou ID: caiyunhaixian

Hometown: Lianyungang City, Jiangsu Province

Age: 30

Education: junior middle school

Topic: seafood

Production style: a spirited internet celebrity who is able to persuade his loyal followers to buy, buy, and buy some more as soon as he opens his mouth

Message to his loyal fans: You won't feel pressure if you promote your goods in good faith. And if you want to eat, you must eat the freshest.

Business model: promote goods through livestreaming on Kuaishou, and sell locally caught and processed seafood through the Kuaishou Store

Narrator: Kuang Lixiang

I am the person who runs the Kuaishou account called "Caiyun Seafood". My short videos and livestreams tend to be of a vigorous, spirited style, which is quite a mismatch with my account name. Actually, Caiyun is my wife's name, and Little Caiyun is my daughter's name. My real name is Kuang Lixiang, while several of my loyal followers on Kuaishou like to call me "Boss Kuang" or "Brother Kuang."

I am an ordinary fisherman from Haiqi Village, Haitou Town, Lianyungang City. I grew up by the sea in a village of many generations of fishermen. I started using Kuaishou in 2016. At first, I simply watched videos or casually filmed and uploaded a few videos of myself going out to sea or pulling in the nets. However, I slowly began to notice that my videos were making it onto the Trending page and my follower count was increasing. When a follower asked me about the price of my seafood one day, I decided to sell some of my catch online as well.

In the following two to three years, I amassed two million followers on Kuaishou and could thus be considered an internet celebrity. Nowadays, I mainly promote goods by livestreaming on Kuaishou. In doing so, I have helped send fresh seafood caught in these parts to the dining tables of my loyal fans all over China.

In our village of 2000-plus households, basically everyone is a fisherman. In the past, we sold our seafood to fishmongers, so our profits were little, while our sales were also not high in volume. After Kuaishou was discovered here, more than 200 of my fellow villagers became livestreamers, and so there would be people filming short videos, or livestreaming out on their boats or on the docks, at all times of the day. Whenever the tide ebbs, many villagers would livestream themselves gathering seafood on the beach; there would thus be hundreds of livestreams being conducted in my village at 8 or 9 every night.

The purpose of livestreaming is, of course, to sell goods. We have a saying here—as a joke—that people in Northeast China go on Kuaishou to boast about themselves, whereas we people from Haitou go on Kuaishou to sell our goods. In our livestreams, we show our loyal followers the freshly caught seafood and how to properly cook it on the spot, giving everyone an irresistible urge to buy some seafood for themselves.

It is not just our village, but the entire Haitou Town, that is excellent in doing e-commerce. Every family sells seafood, and there are countless livestreamers around town. Many of those who persisted in doing e-commerce over the past few years now enjoy an income of millions—or even tens of millions—of yuan. The changes that e-commerce has brought to the lives of my fellow fishermen and to our entire economy are simply enormous.

Although I was not the first person to sell seafood through livestreaming, I can nevertheless be considered someone who "got a leg of the crab" as well. When talking about the tremendous changes that livestreaming has brought to our village, we have to start from the life of a fisherman in the past.

The Pains of a Fisherman: Making a Living on the Waves

My videos and livestreams on Kuaishou were all recorded at a time when things were already going well in my village. However, they only show a part of a fisherman's life. In the past, the life of a fisherman was very tough—the risks were great, yet the income was low.

I was born into a rural family in the 90s. My father used to be a maritime pilot and navigator, while my mother mended fishing nets. I dropped out of junior middle school and left my village to work for a year. When I returned at 18 or 19 years old, my family pooled together enough money to buy a boat, so I began going out to sea to catch fish, with my father serving as my assistant. This could be considered carrying on the tradition of my ancestors.

As a fisherman, I had to wake up early in the morning and go to sleep late at night. The time when we went out to sea depended on the tide—it could be 6 a.m. today, 6:30 a.m. tomorrow, and 7 a.m. the day after tomorrow. Or, if the tide came in at night, we would go out to sea at night. The work on a boat is very rough. We have experienced strong winds, heavy rains, and storms while out at sea, not to mention the various difficulties of catching fish or handling equipment.

My most dangerous experience took place on a summer day when my father and I went out to sea. Before we set off, the weather forecast predicted rain, but no wind. However, we encountered a Beaufort force 11 storm on our 17-meter-long boat and were caught completely unprepared. Brief thundershowers are very common on the sea, and the weather forecasts are not always accurate.

What did a Beaufort force 11 storm mean for us? I remember thinking back then that we were doomed.

The storm lasted almost 40 minutes before subsiding—had it lasted for another 20 minutes, the boat would have probably flipped over, and the two of us would have been thrown overboard. When it was over, my father and I looked at each other, completely speechless.

While I have never mentioned this incident in my Kuaishou videos, I have done so in my livestreams on occasion, when my loyal followers asked me whether I had experienced any danger out at sea. Once, there were nearly 3,000 people on my channel when I recounted this story with tears streaming down my cheeks and a terrible feeling in my heart. Many followers commented that the story was way too scary.

All fishermen who have gone out to sea for more than 30 years, such as those of my father's generation, would have experienced such winds and waves before. This was how my father's brother died at sea, and there are many similar examples among the people around me.

Although life as a fisherman was very rough, I had no other choice. I got married at a young age and had two children and elderly parents to feed. And so, following that incident, I simply went home and slept for the day, then went out to sea again the next day. As the saying goes, "People who live in the mountains live off the mountains, people who live by the sea live off the sea." If I did not go out to sea, what else could I do to make money?

Once, while I was piloting a boat, I had not slept a wink for two days and nights and was thus very tired. I fell asleep at the helm with the wheel in my hands, so the boat spun round and round on the sea. A nearby boat had to shout at me over the loudspeaker: "What are you doing!? Have you dozed off!?" And it was indeed true—I was so tired that I had fallen asleep as soon as I rested my head on the back of my seat.

Many of my followers have expressed interest in coming to work on my boat with me, to experience the fisherman's life. They think that our life is wonderful because we get to eat seafood and go out to sea every day. In actual fact, they do not know about the hardships and dangers faced by every fisherman.

"You can come," I tell them, "I can take you on a sea trip for one or two days, but no longer than that." In this way, I have taken several fans out to sea for a spin and to catch some fish, but I have never allowed any of them to stay for long.

Livestreaming Has Helped Me Become a "Promotion King" and Establish a Seafood Company

It was a fellow townsman named Sanzi who introduced me to Kuaishou. He is also a fisherman, and he used to have a blog called *A Fisherman's Diary*, where he wrote a lot about the life and at-sea experiences of a fisherman. He was the first local fisherman to publish short videos on Kuaishou and promote goods online, so I learned from him. Back then, few people published seafood videos.

Sometime around February 2017, I began to carefully study how to film videos. Seeing that others had managed to get on the Trending page and increase their followers, I tried to copy them. Later on, I settled on using the account called Caiyun Seafood, and uploaded several videos a day. What I would do was casually film a video whenever I went out to sea to catch fish.

I was overjoyed when my video made it onto the Trending page for the first time. A video I had casually filmed and uploaded about the engine of my fishing boat unexpectedly garnered several hundred thousand views and made it onto the Trending page. Subsequently, I pondered over how to get on the Trending page again. I tried to film various types of content, and I slowly figured things out—sometimes my ideas worked and sometimes they didn't.

It wasn't until June 2017 that I finally got the hang of things. In order to attract viewers to tap on my videos, and subsequently hit the Like button, what I had to do was give them a feel of what it was like to catch fish on the sea. I would show them the process of pulling in the fishing net and the kinds of fish I could catch. They were all fairly curious about the kinds of fish my fishing net could pull in, such as mantis shrimp and octopus. In this way, my followers gradually increased.

Some followers would inquire about the price of a certain fish. We would add each other on WeChat and they would then purchase seafood from me. At first, I received only a handful of orders every day, so most of the fish I caught were either sold to local fishmongers and markets or wholesaled to restaurants. A most memorable milestone was one instance when my popularity suddenly exploded. On the way back to shore after having set sail the night before, I filmed a short video on the boat at around noontime. My father and I lifted a box of freshly caught mantis shrimp and poured its contents into a pot, saying: "When cooking mantis shrimps, we only eat the freshest."

The video garnered two million hits almost as soon as I uploaded it. I quickly began a livestream, which attracted more than 10,000 viewers. I was utterly dumbfounded—I only had 60,000-odd followers back then, and thus, did not expect so many viewers. After livestreaming for a while on the boat, I went home to settle a few other things before continuing to livestream from home. There were still nearly 7,000 fans on the channel, and many of them asked me about the price of my seafood.

Back then, the Kuaishou Store was not yet available, so I could only sell my products through WeChat. At first, I publicized my personal WeChat account, but it quickly reached the friend limit. A second WeChat account also reached the limit in no time. I received nearly 700 orders that day, causing me to become overwhelmed by the shipments I had to make.

Previously, I had only received a dozen or so orders per day at most, and I was happy to get even five orders in a day. But now, those numbers had grown by a hundred times! My father, my mother, my elder sister, my wife, and my mother-in-law all came to help me fulfill the orders. It took us two frantic days to ship all of the packages. Back then, I thought that I had to deliver the goods as quickly as possible or I would lose the customers' trust.

It was just too scary at first. Earning a thousand yuan in one day used to be tough enough, yet the sales I made on this day were worth a few dozen times that.

Thereafter, I gradually developed my own style. The content style of Caiyun Seafood is wild and spirited. In one video, I was preparing seafood in a large pot on my boat when I threw the lid off the pot and put an octopus in my mouth. My followers enjoy this style—I had tried a "charming and handsome" persona at first, but not many people watched those videos. As someone who makes a living on the waves, I have to be able to let things go in order to gain popularity. Besides, what kind of seafood tastes the best? The answer is, of course, the freshest. Hence, I would conduct a livestream right after returning from sea and sell the seafood I had just caught. While certain kinds of seafood, such as conch and octopus, can be directly shipped, others such as mantis shrimp are not easy to ship. I thus found a local food-processing plant to do the necessary processing and preparation before shipping the shrimps.

For my first year of using Kuaishou, I livestreamed while still going out to sea. But later on, when I had amassed several hundred thousand followers and generated a certain sales volume, it became more profitable for me to focus on livestreaming. Moreover, the amount of seafood I was able to catch with my boat was insufficient to meet the rising demand.

Whenever I went out to sea but forgot to livestream, many of my followers would urge me to "hurry up and livestream already." They would tell me things like that they had eaten all the prawns they bought from me and only felt assured buying some more from me. As time went on, I spent more time livestreaming and promoting goods at home, and thus went out to sea less. In March 2018, I established my own company called Zuibaxian.

Nowadays, my work consists mainly of filming videos and clips for a few hours in the afternoon, and then conducting livestreams at 9 every night. Although my videos are very simple and down-to-earth, and do not involve a lot of editing, I have to spend time preparing the seafood and props and also coming up with new content. After all, if I repeated the same content every day, my followers would eventually get bored, and I would not make it onto the Trending page—that would be an even bigger waste of time.

A Small Fishing Village Became a Seafood Village That Sells to the Whole Country

Kuaishou has not only changed my family, but it has also given impetus to the industry chains of our fishing village and town, benefiting the fishermen and couriers alike. As a livestreamer, I have singlehandedly inspired many fishermen to sell their goods on Kuaishou and helped increase their incomes greatly—not to mention that there are several hundred other livestreamers doing the same.

I receive about 1,000 orders during my nightly livestream. I mainly sell octopus, mantis shrimp, conch, scallop, and a few other kinds of fresh and processed seafood. I earn an income of around 100,000 yuan per night on average, and up to 300,000 yuan on a good night.

To cite an example, the octopuses that I sell are all caught by my fellow villagers. There are more than 200 boats in the village, and my relatives are also boat owners—the uncles who I am close to own at least 30 boats altogether. Everyone would deliver the octopuses they caught to me, and I would then freeze the octopuses in my self-built freezer before shipping the frozen octopuses the next day.

Many of my loyal followers have remarked that the fish I sell were not caught by me. I reply to them by acknowledging that this is indeed the case before explaining that if I went out to sea to catch fish myself, I would not have enough seafood to offer everyone. In fact, when the demand is especially high and the supply is insufficient, I have to go and purchase stock from other villages. Nevertheless, I make sure that all of the fish I sell are of the desired quality. After all, if there is even the slightest defect in my goods, my followers would talk about it on my livestream channel for all to see.

I achieved my highest daily turnover one day in April 2019. That was the day when my follower count reached two million, and so I organized a livestream event—in the form of a scallop "flash sale"—to reward my loyal followers. About 5,000 orders were received that day, generating a sales figure of more than 500,000 yuan. As a result, I had to stay up way past midnight just to receive and process the orders.

We usually have five people do the packing and shipping of goods. While this is sufficient for 1,000 orders or so, we have to engage a few temporary workers when the volumes became higher. For 3,000 orders or more, we need at least 10 people in order to finish the work in one day. In the past when we used WeChat to take orders, we needed four or five customer service representatives to handle the hundreds of orders we received on a daily basis. After we started using the Kuaishou Store, however, customer service became a lot more convenient; orders could be directly placed, so we needed only two customer service representatives and one after-sales representative. And during normal times, when we get about 1,000 orders per day, just one customer service representative is sufficient.

We also opened our own online store in the past, but it was too complicated. I had to spend a lot of time traveling around to consult people for advice on how to run it well. Eventually, we decided to focus squarely on Kuaishou.

Over the past two years, many new seafood livestreamers have emerged, bringing with them a little bit of pressure and competition. However, since my principle is to promote goods in good faith, and my goal is to provide affordable products for my followers, it doesn't matter to me how many competitors there are. In the early days, the online seafood market was small and lacked momentum, but now, the entire market has become dynamic.

In 2017, octopuses were sold at 11 yuan per 500 grams. Then, in the winter of 2018, the most expensive octopuses went for 70 yuan per 500 grams. Why was the price so high? The answer is simple: Supply and demand. Because octopuses were showcased and sold on the internet, the demand exceeded the supply, and people were willing to buy them no matter the cost. The promotion of goods via Kuaishou livestreams has given impetus to our village and town by opening up the whole of China as our market.

These days, Haitou Town has become incredible at selling seafood. As long as a product passes the quality inspection and attains a five-star rating, it runs out of stock in an instant.

The changes in Haitou Town's economy are most perceptible to couriers. Before the town started doing e-commerce, SF Express (the second largest courier company in China) would ship only a few hundred orders per day from the entire town. But after the town embarked on seafood e-commerce, daily orders reached more than 10,000. Subsequently, JD Express also began to accept orders from the town. Thanks to the newfound competition between the two courier companies, the costs of express delivery drops whenever the volume is large.

When it's the off season for fishing nationwide, I give myself a break. Nevertheless, I still receive dozens of orders when I do not livestream.

It is actually very tiring to livestream every day. Many people think that my life as a livestream marketer is very easy, but if my livestream channel lacks a good vibe, nobody would enjoy watching my livestreams. Therefore, I have to put in my greatest efforts every time I livestream. My earnings are not completely due to luck, but rather, they depend on hard work.

In any case, the exhaustion from livestreaming is nothing compared to that from going out to sea. I feel that my present life is as wonderful as being in paradise. This is why I treasure all of my followers on Kuaishou so much. My current goal is to manage my own seafood business well. When the summertime fishing off season ends, I will strive to increase my followers by another one million—then I will be satisfied.

CHAPTER NINE

KUAISHOU MCNs: MAKING THE MOST OF THE SHIFT FROM PICTURE AND TEXT TO VIDEO

CHAPTER OVERVIEW

A s the saying goes, "Ducks are the first to know when the river becomes warm in spring." Changes in the ways that data is disseminated have caused multi-channel networks (MCNs) to feel the shift from the era of picture and text to the era of video and, consequently, make the decision to embrace videos. However, the process of transitioning to video will pose many challenges for MCNs. Firstly, the differences in conventions between the era of picture and text and the era of video represent a gap that must be bridged. And secondly, creating videos will not generate income immediately, and thus, patience is necessary.

As a result, most MCNs will opt for a multi-platform strategy and try out all available platforms. Among the various platforms, Kuaishou has a few unique advantages, namely its high volume of private domain traffic, its multiple means of monetization, its relatively fair algorithmic mechanism, and its large user base.

SUCCESS STORIES

Jin Shang Xing: MCNs Must Seize Fleeting Opportunities

May Beauty Makeup: Enabling Ordinary Boys and Girls to Become Internet Celebrities

KUAISHOU MCNs: MAKING THE MOST OF THE SHIFT FROM PICTURE AND TEXT TO VIDEO

Zhang Zhan, head of Kuaishou MCN Operations

As a multi-channel network, May Beauty Makeup was faring pretty well during the time WeChat Official Accounts were on the rise. In 2018, the company suddenly decided to shift to the short video industry. That same year, Jin Shang Xing made the decision to shift its focus to the short video industry as well—it previously had 100 million followers in the picture- and text-based WeMedia domain.

Multi-channel networks are commercial organizations that produce professional content for multiple platforms in order to help them monetize their business. As the saying goes, "Ducks are the first to know when the river becomes warm in spring." Changes in the ways that data is disseminated have caused multi-channel networks to feel the shift from the era of picture and text to the era of video and consequently make the decision to embrace videos. In the face of changing trends, action becomes a necessity.

What Are the Advantages Enjoyed by Kuaishou MCNs?

The process of transitioning to video will pose many challenges for MCNs. Firstly, the differences in conventions between the era of picture and text and the era of video represent a gap that must be bridged. And secondly, creating videos will not generate income immediately, and thus patience is necessary.

As a result, most MCNs would opt for a multi-platform strategy and try out all available platforms. Among the various platforms, Kuaishou has a few unique advantages.

The first is a high volume of private domain traffic. A common pain point among MCNs is the difficulty of monetization. It is an industry-wide consensus to choose private domain traffic over public domain traffic, and Kuaishou is no different.

The second is its multiple means of monetization. Kuaishou accounts can be monetized via e-commerce, livestreaming rewards, Kuaishou Classroom payments, Kuaijiedan, and on-stream promotion of goods.

The third is a relatively fair algorithmic mechanism. Kuaishou's inclusive mechanism serves to eliminate the worries of organizational users by assuring them of fair treatment. More importantly, the platform's large-scale traffic support program is fully in line with the goals of MCNs. At the same time, the platform is continually improving its mechanisms for cooperating with MCNs and making the shift from traditional contract-based relationships to strategic partnerships.

The fourth is a large user base—Kuaishou has more than 300 million daily active users at present.

Kuaishou's Embrace of MCNs

In July 2018, Kuaishou officially began to provide support to MCNs. The results have been remarkable: There are more than 1,000 MCNs on the platform, and together they own more than 10,000 accounts. On average, more than 20,000 MCN videos are published every week, and more than 1.7 billion video hits are recorded every week. Based on follower data, MCNs have received more than 1.8 billion follows in total, and the average follower growth is around 10 million. The value of operating on Kuaishou is further reflected in the fact that these MCNs have gained more than 500 million followers since joining Kuaishou.

Before support was officially provided to MCNs, many of them had already joined the platform on their own initiative. However, they might have encountered a few issues initially and did not know who to contact for help, and thus the growth of their accounts was very slow. Moreover, they did not understand the rules of the platform. Every platform has its own rules and unique laws of survival, as well as a standard by which content is judged. Failure to understand these rules and standards would likely cause a few unnecessary troubles for an account.

During this process, we saw that the introduction of MCNs had a highly significant effect on the supply of rich content. On one hand, it enabled users to see a larger variety of content. On the other hand, it led users to produce corresponding content.

After Kuaishou established a specialized MCN operation department, the following services could be provided:

The first is exclusive operation support. Whenever an MCN encounters an issue with its account, the platform designates specific personnel to help the MCN solve the issue in a timely fashion.

The second is a protection strategy for original content. We know that content production costs time and energy for MCNs, yet plagiarism, appropriation, and other such behaviors are harmful to the development of original content. Our protection mechanism effectively serves the rights and interests of our users and prevent unnecessary losses.

The third is offline public Q&A sessions. By reviewing past cases, the platform provides real-time offline guidance to users on a few trends. We have also built an operation back end for organizations. The livestreaming back end can effectively monitor the on-stream behaviors of every livestreamer and user. After gaining access to the back end, MCNs are able to see the growth status and trend of every piece of content. In addition, while other platforms have only recently authorized videos that are 15 or more minutes long, Kuaishou MCN has authorized these all along. MCNs can post videos that are 15 or more minutes long and can do so either on a computer or a mobile phone.

The fourth is a support program for high-quality content. Aside from providing traffic support, the platform also helps accounts perform a "cold start," that is, to realize the transformation from nothing to something. This thereby helps MCNs achieve reasonable and stable growth. The platform also provides basic features such as buzzword resource exposure and a list of top organizational talents.

The fifth is corporate settlement. Kuaishou's wish for 2019 was to grow together with MCNs and become loyal partners with them. We will continue to improve our products and features in order to offer more methods of revenue distribution, and to enable MCNs to manage their accounts more effectively and directly.

Cooperating with 2,000 Organizations

Kuaishou's plan for 2019 was to build operational cooperation with more than 2,000 organizations. These organizations were not limited to traditional MCNs, but instead included service providers, media outlets, and WeMedia agencies. As long as a user has the ability to create high-quality content, the platform will be willing to cooperate sincerely with them—we have always maintained a very open mind.

At the same time, Kuaishou will continue to open up new modes of cooperation.

The first is tiered traffic support. Every week, Kuaishou will provide one billion views to promote and support accounts at different follower-count tiers. This will help accounts complete their cold starts, get through their bottleneck periods, increase their followers effectively, and improve in efficiency.

The second is exclusive IP cooperation. In cooperation with 10 exclusive IPs, the platform will provide one billion views to support 10 accounts that each have more than one million followers, thereby helping them to promote their brands and, subsequently, to commercialize and monetize.

The third is regional cooperation. We will partner with leading local MCNs to spur the growth of more MCNs and consequently, penetrate more offline scenarios. For example, we will convert the traffic of popular accounts into offline transactions in order to create a closed loop for monetization. Because some users like to watch videos about local anecdotes and stories, the platform will cooperate with local media accounts to work on the localized distribution of content.

The fourth is industry cooperation. Kuaishou will open up the upstream and downstream of the vertical MCN industry in order to deeply explore new modes of cooperation.

In 2019, Kuaishou launched three new sections to help MCNs achieve even more growth on the platform by improving their efficiency, protecting their rights and interests, and speeding up monetization. After a thorough examination of the MCN industry and the platform itself, we found that high-quality content on any platform will always bring in a sizable number of followers and achieve a certain popularity. These accounts are never artificially selected, but instead are naturally grown, from having no followers to having millions—or even tens of millions of followers.

JIN SHANG XING: MCNs MUST SEIZE FLEETING OPPORTUNITIES

Located in Taiyuan City, Shanxi Province, Jin Shang Xing understands that the opportunities brought about by media changes are fleeting. In 2013, the company made the decision to create a WeChat Official Account and gained 100 million followers. But as the lucrative era of picture and text came to an end, the company had to start all over again.

Since June 2018, the company has been producing short video content in domains such as entertainment, cuisine, fashion, cosmetics, and life hacks. It has also become an MCN certified by Kuaishou.

As of September 2019, Jin Shang Xing successfully incubated various high-quality IPs that together have more than 90 million followers and more than 10 billion views of their original short videos.

PROFILE

Company name: Shanxi Jin Shang Xing Technology Co., Ltd.

Location: Taiyuan City, Shanxi Province

Date of establishment: August 2013

Industry: media

Message to their loyal fans: we hope everyone can join the Kuaishou family and assimilate into a real Chinese commercial ecosystem

Business model: Positions itself as an "incubation platform for high-quality online Ips." Cultivates KOLs and empowers merchants. Currently building a commercial ecosystem closed loop for picture and text media, short video, and e-commerce

Narrator: Dong Weiwei (deputy general manager of Jin Shang Xing)

Amassing 100 Million Followers on a WeChat Official Account and Then Returning to Zero

I was born in 1979, and my dream since childhood was to be a reporter. After graduation, I was hired by the *Shanxi Evening News*, where I spent 12 years doing editorial and management work. I then joined Jin Shang Xing in October 2015.

We registered a WeChat Official Account very early on and in a very decisive fashion. I remember receiving a phone call from our company's founder while at an award ceremony hosted by a newspaper company one night in 2013. He invited me for a chat later that night. It was already past 11 p.m. by the time the ceremony ended, but that was when the founding team was in the midst of registering a WeChat Official Account.

Our company's founder has not only managed WeChat and WeChat Official Accounts but has also personally gone through every media revolution in recent history and witnessed the rise of every social media platform. Thus, at a time when the founding team was making a new start, he knew very well that the key to success was to seize opportunities.

At first, nobody knew how to operate an Official Account. What we did was very simple and crude—we tried to hoard as many names as possible. Everyone back then thought that Official Accounts could be sold for money just like domain names, and so we engaged specialists to register Official Accounts in bulk. We ended up registering nearly every single combination of four characters or less.

Subsequently, the team began to operate a large number of marketing accounts, seeking to acquire as much as traffic as possible. By 2014, our WeChat Official Accounts had amassed tens of millions of followers in total, and this number grew to nearly 100 million the next year. At this time, the entire company consisted of more than 100 employees, all of whom were on very stable incomes. However, because of a case of content violation, we also experienced the pain and misery of getting our accounts suspended. We realized that we could not stick to this model in the long term, as it was not sustainable.

In 2016, we began to see that the era of picture and text was past its lucrative period, albeit we did not know what to do and were thus a little confused. During this period, the company was incubating more than 20 projects, but all of them ultimately ended in failure. We had not realized that Kuaishou could be an important opportunity for us.

Our Development Principles of "Focus, Concentration, and Perfection"

In October 2018, we officially joined Kuaishou. Previously, when we first started using Kuaishou, we chose 12 different concepts, covering every category imaginable.

Hoping to produce content that could break the internet, we went through a phase of trial and error. Our first production was a workplace drama; it required personnel for screenwriting, directing, acting, lighting, makeup, costumes, and so on. The difficulties were numerous. The first video we produced was called "Having a Buffet on a Lazy Susan Table"— it garnered barely 1,000 likes. Next, the team produced a video that imitated a relatively popular clip, which unexpectedly garnered more than 10,000 likes, even though the picture quality was rough. The following day, the team reshot the video and greatly improved the picture quality— this time, the video garnered more than a million likes.

Having enjoyed some success in producing popular content, we began to duplicate accounts in large numbers. In September 2018, we became part of the first batch of MCNs to join Kuaishou.

After a period of review and reflection, we came up with the development principles of "focus, concentration, and perfection" and decided to focus our monetization efforts on livestreaming rewards and Kuaijiedan.

Ten months later, we decided to keep only five concepts, namely entertainment, makeup, reviews, food, and cars. The reason was that these five categories could be more directly monetized while keeping in mind our principle that monetization is king.

After four months of experimenting with short videos on a large scale, we finally earned advertising revenue. Some of the company's most successful accounts such as "Mu Zimeng the Photo-lover" and "Little Yueyue's Photo-taking Magic" had amassed two to three million followers by then.

In February 2019, we set up our first account that focused on cosmetics. It broke even the very same month.

We also actively expanded our external cooperation, such as with the largest clothing wholesale market in Shanxi Province. We were seeking to promote goods for wholesale merchants via short video platforms.

MCNs usually operate on multiple platforms concurrently. For us, we are constantly thinking about what Kuaishou's unique aspects are and if it can support our e-commerce strategy.

Kuaishou's user experience gives me confidence that it can indeed support our e-commerce strategy. The platform is able to retain users in a way that no other platform can match. For instance, if I am impressed by a certain Kuaishou producer, I click on their channel and watch all of their videos. Things that are very distant from everyday life are "performances" and can never retain users—users are constantly in search of content that is more real and down-to-earth.

We plan to take a group of people out of our operation department to focus solely on our Kuaishou operations. We hope to reach the top in terms of popularity, build our own influence, and pave the way for our next step in e-commerce.

In July 2019, I took part in Kuaishou's inaugural Guanghe Creators' Conference. This was my fifth time taking part in a Kuaishou event. I saw this as an opportunity for MCNs to develop rapidly—in the following half a year, everyone would be seeking to grab a slice of Kuaishou's 300 million daily active users and 10 billion views. Many of the middling MCNs had come in the hopes of e-commerce monetization. Such an opportunity was fleeting, and nobody knew when a similar opportunity would arise again if they missed out on it.

Two Learning Points from the Transition to Short Video

Nowadays, many people ask me about issues related to the transition to short video. I gained two learning points from this transition: the first is to change my thinking, and the second is that monetization is king.

Let's first talk about changing my thinking. Many people ask me about minuscule points, such as where to begin a transition to short video, how to make money post-transition, how many employees they need, how to structure their organization, or how long it takes to break even. The first question I would ask them is: has your thinking truly changed?

When we have spent too long in a certain industry, we tend to become fettered by crystallized ideas, just like a frog at the bottom of a well. The well actually represents our crystallized thoughts and so-called experience. Sometimes, the more experience one has, the deeper the well is—that is, the harder it is for one to accept new things. Back when we focused on picture and text marketing, we considered ourselves to be highly professional, but we encountered huge problems when we transitioned to short video. Therefore, we warn our team members every day not to become a slave to experience. Instead, we should keep on finding ways to smash the well that we are in.

To make a successful transition, the first thing one must do is smash one's self-imposed limits and not become a frog in the well. Success comes from bold imagination, devotion, and action.

The second point is that monetization is king. During the era of WeChat Official Accounts, I successively worked on several content entrepreneurship projects. My team had 50 people at its peak, but it soon ended in failure.

I gained an important lesson from this failure. Having worked in traditional media for 12 years, I continued to adopt the media's elitist mindset while working on internet content, thereby neglecting the users. Moreover, I only thought about how to produce content and did not have a clear idea of how to monetize it.

For a company, monetization is always the top priority, as it is a matter of life and death.

In the future, there will be more and more MCNs like Jin Shang Xing. All of us are seeds and grass in this ecosystem. I believe that under Kuaishou's fair and inclusive sunlight, we will be able to become the top content producers in China.

MAY BEAUTY MAKEUP: ENABLING ORDINARY BOYS AND GIRLS TO BECOME INTERNET CELEBRITIES

In less than a year since its establishment, May Beauty Makeup has cultivated more than 30 key opinion leaders (KOLs) in the field of cosmetics. Among them, 25 have more than a million fans on a single platform.

The team now consists of nearly 100 people, and it has produced hundreds of popular short videos and amassed 20 million followers on Kuaishou. In March 2019, May Beauty Makeup closed a 10-million-yuan pre-A funding round and planned to increase its total online followers to 100 million.

More and more cosmetics brands have realized the strong advantages of Kuaishou in commercial monetization. With the support of a loyal fan economy, Kuaishou's potential for e-commerce monetization is unlimited. The introduction of professional content producers will also enrich Kuaishou's KOL ecosystem and make Kuaishou even more beautiful.

Company name: May Beauty Makeup

Location: Guangzhou City, Guangdong Province

Date of establishment: 2018

Industry: cosmetics

Message to their loyal fans: May Beauty Makeup wants you to look good; like and follow us so that you won't get lost!

Business model: establish roots as a short video and livestreaming MCN in the vertical field of cosmetics, and produce original and popular content according to the unique selling points of KOLs

Narrator: Gao Gao (COO of May Beauty Makeup)

Transitioning from a WeChat Official Account to Short Videos

In my opinion, the decision that we made to join Kuaishou was certainly the right choice. At that time, Kuaishou was inviting all MCNs to join its platform. We seized the opportunity and became part of the first wave of MCNs to join. Previously, our company had mainly focused on our WeChat Official Account, but we have now made the transition to short videos.

We faced many internal and external challenges in the course of transitioning from the comforts of our WeChat Official Account to short videos. However, everyone knew that the rewards from WeChat Official Accounts were declining, so we resolved to jump on the latest bandwagon that was Kuaishou's short video platform.

We chose cosmetics as our breakthrough product because regardless of the state of the economy, people's beauty needs never change. Furthermore, the generation of young people born after 1995 was growing up, and many domestic brands were on the rise, therefore advertising content and e-commerce content for cosmetics could turn out to be very popular.

Every Detail Must Be Perfect

We insist on using only our fully self-incubated KOLs and performing strong management of our MCN model. Our first batch of incubated KOLs consisted of six people, all of whom were originally editors within our company. They go by the names "Sparkling Alin," "Irritable Duck Senior," "Brother Mala Chicken," "Naughty Princess Xi," "Weird Girl Fries," and "Little Yuan the Magician." Due to the company's "team DNA," "content DNA," and "ability DNA," they had been working in the new media industry for one to four years and, thus, had their own understanding of the industry. Furthermore, they were enthusiastic about the field of cosmetics and approved of the company's direction. These were the reasons why we decided to start our incubation program with them.

Initially, none of us understood the entire short video ecosystem, so things were very tough for us. The growth of going from zero to one follower is always the most difficult phase. As we were still not acclimatized to short video content and had not understood the front end policies, we spent a long time groping in the dark.

We encountered many issues, one of which was that we were receiving very few likes. Once, when a video garnered more than 2,000 likes, our boss gave every employee a red envelope to celebrate the occasion.

Our original picture and text marketing team had the DNA for content production. We chose the initial six KOLs to incubate because they possessed not only the ability to produce content, but also an image that met the criteria for a KOL.

As the saying goes, "The cause of your success is hard work, the fruits of your success are up to destiny." We demand that every detail is done to perfection. From the makeup and clothing of the vlogger, to the editing effects, and finally to the video review, everyone involved must be meticulous about detail. We believe that when all of the details—clothing, makeup, props, video duration, background music, like and follow reminders, prompt replies to comments, etc.—are done right, then an internet-breaking video will naturally be born.

Enabling More Ordinary People to Become KOLs

Some time ago, I got a call from Kuaishou. They told me that the May Beauty Makeup account had entered a bottleneck period and gave me advice on how to improve it.

I felt very excited upon putting down the phone. During a meeting with the editors that same day, I told them we must absolutely get our Kuaishou account done right. The fact that Kuaishou had taken note of the growth and development of our individual KOLs showed me that they were truly in service of content creators.

Being new to the field of short videos during the early phase of our company's development, we tried out many different management models. The biggest problem we found was in the division of labor when building a team.

We spent roughly a month to create the "director responsibility system," which is the management model that our company is now running. Every director is in charge of two or three small groups. They are responsible for managing the entire internet celebrity group (including all internet celebrities, editors, operation planners, and other members under a small group), reviewing content, and unlocking the potential of our internet celebrities.

By September 2019, our short video team consisted of 100 people, had produced numerous popular videos, and had incubated more than 30 cosmetics KOLs, among which 25 had more than a million followers on a single platform. Each KOL has to produce 15 to 17 pieces of content every week, which adds up to nearly 1,000 cosmetics videos by the entire team each month. So far, they have produced more than 6,000 videos in total.

By transforming a group of nonprofessionals into cosmetics KOLs via the Kuaishou platform, we have enabled these ordinary boys and girls to showcase their unique charms on the platform.

Before Sparkling Alin became an internet celebrity, she worked as an editor of a WeChat Official Account. Because she usually likes to recommend various cosmetic products to her friends and colleagues, she was transferred to the cosmetics short video team of our new company. Unexpectedly, she quickly became part of the first batch of KOLs we incubated.

As the "eldest sister of cosmetics" under May Beauty Makeup, Sparkling Alin has consistently ranked in the top 10 on the Recommenders' Ranking, with as much as 70 percent of her audience and followers being females. Aside from introducing various cosmetic products, her videos also provide general knowledge on female sexuality and cover a wide range of topics.

After the success of Sparkling Alin, we established "Alin's Perfume Research Institute" to provide IPs in vertical domains with a higher degree of recognition. This was because we discovered that there were not many influential accounts in the field of perfume, and thus it still held great potential.

"Chen Wennuan the Little Sun" was initially an editor hired by our company. After he had worked for a month for the company, we saw the potential in him—we felt that he was a very natural performer, so we discussed becoming a KOL with him. "Chief Chopper Pig" was also previously an editor in the company who later transformed into a cosmetics KOL.

Aside from keeping strict control on content and paying great attention to our scripts and videos, we also require our vloggers to pay attention to the operation of private domain traffic, to increase the stickiness of their accounts, and to guide users to follow their accounts. At the same time, we require them to have strong interactions with their followers via features such as Kuaishou Talk and the comments section.

Every month, the Kuaishou platform will send us a few event-related messages. For example, we were provided with specific guidance by designated contact persons when we took part in Kuaishou's "Hundred Man Stand" event, as well as a series of events previously organized by Kuaishou's official team. We are always glad to receive a phone call from Kuaishou, as they promptly inform us of the platform's rules and mechanisms and provide us with traffic support. We hope to achieve mutual cooperation and empowerment with them; one of the things we hope to do together with them is personalize our KOLs and enable more ordinary people to achieve their dreams of becoming KOLs.

The Future Has More Exciting Things in Store

I once shared in a Kuaishou public class that, as a woman from North China, I feel that Kuaishou is more down-to-earth compared to other platforms. When I see an interesting and genuine KOL on the platform, I greet them with "666" (an expression that means "awesome" in Chinese culture). In addition, an emoji that I often use is a fist salute to my buddies.

Because Kuaishou is a platform where people are the connections, content publishers can reduce distance with their loyal fans in order to create an image that is even more intimate and genuine. Therefore, I believe that what sets the platform apart is its loyal fan economy. Yet, the platform has never employed strong-handed operation and intervention to spur content production. There is no distance between KOLs and fans on the platform; they can share their daily lives with each other and consequently enhance their mutual relationship.

This is the reason why the platform's conversion is so effective. When fans like a certain one of our KOLs, they are willing to purchase goods recommended by said KOL. Moreover, the purchase process is very simple; all they have to do is add the desired items to the Yellow Cart. Kuaishou has already opened access for many different channels, such as Taobao, JD, Youzan, and Mockuai. This has made it very convenient for us to connect with brands and speed up our cooperation with brand owners.

We have a KOL called "Liang Xiaoxiao," who is a Cantonese vlogger. Although she has fewer than 300,000 fans, her strong ability in presenting content has increased her fans' loyalty and enabled her to promote goods very effectively via Kuaishou livestreams.

Nowadays, we require our KOLs to conduct at least two goods-promoting livestreams every week. We are also planning to bring on more KOLs to conduct livestreams on Kuaishou in the future. Livestreams can not only strengthen the connections between KOLs and fans, but also hone the livestreaming ability of KOLs and uncover their "livestreaming DNA."

We have KOLs who respectively conduct product recommendations, component analyses, cosmetic-themed dramas, and livestreams. This batch of KOLs has not only earned the admiration of brand owners but has also shown glimpses of their potential for e-commerce monetization under the support of their loyal fan economy.

We are now only in the first half of our development. The second half promises to be much more difficult, exciting, and thrilling. This is because the people entering the industry are becoming more and more professional, causing Kuaishou videos to become increasingly fun to watch.

In the future, we will continue to focus on cosmetic products and keep producing high-quality content in the field of cosmetics. This will aid the growth of cosmetic brands and provide service to upstream and downstream industry chains. We strive to become a producer and provider of high-quality digital content in the field of cosmetics. At the same time, we hope that MCNs from more and more diverse fields will join Kuaishou, so that everyone can work together to create a more colorful Kuaishou ecosystem.

LOOKING AHEAD TOWARD THE 5G ERA: THE RISE OF VIDEO TO A LEADING ROLE

On the Value of Kuaishou and the Responsibility of the Times
—Yu Guoming
Executive Dean of the School of Journalism and Communication,
Beijing Normal University

The 5G-enabled internet of everything is becoming a reality that is ubiquitous in time and space. Because 5G is characterized by high speed, high capacity, low latency, and low energy consumption, the 5G era can, in a sense, be called the era when video "becomes prevalent." Video has already far surpassed the role played by traditional entertainment and has become one of the most important media forms of mainstream communication and social cognition.

Kuaishou has undoubtedly emerged as a winner in this era, because it appeared at the right time and in the right place. As an internet product that integrates the charm of technology, the power of the market, and the splendor of the era, it became a leading enterprise in the short video industry of China not long after its founding. Nearly everyone in China has felt the charm and value vividly displayed by its concept of "Enabling Every Life to Be Seen" on the grand stage of social communication.

The advent of the 5G era undoubtedly provides for Kuaishou's development a broader and more imaginative space where life can be unfolded. Let's take a look at the value and role of Kuaishou in this new era by studying what 5G is all about.

I. VIDEOS IN THE 5G ERA WILL FORM A BROAD-BASED PARADIGM OF EXPRESSION

In the past, although people were the communicators on the internet, the main form of expression was written language, which—judging from a deep logical perspective—is a paradigm of social expression that gives precedence to the expressions of elites. Therefore, during the era of written language, the people who could express their thoughts and opinions on the internet were a small group of elites in society, while more than 95 percent of the population were merely bystanders, "likers," or "reposters." Instead, video is a broad-based form of communication that is different from earlier forms of media expression. Since the 4G era, video has empowered the general public by providing more and more ordinary people with the right to express themselves in social discourse. By making use of the concise and intuitive form of expression that is video, anyone can share their ideas with other people and society—this is a change in communication with revolutionary significance.

At the same time, new technology brings new problems. It is therefore necessary for the government, enterprises, and various parties in society to work together on actively exploring various problems in new technological fields, providing targeted solutions, and achieving the outcome of technology for social good. During this process, we need to further improve the communication between the broad-based expressers and the elite expressers, form a media ecosystem, and develop a framework for broad-based expression.

This is one of Kuaishou's social values and responsibilities for the present and the future.

II. IN THE FACE OF A LARGE NUMBER OF VIDEOS, WE NEED TO FURTHER IMPROVE AI TECHNOLOGY

The 5G era has given birth to forms of communication that are based on the internet of everything. This will inevitably be followed by the emergence of a large number of videos. Due to the dramatic increase in video transmission rates, the number of medium-length and long videos will increase greatly. In the future, videos of various lengths will constitute a rich internet ecosystem.

Faced with the emergence of a large number of videos, Kuaishou needs to do two things right.

The first is to form classifications and connections similar to the knowledge graph methods for textual communication. This is so that when people come into contact with a point of information, they also come into contact with a video connection structure on one plane that is provided by the supplier and built based on a knowledge graph. In other words, we have to provide a systematized video combination and form links that enable videos to complement, elevate, and be compared with one another.

The second is to further improve AI technologies that understand videos and users and perform precise matching. By making use of AI technologies, we can continually lower the barriers to entry for users to gain followers, increase our users' ability to explore the world, and build a more inclusive community.

III. THE 5G ERA IS AN INNOVATION-LED ERA

The emergence of video as a means of communication marks a major change in the methods of social cognition, decision-making, and technological empowerment. In my opinion, as a part of this industry, we should contribute to the industry's efforts in institutional innovation and rule innovation. We know the requirements and rules in the field of communication better than anyone else. If we do not strive to innovate, we will face external constraints from other aspects.

For example, with the development of the internet today, how can we achieve a balance among content originality, platform distribution, and the interests of other content providers? That is an important issue we should consider. In the internet era, the internet imposes a wide range of micro-sized, era-pertinent demands on content. Can content copyrights be micro-processed to suit the requirements of content services, subject matter usages, and value services in the internet environment *and* increase the liberation of the market for content copyrights? This is precisely what is proposed by the innovation that is micro-copyrights.

For example, a family member wants to make a video featuring well wishes from celebrities for his father's birthday. If each celebrity's copyright has to be purchased as a whole, the cost would be enormous. But, if video indexing is done well with the help of AI, then using the concept of micro-copyrights and clever editing, the video could feature each celebrity for only a second or even half a second. For instance, if Tom Hanks says "Happy," Jackie Chan says "Birthday," Brad Pitt says "to," and so on until the full "Happy Birthday to You, Dad!" is jointly said by different celebrities, then the copyright cost of the video might be as low as a few cents. In fact, for the copyright owners, the return rate of monetizing their copyrights would be much higher.

Based on this reasoning, if copyright can be micro-processed, a new form would emerge in the field of communication: micro-editing. Through creative video editing, it would be possible to create more works, implantable advertisements, and native advertisements. The creative energy that would be released by this new form of editing is as yet unimaginable today.

In the future 5G era, when video has garnered widespread attention, we will need to be creative in order to welcome new market opportunities through institutional innovation and rule innovation. Only we can liberate ourselves.

As a pioneer of the video era, Kuaishou must create a world in which society and itself can thrive. It is only with the right timing and personnel—and through its own innovation and creation—that Kuaishou can achieve its ideals and excellence.

IV. A NEW FIELD FOR FUTURE SOCIOLOGY AND A LABORATORY FOR FUTURE COMMUNICATION STUDIES

With the advent of the 5G era, the academic structure of communication studies is undergoing revolutionary changes. At its base is telecommunication studies, which is the study of how communication technology affects the modes of communication, the types of communication, and so on. Next is semiotic communication studies, which examines all kinds of symbols that can become carriers of communication and engender problems in mechanistic patterns and role-playing. This is followed by interpersonal communication studies; here, interpersonal communication refers to different levels of social communication, including person-to-person, person-to-people, and person-to-society. The next higher level is human-computer communication studies, which is the study of how people communicate with machines and things.

These disciplines will form the basic structure of communication studies in the future.

As a leading internet technology enterprise, Kuaishou represents not only a new field for future sociology, but also a laboratory for future communication studies.

———

Yu Guoming is a distinguished professor at the Changjiang Scholars Program under the Ministry of Education of the People's Republic of China; executive dean of the School of Journalism and Communication, Beijing Normal University; and chairman of the Committee of Media Economics and Management, the Chinese Association for History of Journalism and Mass Communication.

THE POWER OF KUAISHOU

"Profound, yet, easy to read." That was our ambition and expectation when we set out to write this book.

The online world was originally dominated by text. However, due to the popularity of smartphones and 4G networks, the application of video understanding (i.e., a deep-learning technology for analyzing videos), and distribution technologies over the past few years, video has supplanted text in the new era. This represents a paradigm shift that will lead to the birth of countless new things.

Kuaishou is a new application of AI technology in the video era, and its ecosystem is still rapidly evolving. We will strive to showcase the community ecosystem of Kuaishou as comprehensively as possible. Hopefully, this will allow the government, the academic world, and enterprises to better understand Kuaishou and, subsequently, the unwritten laws of the eras of AI and video.

We also have another ambition, which is for this book to be easy to read and useful for people of all ages. A scenario that we have envisaged is that a reader would casually flip open this book out of curiosity or desire to seek out new business opportunities, and consequently gain some inspiration from one of the vivid examples we offer.

PART ONE

Kuaishou's creator ecosystem is an ever-evolving process.

It was a few fortunate individuals who were the first to find business opportunities on Kuaishou, and they often did so inadvertently.

Xueli the Smile-a-Lot failed to get into college, and thus worked as a farmer back in her hometown, which is located in a poverty-stricken yet ecologically rich region. Once, when herding cattle, she filmed and uploaded a video to Kuaishou and inadvertently catapulted to fame. It was only thanks to Kuaishou that she had the opportunity to showcase her hometown to the whole of China. Today, she is helping her fellow villagers escape poverty and attain wealth.

Two years ago, a video on kiwifruit that Luola Run casually filmed in his landlord's house made it on to Kuaishou's Trending page, causing a large number of orders to pour in. This prompted him to drop his ceramic tile business and focus on selling fruit on Kuaishou. Today, he has his own fruit brand.

In 2017, a street vendor in Yiwu City, Zhejiang Province, by the name of Yan Bo increased his monthly sales of woolen sweaters from 100,000 to 350,000 by using Kuaishou. His "miracle tale" rapidly spread throughout Kuaishou's business community. In Beixiazhu Village of Yiwu today, 5,000 people livestream every day to sell their goods.

An increasing number of individuals and enterprises are beginning to use and study Kuaishou. After Sany Heavy Industry opened an account on Kuaishou, they unexpectedly sold 31 road rollers in a one-hour livestream. Meanwhile, we have also included the story of a mobile-home business that gets one-third of its orders from Kuaishou.

As of September 2019, more than 19 million people earned an income on Kuaishou, and this number is growing by the day.

PART TWO

What gives Kuaishou its power? There are at least two aspects of Kuaishou that deserve to be highlighted, namely its use of technology to lower the barriers to entry for filming and distributing videos, and its principle of inclusivity.

Many people think of Kuaishou as a platform that specializes in short videos, as well as a platform that can help people film better short videos. This understanding is actually incorrect. The benefits of lowering the barriers to entry for filming videos far surpass those of teaching people how to film good videos.

To cite an analogy from history, there are probably many people who do not recognize the critical importance of the invention of the paint tube in the history of fine art. In the early days, painters concocted their own paints with their own formulas. After standardized tube paints came about, the barriers to entry for painting were greatly lowered. Access to painting materials was made easy for painters and young students alike, thereby affording more people the opportunity to showcase their talent in painting.

In a similar way, Kuaishou has lowered the barriers to entry for recording and sharing videos, affording everyone the opportunity to film and showcase their lives. From the perspective of the entire community, this represents a dramatic expansion of the production capacity for videos and a tremendous enrichment of information. When recommendation technologies are then added on top of this, what we get is the Kuaishou community.

There is a popular saying that in the past, people used to search for videos, but today, it is the videos that search for people. The difference between the two halves of that sentence lies in the degree of richness of videos.

After the Kuaishou community was formed, it constituted an enormous market on its own. In 2020, Kuaishou's daily active users reached 300 million. As a saying in Yiwu goes, "Where there are people, there is business." Two to three million people gather in the community on a daily basis, naturally constituting an enormous market. Many of them have also discovered business opportunities on the platform and have consequently improved their own quality of life.

Our principle of inclusivity offers opportunities to ordinary individuals. As Su Hua, Co-founder of Kuaishou, once said, "Kuaishou hopes to distribute attention to everyone equally, as though it were sunlight."

Authenticity is the main theme of Kuaishou videos, and an effect it generates is the idea that *I can do it, too.*

A typical example of this is a girl who grows snow fungi in Gutian County, Fujian Province. It was after she downloaded the Kuaishou app that she saw the lives of people who live in the grasslands for the first time. She thought to herself that, if those people could film Kuaishou videos, then so could she. Thereafter, her Kuaishou videos allowed many people to see fresh snow fungi for the first time, and that was how her business expanded.

The effects of "I can do it, too" are ubiquitous on Kuaishou.

PART THREE

Kuaishou is a complex community that is continuously propagating and developing. Aside from short videos and commerce, it also has many other aspects.

Kuaishou is a trust-producing machine. By following a livestreamer for a long time, you gradually get to know them better until they essentially become your neighbor. Spatial distance in the real world does not exist in a video community, and thus the Chinese idiom, "neighbors at different ends of the world," is made real.

Prior to the Industrial Age, most people lived in villages and would often go to their neighbors' homes to buy things. If their neighbors sold chickens, they would know whether the chickens were given free range and what fodder the chickens were fed. Thus, there was a lasting trust among neighbors. The cost of cheating a neighbor was very high, because everyone else could see when the cheated neighbor talked things out with the cheating neighbor.

In Kuaishou livestream channels, when there are several hundred viewers, the cost of selling counterfeit goods is extremely high. Once the fact is pointed out by someone among the audience, the trust that the livestreamer has painstakingly built is broken instantly.

The trust economy exists in a new form. It is almost as if we have returned to an era prior to the Industrial Age, when people bought goods from their neighbors' homes or roaming peddlers.

Canadian scholar Marshall McLuhan proposed the concept of the *global village*, which refers to the fact that with the development of new technologies, it increasingly seems like everyone is living in a village where we can have face-to-face interactions. The emergence of short videos has caused the global village to truly become a reality.

This concept is very instructive for future forms of commerce. In existing businesses, there are many chains between the producers and the end buyers, and many of them are the result of spatial distance. When you are in a different place from your customer, the costs of communication are very high.

In a short video community, however, spatial distance does not exist. Everyone is neighbors with everyone else, and so producers can intuitively showcase their goods and conduct face-to-face transactions with end buyers. Many chains that are caused by distance will disappear in the future—this could be an important direction for business development.

Kuaishou is a platform for knowledge production and dissemination. Many people in China have never eaten kiwifruit or seen how it grows. On Kuaishou, Luola Run has thus produced knowledge regarding the kiwifruit by filming videos of them.

Many people in China have eaten seafood but have never seen how seafood is caught. Kuaishou has thus enabled many Chinese people to see live seafood for the first time—this is also a process of knowledge production.

When television became popular in the United States 70 years ago, McLuhan proposed the relationship between process and result. Previously, people learned about a matter through text, but the dynamic process of its development could only be intuitively experienced through video. Compared to text, video recording is, in itself, a process of knowledge production and dissemination.

Kuaishou is an AI community. Every day, more than 15 million short videos are uploaded to Kuaishou and accurately distributed to more than 200 million users. This necessitates leading-edge technologies of accurate distribution, as well as a superb ability to understand videos and users.

Through inclusivization, Kuaishou has made sophisticated technology accessible to every ordinary person. For instance, in the past, only the most advanced smartphones could film certain special effects, but through technological research and development, Kuaishou's engineers have made all special effects available to every smartphone.

As Su Hua once said, "Kuaishou's goal is to make AI technologies usable by ordinary laypersons."

Kuaishou is a weapon for poverty alleviation and the best tool for protecting intangible cultural heritage. There are many causes of poverty, but from an economic perspective, the cause is either an inability to produce things that are accepted and well-received by the market, or an inability to find a market. As an enormous market of more than 200 million people, Kuaishou allows products to be showcased to a huge audience in a sufficiently intuitive manner, and greatly lowers the costs of transactions. Furthermore, the seller can earn money as soon as a transaction is made. Therefore, Kuaishou has naturally become an effective tool for poverty alleviation.

For example, the region of the Daliang Mountains is relatively poor, but it produces apples that are extremely delicious. The local people have sold so many apples via Kuaishou that they are now willing to pool their money together to build a road for shipping the apples. This is something that could hardly have been imagined in the past.

Kuaishou is not just a short video platform, but even more so a three-dimensional network and an ever-evolving ecosystem—its power is being seen by more people as we speak.

INDEX

Page numbers followed by *f* indicate figures.

cosmetics, 29, 90–91. *See also* May
    Beauty Makeup
cultural heritage. *See* intangible cultural
    heritage

D

DAUs (daily active users), 11, 12
David, Professor, 14
    aims of, 27
    background of, 26, 27, 28
    on British and Chinese students, 31
    on chemistry safety, 32
    on China, 28–29
    China's improvements from, 29
    on cosmetics, 29
    first videos of, 30
    on inclusivity, 33–34
    loyal fans of, 31, 32–33
    "Magical Experiments" from, 30
    mentoring by, 33
    messages to, 27–28
    production style of, 27
    profile of, 27
    on questioning, 32
    Royal Society of Chemistry and,
        29, 33
    science popularization by, 30–34
    on summer camp, 33
    uniqueness of, 34
description
    AI in, 4–6
    attention gap in, 1–2, 8–9
    China's long-term investment in, 2–4
    digital divide and, 1
    inclusivity in, 2, 7
    Matthew effect and, 1
    milestones in, 11–12
    seen world in, 9–10
Detail Seller Rating (DSR), 54–55
development bottleneck
    content categories and, xxviii–xxix
    financing in, xxix–xxx
    team in, xxx–xxxii
    transition in, xxix
digital divide, 1
distribution curve, 7
dolphins, 157–158
Dong Huagai, 230, 236

DSR (Detail Seller Rating), 54–55
durians, 65–66

E

e-commerce, 10, 11. *See also* Kuaishou
    Villages; Luola Run; Wawa and
    Xiaoliang
    beginnings of, 52
    brand businesses for, 53
    content creation in, 52, 53–54
    development of, 49–52
    driving force of, 49
    ecosystem co-prosperity for, 55–56
    ecosystem prosperity for, 55
    ecosystem security for, 54–55
    Kuaishou Store for, 53–54
    loyal fans of, 53–54
    market development for, 54
    operational capabilities of, 53–54
    purchase assurance in, 52
    success stories on, 50
    traditional, 246, 247
    transaction convenience in, 52
    for Yugouliang Village, 209–210
E-commerce Accounts, 150
e-commerce enterprises, 150
ecosystem co-prosperity, 55–56
ecosystem prosperity, 55
ecosystem security, 54–55
ecosystems, 156–157, 281
    of Kuaishou Education, 98–99
    of Kuaishou Villages, 241
    of poverty alleviation, 171–173
Edison, Thomas, 20, 34
education, x. *See also* Kuaishou
    Classroom; Kuaishou Education
    availability of, 10
    of 87 percent, xii, xviii
    of Handy Geng, 21
    in poverty alleviation, 172
    of Zhu, 35
efficiency increase, xxii
elders
    old man, xvi–xvii
    of Seven Fairies, 186
    with Xueli, 177
    in Yugouliang Village, 201–202,
        205–206, 208